14.95

Private Foreign Aid

Also of Interest

† *From Dependency to Development: Strategies to Overcome Under-development and Inequality*, edited by Heraldo Muñoz

Future Dimensions of World Food and Population, edited by Richard G. Woods

Food Security for Developing Countries, edited by Alberto Valdés

Agricultural Credit for Small Farm Development: Policies and Practices, David D. Bathrick

† *Transnational Enterprises: Their Impact on Third World Societies and Cultures*, edited by Krishna Kumar

A Select Bibliography on Economic Development: With Annotations, John P. Powelson

Economic Development, Poverty, and Income Distribution, edited by William Loehr and John P. Powelson

Protein, Calories, and Development: Nutritional Variables in the Economics of Developing Countries, Bernard A. Schmitt

Crisis in the Sahel: A Case Study in Development Cooperation, Noel V. Lateef

† *The United States and the Developing Countries*, The Atlantic Council Working Group on the United States and the Developing Countries and Edwin M. Martin

New Directions in Development: A Study of U.S. AID, Donald R. Mickelwait, Charles F. Sweet, and Elliott R. Morss

Development Strategies and Basic Needs in Latin America, edited by Claes Brundenius and Mats Lundahl

† *Managing Development in the Third World*, Coralie Bryant and Louise G. White

Food, Development, and Politics in the Middle East, Marvin G. Weinbaum

† *The Third World and U.S. Foreign Policy*, Robert L. Rothstein

† Available in hardcover and paperback.

About the Book and Authors

Private Foreign Aid:
U.S. Philanthropy for Relief and Development
Landrum R. Bolling, with Craig Smith

Over the past 150 years, Americans have responded repeatedly to the needs of people in foreign lands, providing aid in times of natural disaster, in the wake of war, in the development of resources, in the eradication of disease and poverty, and in the battle against hunger. This challenging task has been tackled again and again by churches, corporations, labor unions, foundations, hundreds of private voluntary organizations, and millions of individuals. They have donated money, goods, and labor to overseas relief and to help promote economic and social development at the grass-roots level. The U.S. government has also been active in providing much-needed foreign aid through different agency channels.

This book is a record of what private groups and individuals have accomplished, as well as a candid analysis of some of the problems, disappointments, and frustrations associated with foreign aid, both public and private. It is fundamentally a success story. The authors document the foundation policies and program interests behind aid in the international arena and trace the shifts that have occurred since the Rockefeller Foundation initiated the projects that helped eradicate hookworm, yellow fever, and malaria around the globe more than 60 years ago. They also offer examples of the joint efforts of private volunteer organizations and U.S. government agencies such as AID as proof of the positive results that can be obtained through cooperation between the private and public sectors.

Landrum R. Bolling is research professor of diplomacy at the Institute for the Study of Diplomacy at Georgetown University's School of Foreign Service. He has also served as president of Earlham College and chairman of the Council on Foundations. **Craig Smith** is an independent consultant based in Washington, D.C. His clients include the White House and the UN, for which he is engaged in an effort to build ties between governments and philanthropic organizations.

PUBLISHED IN COOPERATION WITH
THE COUNCIL ON FOUNDATIONS

Private Foreign Aid

U.S. Philanthropy for Relief and Development

Landrum R. Bolling
with Craig Smith

Westview Press / Boulder, Colorado

Copyright © 1982 by the Council on Foundations, Inc.

Published in 1982 in the United States of America by
Westview Press, Inc.
5500 Central Avenue
Boulder, Colorado 80301
Frederick A. Praeger, President and Publisher

Library of Congress Cataloging in Publication Data
Bolling, Landrum Rymer.
    Private foreign aid.
    Bibliography: p.
    Includes index.
    1. Economic assistance, American. I. Smith, Craig. II. Title.
HC60.B636   361.7'0973   82-1867
ISBN 0-86531-393-8   AACR2

Printed and bound in the United States of America

Contents

Preface

This report is an attempt to examine the issues related to past, present and future U.S. involvement in foreign assistance, and particularly the role of private, voluntary, nongovernmental organizations in those endeavors. It is not an exhaustive, scholarly study of private initiatives in foreign aid, nor is it a philosophical treatise about foreign aid. We seek simply to throw some light on the problems of private grantmaking for international development and to define some of the options. Accordingly, we set down certain basic facts and informed opinions on such questions as these:

- What foreign relief and development services do U.S. voluntary agencies, institutions, and organizations provide, and how?
- Where do private organizations get their funds and how accountable are they for their spending?
- What, if anything, are private organizations doing in the foreign assistance field that government agencies aren't doing just as well or better?
- What, if any, of the foreign assistance activities of government could be just as well or better done by private agencies?
- Do the recipient peoples draw any distinction between, or show any preference for, one form of foreign aid, public or private, over the other?
- What problems have grown out of the increasing use of private organizations to administer aid programs funded by the government? What can be done about them?
- Should the government do more or less to encourage the involvement of private organizations in relief and development programs?
- Are there practical ways in which the various private bodies engaged in foreign aid can work together more effectively?

- Should foundations, corporations, and individual givers expect continuing appeals for contributions to foreign relief and development projects? How can they go about evaluating such appeals?
- Finally, how much good does U.S. assistance, from both government and private sources, do for those who receive it?

Such questions point to the need for more information to back deliberate choices on public policy decisions in determining how the always limited resources, public and private, can be used most effectively. The answers may suggest something about the desired levels of assistance from both private and government agencies. They should also shed some light on what kinds of projects are worthy of support, if and as foreign assistance programs are continued, and what kinds of organizations should undertake them.

We need far more precise knowledge than we now have about what has been accomplished through foreign assistance. We need to know more about which forms and techniques of foreign aid work well and which ones do not. If assistance from developed countries to less developed ones is to continue, that work should be better done. We need practical suggestions about how those desired improvements can be brought about. We also need to arrive at some clear distinction between the national security and the humanitarian reasons for aid and to examine how both purposes can be served effectively and with integrity.

Perhaps of greatest importance, we need a heightened awareness of the human suffering, hunger, poverty, festering resentments, and unfulfilled hopes that lie behind the call for foreign assistance. The administrative and financial issues must be examined somehow against the backdrop of growing understanding of Third World turmoil and Fourth World despair, of the problems of the North-South dialogue and struggle, and of the revolutionary forces that threaten individual states and whole regions. This report is essentially journalistic, based upon extensive interviewing and a review of the literature. We have deliberately sought out a variety of interested participants and observers. We have drawn from them a diversity of facts and opinions. Obviously, they do not all agree on some of the basic issues.

A number of individuals with experience working abroad in an assortment of private voluntary organizations, and representatives of a few foundations and corporations that support them, encouraged us to undertake this study. Part of that encouragement came from a two-day seminar organized under the leadership of the Overseas Development Council and attended by 40 representatives of foundations, corporations, and PVOs. Funding, in part, was provided by the Ford Foundation, for whose advice and support we are grateful.

Whatever conclusions may be drawn from this report, we hope it will stimulate a broadened discussion of various facets of U.S. involvement in overseas development and will encourage still more comprehensive and intensive research on the results of the foreign assistance programs, both public and private.

Landrum R. Bolling
Washington, D.C.
(Chairman, 1978–1980,
Council on Foundations, Inc.)

Acknowledgments

Within the conventions of publishing, it is sometimes a bit puzzling to know how to designate precisely the authorship of a book. This study probably would not have been written had it not been for the initial work of Patrick Kennedy, former editor of *Foundation News* and long-time staff member of the Council on Foundations, and the help of Shelly Kessler, who interrupted her research activities as a staff member of the Overseas Development Council. Both devoted many weeks to gathering basic materials and conducting interviews with representatives of a number of foundations, corporations, and private voluntary organizations. When they went on with their other duties they turned over to me an invaluable set of notes, tape recordings, and early drafts of materials, which in various ways have been drawn on for segments of several chapters.

Craig Smith came along at just the right time to assist in pulling together the assorted strands of this project. He did a considerable amount of fresh research and an updating of some of the information already in hand. Several chapters, particularly those dealing with PVOs and governmental organizations, are essentially his work. In addition, he gave many useful criticisms and insights overall, drawing upon his experiences in working with and writing about the intergovernmental agencies concerned with development. I am grateful to all three for their assistance.

L.R.B.

Introduction

Assistance to people in need in distant lands is a long-established U.S. tradition. Over many generations, millions of Americans have gathered food and clothing, collected money, or volunteered their time and skills to help the hungry, the sick, the poor, and the homeless in faraway countries. Often, these have been spontaneous responses to man-made or natural disasters. Also, they often have been expressions of sustained concern for the long-term welfare and advancement of other peoples and nations—and of ongoing U.S. relations with them. Numerous intertwining activities by thousands of churches and secular institutions have evolved from that concern.

There has never been any grand design for the many private initiatives to benefit peoples abroad and to build understanding and cooperation between us and them. Yet the complementary nature of these endeavors is remarkable. Despite occasional jurisdictional disputes and inevitable competition for funds, the U.S. private institutions and agencies involved in international activities constitute a very loose "network" that has had an enormous impact upon the affairs of the Third World.

Churches, private foundations, universities and research institutes, multinational corporations, and thousands of private voluntary organizations (commonly called PVOs) are the distinct but interacting segments of that network. Rarely are they discussed as a "system," yet it is impossible to see and understand the full sweep of private foreign aid without taking into account all of these actors and their relations to each other. Moreover, it is essential to examine their relationships with governmental agencies both at home and abroad.

The U.S. government is now involved in foreign disaster relief, somewhere, every year. It also provides several billions of dollars of development assistance to Third World countries every year. Its foreign aid programs operate in so many countries, and for so many reasons, that foreign assistance has, inevitably, taken on controversial political overtones. The issue of foreign aid is frequently debated in the United States, with varying degrees of passion and with different voices raised in denunciation of "giveaways" to "ungrateful" or "hostile" recipients. Yet, year after year, the U.S. Congress allocates more billions to these assistance programs, justifying them primarily in terms of their purported usefulness for U.S. national interests. To some, in and out of Congress, official U.S. economic and technical assistance must be linked to or merged with military aid and can be justified only as it contributes to national security. In practice, the government frequently mingles its economic aid with military assistance and, at times, gives or withholds assistance out of political or security considerations. Even those who downplay the security angle, viewing U.S. involvement in development abroad as a worthy humanitarian goal in itself, often link foreign aid to broad political objectives of opposing communism and winning friends and allies for the United States. Both at home and abroad, people argue endlessly over the motivations behind U.S. foreign aid—and over the results.

The history of U.S. government participation in foreign assistance goes back a long way. The first official U.S. foreign aid shipment, paid for by tax funds, arrived on the coast of South America in 1812, when Yankee sailing vessels delivered several thousand barrels of flour and other supplies to earthquake victims in Venezuela. Countless similar shipments have crossed the seas of the world since then, especially since the beginning of World War I. All along the way, government representatives and funds from the public treasury have had a variety of links with private organizations and their international activities.

During much of our history, churches organized and financed most U.S. relief and reconstruction activities abroad, treating these benevolences as natural extensions of their basic programs for spreading the Christian gospel. American missionaries working in remote places found themselves constantly drawn into efforts to provide medical care, basic education, and practical training for agricultural and industrial modernization. In place after place, they were the first carriers of community development assistance. They were there long before the Peace Corps volunteers, before the U.S. AID (Agency for International Development) representatives, often before any of the native elites from the local urban centers. Most missionaries saw their function as broader than that of seeking religious converts, however strongly convinced they may have been that evangelizing was their prime task. Although not always successful in gaining converts—this was notably the case in Muslim areas—they nevertheless stayed on to carry out humanitarian services as expressions of their religious commitments. Various church bodies eventually set up relief development services—e.g., Catholic Relief, the American Friends Service Committee, the Unitarian Service Committee, and the interdenominational Church World Service—that were and are not involved in evangelizing activities.

Foundations gave substantial sums for the relief of war victims during World War I and afterward. A few of the major ones, starting with the Rockefeller Foundation and its affiliates, took a substantial interest in international health programs and embarked on ambitious and highly effective campaigns to control some of the major diseases that were a heavy burden on millions of people in less developed lands around the globe. During the last half of this century, Rockefeller, Ford, and a few other foundations have become involved in the initiation and support of multifaceted efforts to promote improvements in agriculture and other basic aspects of life in developing countries.

Universities and colleges in the United States have received many generations of young people from overseas for undergraduate, professional, and graduate training—tens of thousands of them from the emerging new nations that had, initially, very limited opportunities for higher education. The American contribution to the national development of those new countries through the education of their leaders has been enormous. Moreover, the larger universities have engaged in extensive research on problems of the developing world, at times entering into contracts to aid development directly by setting up indigenous educational services and institutions. One should not overlook the contributions of American specialists who have come to know intimately the problems and needs of the Third World and who have used that knowledge to help find realistic solutions.

The private voluntary organizations (PVOs) working on international issues and needs are legion. They come in all sizes and shapes, varying greatly in resources, in programs, and in effectiveness. Some of them have been around since World War I or before, and there has been a great proliferation of them since World War II. Although the need to distribute emergency relief often provided the original organizing motivation, a large percentage of them have by now moved into development activities as their primary objective. The training of farmers and nurses, the drilling of sanitary wells, the setting up of demonstration farms, the operating of birth control clinics — these are but a sampling of the myriad services provided by PVOs. Increasingly, both U.S. AID and UN assistance agencies have turned to the PVOs to carry out grass-roots applications of some large governmental policies.

Multinational corporations, subject to attack in some circles, are also an undeniably important segment of the network of private instruments for international development. Their normal profit-seeking activities in mining, manufacturing, or trading, for example, give them crucial roles in the economic life of the countries where they operate. The less developed the country or the greater its dependence on high-level technology for the exploitation of some precious natural resource, the more it needs the skills and marketing connections of the foreign corporations. Once established within a country, the transnational firm becomes involved in a variety of local problems and may help fill needs beyond those directly related to its primary business. Although most firms make a point of avoiding publicity about their philanthropies abroad, there are numerous cases of profit-making businesses carrying out social projects or contributing money, technical personnel, or in-kind gifts of machinery and supplies for development programs.

Private-public interrelationships in foreign assistance are inevitably complicated and often perplexing and frustrating, for both the government and the private organizations. Yet the partnership continues and will probably survive, despite the unending arguments over foreign aid, whatever its nature.

Today, PVOs and U.S. government agencies work together in many lands, and "co-financing" of foreign aid by government and private agencies is more and more taken for granted. At times, private aid organizations function in such close coordination with governmental agencies, drawing their financial support extensively, if not completely, from U.S. tax funds, that they almost seem to be official arms of the government. In other cases PVOs and the U.S. government work quite independently of one another.

On occasion, the assistance programs of the PVOs have encountered, even among the people being helped, a backlash of suspicion, criticism, and hostility simply because U.S. organizations run them, whether financed by government funds or not. Groups opposed to the United States, of course, accuse the PVOs of being tools of the U.S. government. The interweaving of the U.S. national interest, as perceived by public officials, with humanitarian concerns, as interpreted by churches and private service-to-mankind agencies, has led at times to misunderstandings here and overseas. Public and private interests are not always compatible, but they often seem to mesh to everyone's satisfaction, as well as to the good of the people they help.

Despite misunderstandings and suspicions, most of the less developed countries still welcome the assistance of U.S. foundations, multinational corporations, and PVOs. These groups continue to participate in development activities in more than a hundred countries around the globe, operating and being accepted on the belief that they still have significant services to perform and that they can perform them effectively.

Nevertheless, searching questions continue to challenge U.S. foreign aid, both public and private: What is the case for U.S. foreign aid today? Is the case for private agency involvement in overseas assistance still sound? What are the development tasks most suitable for private organizations to undertake?

One trouble with foreign assistance may be that it has been around so long, its administration is so clouded by controversy, and the results are so inconclusive that many Americans have grown weary of the whole subject. As our own self-interests have been increasingly affected by inflation, high taxes, crime, unemployment, high interest rates, and other domestic problems, the needs of poor people overseas seem somehow less vital.

What we know with absolute certainty is that the impoverished masses of the world will continue to struggle to rise out of their misery, and that they will continue to demand help from the advanced nations — and not always politely. Moreover, the time is gone when we could shut our ears and our minds to their appeals.

According to ancient wisdom, we will have the poor with us always. For most of human history, however, poverty was experienced as a local phenomenon, visible in our immediate neighborhood, community, or tribe. The poverty in another town or another tribe was *their* affair, and nobody needed to be aware of it, much less feel impelled to do anything about it. Not so today. In an age of instantaneous, satellite-linked communication we see in vivid color the wounds of those who have become the victims of man-made or natural disasters. We look through a lighted tube into the faces of the sick and the hungry. We hear the very explosions of shells fired in anger half a world away, and we watch the destruction of people and their possessions by the violence of men and of nature. We no longer have the protection of unawareness.

Down through the ages all the great religions of the world have tried to make their followers sensitive to the needs of the poor and to inspire acts of generosity to help them. Only in the modern era, however, have those teachings been translated into broad social policy goals that trouble the consciences of many peoples in many lands and help to determine some of the work that governments do. Moreover, with growing awareness of the economic and political inter-relatedness of all people, the more developed nations have begun to see significant elements of self-interest in helping the people of the less developed countries—particularly in helping them to help themselves. Two world wars and the freeing of hundreds of millions of people in Asia and Africa from colonial status have been major factors in developing our current awareness of great needs and of the challenge to help.

PART ONE

The Long Emergence of Private Foreign Aid

1

War Relief Activities and Their Aftermath

World War I and World War II altered many things in the relationships among nations and peoples. Those global upheavals gave rise to the broad, prolonged, though fluctuating foreign assistance involvements of the American people with the human service needs of many foreign lands, as well as with an assortment of other international issues and causes.

Consider private U.S. efforts to stay out of World War I. Long before the United States itself became a belligerent, American pacifists of various persuasions tried to stop the "Great War" and to define and promote the principles on which a lasting peace could be established. In 1915 Henry Ford chartered a Peace Ship, at a personal cost of about $500,000, and sailed to Europe to dramatize the need for mediation to settle the conflict. With him went ministers, college professors, feminists, social reformers of diverse views, journalists, and a few prominent business people and professionals. They were by no means united in what they hoped to accomplish, and the press, predictably, ridiculed the expedition. Clearly, they did not stop the war. However, out of this curious adventure came a "Conference for Continuous Mediation" and a number of peacemaking ideas such as "self-determination, disarmament, and a league of nations," well before Woodrow Wilson incorporated them into his Fourteen Points. (For a fascinating treatment of this period, see Merle Curti's *American Philanthropy Abroad*, Rutgers University Press, 1963.)

It would be absurd to suggest a direct link between Henry Ford's Peace Ship of 1915 and the globe-circling activities of the Ford Foundation after the 1940s. And yet, there is at least an intriguing symbolic omen here: the rugged individualist automaker, Henry Ford,

9

caught up in his first major public philanthropy in the midst of World War I, foreshadowing the vast international programs of the Ford Foundation after World War II.

The kind of foreign aid involvement that touched Americans most significantly at the beginning of the twentieth century was, of course, emergency relief for the sick, wounded, and hungry victims of war. Beginning immediately after hostilities broke out, the American Red Cross sent supplies, teams of doctors and nurses, and whole hospital units to aid war victims in Russia, Germany, Austria-Hungary, Serbia, and France.

The Rockefeller Foundation created a War Relief Commission before the end of 1914 and during the following four years spent many millions of dollars on such projects as food supplies for Belgium, an anti-typhus campaign in Serbia, the care of prisoners of war on both sides, and medical services for the sick and wounded. In time these relief activities, which had always been heavily weighted on the side of the Allies, shifted entirely to that side when the United States joined them as co-belligerent in 1917.

Both before and after the beginning of direct U.S. involvement, World War I brought an amazing outpouring of American concern, gifts of money and goods, and volunteers to minister to people in need abroad. Numerous special war relief associations, set up on a national or ethnic basis, were created to help the Belgians, the French, the Serbians, the Persians, the Romanians, the Russians, the Armenians, the Syrians, the Poles, the Jews, and just about any other group in Europe or the Mediterranean Basin that was touched by the war. The impetus for these activities came, naturally, from the immigrant communities that had settled in America during the previous century that wanted to give aid to their relatives and co-religionists in the "Old Country."

The greatest expression of American concern, however, was directed toward the Belgians, overrun by German armies invading France and threatened with mass starvation because of the Allied blockade. The Belgians were so clearly innocent victims of un-provoked aggression that their plight evoked immediate sympathy in the United States. A Commission on Belgian Relief was created, headed by Herbert Hoover, who was catapulted overnight into a position of world prominence that steered him on the path to the White House. Local organizations and fundraising campaigns to help the Belgians sprang up across the country. Newspapers and magazines aided the crusade, as did churches, chambers of commerce, wealthy individuals, the Rockefeller Foundation, and the governments of the United States, Canada, Britain, and other nations.

Belgian relief was a demonstration of the huge potential for private charitable responses to the clearly perceived needs of unknown people in a small and distant land. It gave proof of the workability of "co-funding" by private agencies and government for international activities. It also provided valuable practical lessons and inspiration for other relief programs that carried over into the postwar period and involved the problems of refugees, war orphans, amputees, and the reconstruction of homes, schools, and cultural monuments. At the end of the war, Herbert Hoover, acting through the American Relief Administration, assumed broadened responsibilities for U.S. relief activities throughout Europe, including Germany and the Soviet Union.

A partial list of the ways in which private organizations in the United States engaged in overseas assistance during World War I and the years immediately following indicates the extraordinary diversity of philanthropic activities in this country: The Amalgamated Clothing Workers and the International Ladies Garment Workers Unions organized their members and those of the other unions to give one day's pay for foreign relief; the Daughters of the American Revolution and many other women's groups prepared millions of surgical dressings; Gertrude Stein went in person to deliver medical supplies to hospitals in the provinces of France; Julius Rosenwald made gifts of more than two million dollars during one year in connection with a Jewish Relief campaign; the Smith College alumnae set up their own Smith College Relief Unit, which they staffed and funded to work in France; Drew Pearson and other young people attached to a Friends unit helped build houses for homeless Montenegrins in the Balkan Mountains; the Carnegie Endowment for International Peace and John D. Rockefeller, Jr., gave several million dollars to help restore damaged architectural treasures in France; the Commonwealth Fund provided grants for the relief of Armenian refugees; the Italian War Relief Fund of America worked with organizations in Italy to carry out a campaign against tuberculosis; Nicholas Murray Butler, president of Columbia University, mobilized thousands of school children and college students to gather gifts to help rebuild the destroyed library at the University of Louvain. The story is endless.

Many of the organizations active during World War I and its after-

math have, of course, disappeared. Others continued through the
1920s and beyond, and some are today more active than ever. The
American Red Cross, linked to other Red Cross organizations, continues to be a major channel for American assistance abroad. The
American Friends Service Committee, launched in 1917 with a unit
of Quaker relief and reconstruction workers attached to the civilian
branch of the American Red Cross, came into its own with an
assignment from the American Relief Administration in 1919 to
handle a large-scale food program for undernourished children in
Germany.

Since then, other church-related international service agencies
have been set up by the Mennonites, the Brethren, the Unitarians,
the Lutherans and the Catholics. The Quakers, the Mennonites and
the Lutherans gained much of their expertise for administrating
relief programs and other international activities from their work in
Germany immediately following World War I—work that evoked
considerable controversy because of lingering public bitterness
against the Germans and the widespread feeling that their postwar
suffering "served them right."

The political ambiguities of U.S. assistance to foreign people in
distress have been nowhere better illustrated than in connection with
post-World War I relief help for the Russians. As described by Merle
Curti, "Of all American overseas relief programs in the aftermath of
the war, the largest and most complex in character was that inaugurated for the Soviet Union in the summer of 1921."

As far back as 1917, long before the war had ended, representatives of the United States had negotiated with the newly installed
communist leaders in the hope that promises of U.S. aid would
bring a promise by Lenin's revolutionary government that it would
continue a second-front war against the Germans. This Lenin refused to do. Later, as Russian counterrevolutionary forces maintained their struggle against the Red Army, American food and other
supplies came to be used as a kind of political weapon to aid the
White Russian efforts to overthrow the Bolsheviks. Those efforts
failed. By early 1921 there were clear signs of a rapidly spreading
famine in various parts of Soviet Russia. Whatever their politics,
millions of Soviet citizens faced starvation. Thousands died, and
there were gruesome reports of cannibalism.

The United States had no diplomatic relations with the revolutionary leaders in Moscow, but the new government of President
Warren Harding was willing to consider sending relief supplies as a
humanitarian gesture. Herbert Hoover, by this time Secretary of

Commerce, had retained nominal control of the American Relief Administration, which, though winding down in Western and Central Europe, still had about $10 million that could be transferred to Russian relief. The U.S. Congress appropriated funds to purchase grain for Russian relief; $4 million worth of army surplus goods and medical supplies were funneled through the American Red Cross. Encouraged by Hoover, many private American groups were stimulated to raise money; to collect clothing, blankets and other goods; and to send volunteers to supervise the massive relief program. Altogether, more than $80 million worth of U.S. assistance flowed into the Soviet Union during this period, and more than ten million Soviet citizens received food supplies. Meanwhile, the Soviet government contributed over $25 million to the relief effort, drawn from its gold reserves and local currency.

In addition to the American Red Cross, the private organizations that played significant roles in the collection of money and gifts in kind included: various trade union organizations, particularly those in the garment, furrier and hat-making trades, which had many members from Russian-Jewish immigrant families; various religious groups such as Southern Baptists, Lutherans, Mennonites, and Catholics; the YMCA and the YWCA; special *ad hoc* committees, clubs and associations established to promote private giving for Russian famine relief; and several leftist and communist groups devoted to propagandizing for the Bolshevik Revolution and for American friendship with the Soviet Union. The activities of these leftist and communist organizations upset many Americans; some denounced the whole idea of helping feed people who, willingly or not, lived under a government dedicated to the spread of communism throughout the world. And there was understandable annoyance over the ways in which the suspicious and doctrinaire Soviet bureaucracy often created difficulties for the Americans who had gone there to help. Moreover, in America it was a time of recession and anxiety and a so-called Red Scare in many part of the country. Yet, in spite of these inauspicious circumstances, the U.S. government carried through its humanitarian commitments to the people of the USSR, as did the numerous private voluntary agencies that worked in partnership with both the U.S. government and the Soviet authorities. Throughout the period of U.S. involvement in Soviet relief, special roles were played, with strong official backing, by the American Jewish Joint Distribution Committee and the American Friends Service Committee.

Beyond the immediate postwar years, the 1920s and 1930s were not a time of extensive U.S. involvement in foreign assistance. Yet private foundations and church groups did continue to enlarge their overseas activities in education and health services, particularly in India and China (prime missionary fields, it was then thought), and also in parts of Africa and Latin America. Following the Versailles Peace Treaty commitment to implement the Balfour Declaration, which promised Jews a homeland in Palestine, American Jewish organizations became increasingly active in raising funds to support Zionist settlers in the Holy Land and enhance their economic and social development.

In general, U.S. endeavors on behalf of peoples in the under-developed and largely colonial areas of the world had not yet been undertaken on any substantial scale beyond the work of various missionary bodies and the expanding public health activities of the Rockefeller Foundation. The French, British, Dutch, Belgians, Por-tuguese, and, in small measures, the Italians and Spanish were im-perial powers and, as such, had whatever responsibilities ("White Man's Burdens") the advanced nations might be expected to carry for most of what eventually became known as the Developing World. For the United States to have shown much interest in the peoples of these regions in those years probably would have been resented and resisted by the colonial powers, our recent allies. Moreover, with American isolation following World War I, and preoccupation with domestic problems that culminated in the Crash of 1929 and the Great Depression, the American people were in no mood for noble adventures abroad or the costs that went with them.

The Japanese invasion of Manchuria (1931) and the beginning of the long Sino-Japanese war, the Italian conquest of Ethiopia (1936), and the Spanish Civil War (1936–1939) triggered sporadic expres-sions of U.S. indignation, but little else. Some private assistance flowed from the United States to the victims of those wars, but not much. The best-publicized form of U.S. foreign assistance during this period was perhaps the civilian and military help that several politically activist liberal and leftist groups provided the Republican forces in Spain who were struggling against the troops of General Francisco Franco.

Even the progressively horrible evidence during the 1930s and 1940s of persecution of the Jews in Germany, and in other countries to which Hitler's influence extended, did not produce as much car-ing concern and financial assistance as might have been expected from the United States. Jewish organizations and some Christian churches did find ways to assist many individual Jews and family groups that managed to escape. Distinguished Jewish scholars, writers, and artists were helped to continue their careers in this country, enriching many university faculties, research laboratories, and symphony orchestras. U.S. private agency activities on behalf of refugees, to this day, are in large measure the outgrowth of emergency assistance programs developed to aid Jewish emigrés in the 1930s. Yet, the half-hearted efforts to rescue the millions of threatened Jews before their fates were sealed, and the cautious haggling over changes in U.S. immigration laws and regulations to admit larger numbers of European Jews created doubts about U.S. claims of compassionate commitment to foreign peoples in need. Nevertheless, it was during this period of neutrality and ambivalence that the organizational structures and public sympathies were developed for the later massive assistance to Israel and to all kinds of refugees around the globe.

The isolationist mood that prompted the United States to refuse to join the League of Nations was confirmed for many by the ineffectiveness of the league in dealing with wars of aggression launched by Italy and Japan and by its total paralysis in response to the rise of Hitler. Moreover, during the 1930s, journalistic exposés and congressional investigations of the international arms industry led to legislative restraints on the actions of private organizations and government agencies that might seem likely to involve the United States in a foreign war. When World War II broke out in 1939, the North American people were overwhelmingly hostile to Nazi Germany and sympathetic to Britain and France; they were also pro-China and anti-Japan. Yet the "neutrality laws," theoretically, placed inhibiting controls on the impulse to rush again to aid our friends and former allies. Nevertheless, both the govenment, under an interventionist President Franklin Roosevelt, and a variety of established and *ad hoc* private relief agencies began to raise money, roll bandages, collect clothing, and send supplies to distant peoples caught in another great war. (However, when it was proposed that Congress modify the immigration laws to admit 20,000 German Jewish refugee children over the regular quota, the bill was not even voted out of committee.)

Despite widespread determination to stay out of World War II, and despite the laws that encouraged neutrality, the human suffering produced by war had a profound emotional effect upon the American people. Both Catholics and Protestants set up national war relief committees. Trade union groups became involved in overseas relief again, as they had during World War I. Hollywood stars and other entertainers held benefit performances, and millions of individuals came forth with gifts to support the work of such organizations as Bundles for Britian, the British-American Ambulance Corps, the American Friends of France, the Finnish Relief Fund, the Commission for Polish Relief, the American Committee for Medical Aid to Russia, United China Relief, the Greek War Relief Association, and many others. More than 350 U.S. war-relief agencies registered under the Neutrality Act before the war was one year old. Meanwhile, the U.S. government began to pour food supplies and funds into relief programs for the benefit of civilian war victims—circumventing in various ways the restrictions on helping the military effort of the side we favored.

As private relief agencies proliferated in the United States, and particularly after the Pearl Harbor attack brought the country into the war, the government moved to establish substantial controls over the many nongovernmental relief organizations. The President's War Relief Control Board took on the task of maintaining comprehensive oversight, defining ethical standards for relief solicitation, setting accounting procedures, and registering fundraising groups. One of its main responsibilities was to reduce the number of relief organizations through mergers—only one per foreign country, if possible—and to coordinate the timing of fund drives. For example, no foreign relief agency solicitation could take place during drives for the American Red Cross or for the sale of U.S. war bonds. Moreover, pressure was exerted to get various private agencies to change their names to incorporate the word "American." The French Relief Fund was renamed American Relief for France; the Queen Wilhelmina Fund became American Relief for Holland. With government prompting, the National War Fund, a private organization with strong government ties, was established to provide one comprehensive, coordinating mechanism to reduce competition, cut overhead, and promote the widest possible public support for a variety of charitable programs administered by agencies certified by the War Relief Control Board. In short, private philanthropy abroad became an integral part of the overall U.S. war effort.

Partnership between the U.S. government and U.S. private agencies working overseas, hammered out under the strains of war, was also the pattern for much of the relief and rehabilitation work that gained its full momentum only after the tides of battle had passed. At the end of 1942 the U.S. government committed itself to a massive, long-term effort to aid the needy survivors of war by creating the Office of Foreign Relief and Rehabilitation Operations (OFRRO).

Governor Herbert H. Lehman of New York, at President Roosevelt's urging, resigned his state post to take charge of OFRRO and lead the national drive to gather food and other supplies for the millions of needy people in the war-ravaged areas. As the conflict moved toward a climax, the allies intensified their efforts to create a framework for postwar cooperation and to plan the United Nations structure. One of the first practical results of these efforts was the creation at the end of 1943 of the United Nations Relief and Rehabilitation Administration (UNRRA), into which OFRRO was absorbed and for which Governor Lehman became the director-general. Of course, UNRRA, financed primarily by U.S. tax dollars, vastly overshadowed the combined activities of all the volunteer agencies that had provided most of the civilian relief supplies during most of the war. Yet neither the massive deliveries from UNRRA nor the civilian relief role the U.S. Army came to play in areas it occupied ruled out the work of the voluntary agencies. On the contrary, they greatly enlarged their activities in the last two years of the war and in the immediate postwar period. According to a report of the War Relief Control Board, the total funds sent abroad by the voluntary agencies rose from $44,893,933 in 1943 to $72,072,934 in 1944 and to $87,416,654 in 1945. During those three years, the value of gifts in kind — foodstuffs, blankets, clothes, medicine — acquired by private donations rose from $11,250,027 in 1943 to $26,933,033 in 1944 to $141,997,374 in 1945. Naturally, the ending of the war opened the way for the delivery of relief shipments throughout Europe and made it possible to gain wide public awareness of how great the need was.

Although most of the expanded U.S. voluntary assistance went to the western Europeans who had been our allies, substantial assistance also went to the Germans, Austrians, and Italians. Again, as after World War I, there was also the controversial question of relief supplies to the peoples of the USSR. Because they fought the war on our side, and because they suffered greater casualties than all the other allies combined, sympathies in this country toward the people of the Soviet Union produced a substantial outpouring of clothing, food, agricultural seeds, medicines, and money. Russian War Relief and the Jewish Council for Russian Relief were two of the principal organizations that organized and carried through the solicitation campaigns. Despite its great wartime losses, the Soviet Union provided shipping for much of these supplies in its own ships and set up distribution through its own social service agencies. American relief workers were not needed or wanted this time.

Meanwhile, the needs of war victims in the other great theatre of World War II, Asia, were also being addressed by certain special voluntary agencies such as United China Relief, the Mennonite Relief Committee of India, and American Relief for India, and by global-minded organizations such as the American Red Cross and the American Friends Service Committee. Still other voluntary agencies sought to aid people in need in Ethiopia, the Greek Islands, Poland, Morocco, Libya, Tunisia, and Algeria.

Of all the special groups attracting the assistance of voluntary organizations, none stirred deeper emotions than the Jewish survivors of the Holocaust—those found still alive in the concentration camps and those who had fled from Nazi-occupied territory to sanctuaries around the globe: China, Sweden, Portugal, Switzerland, Mexico, Iran, Brazil, Argentina, Palestine. To feed, clothe, retrain, transport and resettle them in permanent homes was a task that required enormous sums of money, great resourcefulness and organizational skills, and high diplomacy. (Millions of dollars raised during the war went to the ransoming of Jews from Nazi officials themselves.) It is not appropriate here to summarize the story of the American Joint Distribution Committee and the other agencies associated with the United Jewish Appeal. It must be noted, however, that of all forms of voluntary foreign assistance provided from the United States to people in need abroad, the most generous giving per giver and per recipient, year after year, has been directed to the benefit of a people Adolf Hitler marked for extinction. Those who had been destroyed could not be brought back to life, but those who had survived could be helped—not just to survive, but to rebuild a good life and develop a new homeland.

2

From War Zone Relief to Global Development

Even as the world struggled with the vast relief and reconstruction of the countries devastated by World War II, other foreign-assistance ideas were beginning to emerge. Long-term U.S. strategies for aiding many nations with their economic and social development problems came to the fore. Loans, credits, and gifts of war surpluses flowed to our allies to help them through the first arduous months of peace. The PVOs distributed food and blankets and brought in seeds and tools. The U.S. military forces provided many types of reconstruction assistance, particularly in occupied territories. UNRRA expanded its help in the form of food, machinery, and reconstruction supplies. Eventually the Marshall Plan emerged with its massive credits to bring about a comprehensive rebuilding of Western Europe. (The Soviet bloc countries were offered the opportunity to participate, but the Soviet Union demanded that they all refuse the proffered "capitalist" assistance.) Finally, plans for global social and economic development evolved, made possible by U.S. financing, know-how, and idealistic good will.

The United States' primary world leadership position encouraged a belief that virtually all of mankind's problems could be solved by the use of U.S. power, influence, and money. It was thought that our military strength could prevent violent revolutions and war and could be used to build world stability. Our advice, our loans, and our gifts, it seemed, would promote economic and social progress everywhere. The daring and generosity of Lend-Lease and the Marshall Plan and the implications of the Truman Doctrine and the Bretton Woods monetary system all heralded what some briefly called the "American Century." Optimism and idealism were triumphant—nothing seemed impossible.

At the same time, there was an acute apprehension about the intentions of the Soviet Union and about the possibilities of communist inspired revolutions in many lands. The wartime alliance of Western Europe and America with the Soviet Union was beset by deep suspicion and tensions even before the military victory was won. These intensified as the problems of the shared occupation of Germany and Austria became clear and congealed into the Cold War; rivalries for postwar influence showed up in virtually every quarter of the globe. Western fears of communist expansion followed swiftly on the heels of victory. Soviet fears of America's industrial superiority and the atom bomb monopoly grew in tandem.

The United States and its Western allies were disturbed over the prompt and ruthless manner in which communist or procommunist regimes came to power in the countries the Red Army occupied or helped to liberate: Poland, Bulgaria, Hungary, Czechoslovakia, Yugoslavia. They were alarmed by the way an aggressive, Soviet-blessed faction struggled to seize control, and almost succeeded, in Greece just before and immediately after the war was over. They were sobered by the determined postwar drive toward influence and power by communist parties throughout Western Europe. The spectre of communist-led revolutions spreading westward to the shores of the Atlantic and beyond may, to some, have seemed far-fetched many years later, but in 1945 and for some time thereafter, the threat was very real to many Western leaders. The Truman Doctrine, offering economic and military assistance to Greece and Turkey, was proclaimed in 1947 to check a perceived communist threat in the eastern Mediterranean. The Marshall Plan, initiated in 1949 with billions of dollars of assistance for the restoration of Western Europe, spurred economic recovery at a remarkable rate; Winston Churchill praised it as the most generous act in the history of intergovernmental relations. Meanwhile, the North Atlantic Treaty Organization (NATO) was created as an anticommunist western defense alliance. In the United Nations, backed by a huge majority, the United States largely had its way.

Events in 1949 and 1950 began to threaten America's international dominance. The victory of the Communist Chinese in mainland China, the Soviet detonation of an atomic bomb, and the North Korean attack on South Korea challenged any assumption that the United States could control the course of history in all parts of the world. These events also helped to make foreign aid unmistakably an adjunct to defense policy. Military assistance came to overshadow economic assistance, even in some developing countries with no immediately discernible military needs.

Foreign aid thus became a tool in fortifying the world against Soviet and Communist expansion. Who received what became dependent, in part, on the quirks of geography that gave one nation greater strategic importance for the United States than another — and the quirks of politics that gave one country more of an internal communist threat than another. Cynics sometimes said that unless a country had a substantial communist party, it had little chance of getting much American aid.

The argument, widely accepted, was that the promotion of economic well-being was one of the most promising ways of immunizing a people against communism. Judging by the success of the Marshall Plan in speeding Western Europe's recovery, and the failure of the communists to gain control in any of the Marshall Plan countries, the argument seemed to have merit. In any case, the worldwide American foreign aid program — administered by a succession of such agencies as the Economic Cooperation Administration, the Mutual Security Agency, the Foreign Operations Administration, the Technical Cooperation Administration, the International Cooperation Administration, the Development Loan Fund and the Agency for International Development — has reflected a combination of motivations not unrelated to the motivations that prompted the immediate postwar assistance to Western Europe. Concern for checking the spread of communism has been real; the desire to acquire dependable allies in strategic parts of the world also has been a factor. Yet other elements of self-interest have been present as well. The U.S. economy is, in important ways, dependent on a number of other countries, many of them underdeveloped, for crucial raw materials and energy supplies. Moreover, the developing countries, as they progress, have increasingly become profitable markets for U.S. manufactured goods and, at times, for farm surpluses. For those countries to be stable and advancing toward their development goals is advantageous to the United States economically and politically.

Although U.S. foreign aid concentrated on military assistance throughout the 1950s, there were exceptions. The major exception was Public Law 480 of 1954. Called "Food for Peace," it permitted surplus food from the United States to be sold for local currencies, which were then spent locally for nonmilitary and military projects and programs. Public Law 480 has continued to be an integral part of U.S. foreign aid ever since, although its purpose and long-term impact are still controversial. Much of that food has been distributed by U.S. PVOs.

The emergence in Asia and Africa in the 1950s and 1960s of more than eighty independent new nations, encompassing 800 million people, challenged the United States with an almost unlimited opportunity to become the guiding force of the developing world. Max F. Millikans and Walter Rostow, in their book *A Proposal: Key to an Effective Foreign Policy*, published in 1957, urged an expanded U.S. assistance program for the "economic development of the underdeveloped areas." "Such a program," they argued, would make the peoples of the world see that "their goals and those of the United States were identical and would lead to viable, energetic and confident democratic societies through the free world."

The opportunity for such world leadership and power was a heady prospect, and one that inspired hope and idealism. President Kennedy, at the beginning of his administration, initiated a series of steps to intensify U.S. global involvement and put increased emphasis on the Third World. Kennedy saw the 1960s as "an historic opportunity for major economic assistance efforts by the free industrialized nations to move more than half of the people of the less-developed nations into self-sustaining economic growth."

The Truman administration's position on foreign assistance had been primarily one of benevolent protection: low level assistance with the assurance of defense against communist takeover. The Eisenhower administration had concentrated on strengthening relations with existing friendly regimes so as to create effective military allies. Kennedy, however, readjusted the focus of foreign aid and brought the social and economic development needs of the Third World to the fore among U.S. foreign-policy objectives. The hope was that by helping the underdeveloped nations they would, one by one, eventually achieve steady self-sustaining economic growth within a democratic political structure, and be part of a network of noncommunist, pro-Western developing countries.

In June 1961, the President's Task Force on Foreign Economic Assistance, in a summary presentation to Congress, explained the administration's proposed Act for International Development. It stated: "One of the most critical circumstances of today is that the underprivileged masses in less developed areas of the free world have a passionate aspiration toward economic, social and political change. . . . This is a 'Decade of Decision' . . . the only acceptable course for industrialized nations of the free world is to provide external aid to the underdeveloped world and thereby to help turn a decade of crisis into a decade of development of growth within a free society. . . . "

The Agency for International Development (AID) was created to administer enlarged and new foreign aid programs. The first major foreign policy initiative of Kennedy's New Frontier was the Alliance for Progress and the subsequent pledge in the Charter of Punta Del Este to begin massive economic restructuring in Latin America, to mend the ragged relationship between the U.S. and its neighbors south of the border, and to secure them against violent insurrections. Soon the alliance was seen to be a failure, partially because of unrealistic expectations, partially because of the inability of the partners to work in concert, and partially, perhaps, because of waning U.S. attention and commitment. Kennedy admitted that it "failed to some degree because the problems were insuperable. . . . The road seems longer than it was when the journey started." This sobering discovery was an early indication to the policy planners that development was a slow and arduous process, the best means for which were elusive.

Another Kennedy foreign aid initiative, the Peace Corps, with its army of young volunteers sent to remote rural areas of the world, proved more enduring. Its success came not from big budget programs (seldom more than $100 million annually), but from the impact upon the volunteers who returned home with some better understanding of foreign cultures than could be attained from books, films, and the daily news. Moreover, some tangible benefits for the local people came from the work attempted and, in most cases, some human good will was left behind. (Long years afterward, some Reagan administration advisors urged sharp cuts in the Peace Corps on the grounds that its contributions to development were dubious—that the chief beneficiaries were the Peace Corps volunteers themselves.)

Although well-intentioned, Kennedy's New Frontier hit the same kinds of snags in trying to convince the country of the validity of development assistance that frustrated earlier (and later) administrations. Again and again, Cold War fears were decisive in overcoming public resistance and congressional opposition to foreign aid.

At the same time, some proponents of foreign aid, notably Senator Hubert H. Humphrey, repeatedly expressed genuinely altruistic, ethical, and moral purposes that led them to sponsor legislation and annual appropriation measures to strengthen and extend U.S. governmental assistance to needy and developing nations. From these idealistic impulses, as well as certain practical administrative considerations, fresh attention was given to PVOs as effective instruments for promoting development and dispensing relief. Moreover, the PVOs, in their voluntary endeavors abroad, helped convey the image of Americans moved by a desire to respond to human need without regard for national political self-interest.

With both private and governmental foreign assistance since World War II there has been a growing shift from programs of relief to long-term programs of development; government funds have become available for development projects. Given the capriciousness of natural disasters, short-term relief will continue to be needed from time to time in both developed and underdeveloped countries. Yet most foreign assistance is and will continue to be directed toward broad development programs in the Third World for bringing about technical, social, cultural, and economic changes to advance the general well-being of the people. Significantly, assistance will be directed at helping people help themselves.

That goal, too, has proved to be elusive. It is often difficult to give or receive help without creating dependence and resentment, and frequently new problems arise in place of the ones for which assistance was given in the first place. This is one of many lessons from the last quarter century of experience with foreign aid.

Foreign assistance programs have helped to expand food production, to eliminate or control certain diseases, and to reduce death rates. But such changes, if there is no drop in the birth rate, may simply compound the problems of poverty, with still too many mouths to feed from the too limited supply of food. Such is one of the most generally noted dilemmas of development.

The great drought of the early 1970s in the Sahel region of western Africa may have been related in part to the success of development among the primitive nomadic tribes in Niger, Upper Volta, Chad, and Mali. Foreign assistance there introduced modern medical and technological improvements that made possible dramatic increases in the populations of both cattle and people. Pest control, vaccination, and the drilling of more wells in the scrubby rangeland led to great expansion in the herds that the land was expected to carry. For the herdsmen tribes this was progress, but such success brought its own tragedy, made worse by cyclical changes in the scanty rainfall pattern. The enlarged herds cropped the grasses, weeds, and bushes closer and closer, destroying fragile root systems and turning vast areas into barren sand dunes, particularly around the new water holes. As the vegetation disappeared hundreds of thousands of cattle died. Many people went hungry, became sick, and perished. Mass starvation was averted only by merciful (and outrageously expensive) airlifting of grain and dried milk from America and other distant lands.

Despite such difficulties and ironic dilemmas in development, the search for a better life goes on in all the developing countries, and the technologically advanced nations continue to offer help. To help intelligently and effectively we need to know more than we have known or understood in the past about what assistance programs really work, and we need to be flexible enough to make the necessary changes. What are the realistic development prospects for the near and longer future? What are the true needs and desires of the peoples of the developing Third World? Limitless, almost. Unfulfillable, for sure. But they are needs and desires that they, and most likely we, will continue to try to meet in some measure.

As a generalization, it can be said that the less developed countries (LDCs) want to bring to their people the benefits of science and technology. They want to extend modern health care, even if they cling to certain primitive traditions in medicine. They want to improve and expand services in transportation and communication. They want to be able to run whatever industries have already been erected, and to establish more. They want to expand their food production and make their farming methods more efficient. They want a great increase in educational opportunities for their young people, and they have demonstrated the reality of that interest with national budgets that make remarkably large allocations to education. In all these matters they want substantial assistance from developed countries, but they want it without strings.

There are some things that they and people of the advanced countries can do rather well working together: Roads can be built, electric power lines can be strung, schooling can be expanded, food production can be increased, medical services can be extended, GNPs can be enlarged. All these things they are working to achieve. For all the billions invested in Third World development by the United States and other advanced countries, by international agencies such as the World Bank, and by voluntary agencies and their donors, far and away the largest investments in development have been made by the developing countries themselves. Except for the oil-rich few among them, they are forever short of capital. They save what they can, they borrow all that foreign bankers will lend them. But it is never enough.

The money and labor expended have produced many tangible results—sometimes spectacularly impressive results. Yet enormous problems cast dark shadows over the development efforts of most Third World countries.

Political stability among them is rare, and human rights violations are commonplace. Often it is violence that brings changes of government, not free elections. Corrupt behavior by government officials, something widely experienced in various advanced countries, is a special curse on many of the developing countries. Military men often hold the dominant power and, on occasion, they feud among themselves. Yet, for all these domestic troubles, Third World peoples proudly assert their right of self-determination and most of them are making progress in the training of their own leadership, including civil servants, various professionals, and top administrators. Whatever the nature of their troubles, all people prefer to be ruled by their own.

Being ruled by one's own, however, has not come about automatically for all peoples in the developing world with the end of imperial control. Many former colonies are now artificially constructed polyglot states. The boundaries the colonialists drew were not always in accord with linguistic or tribal realities. Many ethnic groups, some with a profound sense of their distinctiveness, find themselves parcelled out to two or three different nation-states. In some cases a particular ethnic group may be entirely within a given country but feel that it has inferior status compared with one or more ethnic groups that have predominant power. Development programs are sometimes unevenly carried out or handicapped by such internal divisions.

For all the egalitarian talk by the leaders of new nations about "African socialism," "Arab socialism," or other formulations of national goals, the harsh reality is that some individuals and groups profit from the system, whatever it is, a lot more than others. The gap between rich and poor—in their possessions, their life styles, their privileges—is shocking in some economically disadvantaged countries. The elites have sometimes profited tremendously from development, legally or illegally, while the very poor remain very poor indeed, with barely discernible benefits, if any, from foreign assistance and long-established development programs. Seeing this problem, some of the American PVOs have committed themselves to try to bring the benefits of development directly to the grass-roots poor. Such efforts are not always welcomed by the ruling elites. Where such initiatives are attempted on any sizeable scale through U.S. governmental agencies, suspicion, friction and charges of "interference" are almost inescapable. PVOs working on limited-scale projects with grass-roots local organizations often seem able to make significant and practical contributions to help the very poor move a bit forward where vast government programs cannot.

Another tragic problem with which some developing countries have been struggling is armed conflict. Few handicaps to development could be greater than those imposed by civil or international wars. Yet such wars continue, thanks to Big Power rivalries, the abundant supplies of arms and easy credit with which to purchase them, the maddening influence of simplistic revolutionary dogma, nationalistic ambitions of some of the developing states and their rulers, and conventional power struggles between competing political, linguistic, and tribal factions. Deep intractable ethnic rivalries can stall development and produce senseless violence, as has been seen in Nigeria, Pakistan, and India. Other developing countries that have been wracked by war or internal violence include Cambodia, Laos, Vietnam, Afghanistan, North Yemen, Angola, Ethiopia, Somalia, Uganda, Zaire, Chile, Lebanon, Nigeria, Chad, Morocco, Iran, and Iraq. Already impoverished lands that need all the internal and external resources they can draw upon to enable their people to survive and improve their condition have been sucked into the whirlwinds of violence. The scale of human suffering in some of these places has been staggering, and the setback to orderly development is beyond calculation.

Some of the violence in the Third World has been related to the unfinished struggles that accompanied the movements for liberation from colonial rule. Some of it represents popular outbursts against corruption and incompetent or tyrannical rule. Some of it has been produced or enlarged by the competition between the United States and the Soviet Union or between China and the Soviet Union. That these Big Power struggles are fought on the soil and over the broken bodies of the poor people of the Third World is an indictment of all the factions and nations involved; it is a discouraging commentary on the feebleness and malfunctioning of the peacekeeping machinery of the world community, even in relation to weak countries. Man's capacity for inhuman behavior is not softened by arguments that the developing countries can't afford such madness. It can not be claimed that poor, developing countries, freed from the wicked influence of colonialism, are somehow too pure and too noble to engage in mindless violence that blocks their own development.

However, it must be stated that since World War II, competition between the communist and noncommunist power centers has produced in some developing countries capital and technical services, and even educational opportunities, that probably would not have been available without the national and ideological rivalries of the Big Powers. In spite of—maybe even because of—the armed conflicts that drew the support of the Big Powers, some aspects of development in some places, for a time, have been accelerated. But what a price to pay!

Of all the handicaps to development, few are more difficult to deal with than the towering problems of psycho-social destabilization that come with modernization. However passionately the peoples of the developing world want to acquire the skills, the technologies, the educational resources, the practical know-how, and the symbols and household conveniences of the developed world, many of them go through great trauma along the way. One example is the social degradation symbolized by the appalling shanty-town slums on the outskirts of Kampala, Beirut, Bombay, Cairo, or Lagos, where young people from the hinterland have drifted in looking for work and urban excitement. Often they become the "de-tribalized" victims of social change, rejecting the old ways and the old family and village structures, but with no new rootage for their lives.

That trauma is also reflected in the strident and often violent attacks on existing power structures by religious "fundamentalists" of one kind or another who appear to want to stop social change in its tracks and return to ancient ways and beliefs. Such attitudes seem to have motivated the attack by schismatic Saudi Muslims on the Great Mosque in Mecca in late 1979. Such feelings also were exploited by those who led the street mobs in the overthrow of the Shah in Iran and, later, the seizure of the American Embassy.

Whatever may be said about the turmoil in Iran, Shah Reza Pahlavi and the Ayatollah Khomeini are highly instructive symbols of the psycho-social destabilization in development. The Shah was for many years a kind of Exhibit A for modernization and industrialization of a developing country, backed fully by the U.S. government and aided by thousands of American experts of every conceivable kind. The Shah produced a great deal of modernizing, westernizing "progress." Yet much of what accompanied that "progress" was bitterly resented and resisted as subversive of the local culture. There are many lessons to be learned from the Iranian revolution, but it is important that serious efforts be made to explore in depth the relationships between that particular model of development, as it was carried out, and the upheaval that occurred.

From the accumulated criticisms of development in many lands, there emerge several lessons about development that must be weighed in planning foreign assistance for the future:

- The pace of effective social change, certainly not the same in any two countries, can backfire if forced too fast by impatient social planners, foreign or domestic.
- The upholders of traditional values, wherever possible, should be made the *partners* of developmental change, not the *enemies* of change — although, clearly, that will often not be achievable.
- Foreign advisers and technicians, however honorable their motives, almost inevitably produce suspicion and resentment. The greater their numbers, the higher their visibility, the more blatantly their imported life styles contrast with local norms, the greater the certainty of suspicion and resentment.
- Initiatives in developmental decision making should remain as much as possible in the hands of the local people, who should themselves be the visible and effective agents of their own advancement.
- Assistance programs that are shaped by military considerations linked to U.S. foreign policy objectives — however popular they may be with the U.S. Congress — are severely handicapped and can be easily be made into targets of active local hostility.
- Government assistance programs are likely to concentrate, understandably, on large-scale projects related to building the infrastructures of the modern, technologically advanced society: roads, airports, power stations, communication systems. The payoff in terms of improved standard of living for the people may be a long time coming.
- Many small-scale, village-based experiments in development need to be undertaken and critically appraised. Private voluntary agencies may be better able to assist local people with such projects than the civil service representatives of a foreign government are.
- Government-to-government assistance continues to be important for dealing with many of the major dimensions of development. People-to-people assistance — if it is sensitively

done on a genuinely cooperative rather than paternalistic basis — can bring tangible benefits to the most needy at the grass-roots level.

It is important to recognize that most investment capital in development programs in virtually every developing country comes from the human and physical resources of the local people themselves — not from foreign governments, international organizations, or private donors. It must also be recognized that there are important ways of promoting development other than external loans and grants. In the long run, the growth of the local economy, the achievement of self-sufficiency in food supply, and the expansion and proper balancing of international trade are all highly important factors in achieving the nation-building goals of any developing country. Trade negotiations may, on occasion, have more far-reaching significance than negotiations for a foreign assistance grant or loan; these are issues to be dealt with elsewhere.

PART TWO

Private Support for Foreign Assistance

Introduction

The private agencies that carry on relief and development programs abroad greatly value the private giver. They view volunteer financial contributions as absolutely essential for their current activities and for their continued existence. They want a lot more private gifts than they are getting. They worry about holding the nongovernmental support they have had in the past. They have grave doubts about being able to expand either private or government support in the future.

For organizations that refuse to accept government funding, private gifts, of course, are indispensable. Others that accept government support, whether grudgingly or enthusiastically, find it important to maintain a substantial component of private funding in order to keep their credibility as nongovernmental agencies, if for no other reason. And there are other, perhaps more important reasons to press hard for continuing and expanding private gifts.

From many quarters come essentially the same judgments about the basic significance of private support for private voluntary agencies working in the foreign assistance field. Private support is crucial:

- to enable PVOs to be more flexible and more promptly responsive to emergency needs and unusual program opportunities;
- to strengthen the sense of people-to-people concern and communication that can help maintain a friendly atmosphere for building cooperative, constructive attitudes and working relationships between givers and receivers of assistance;
- to maintain credibility for private international initiatives and private institutions working abroad as truly nonpolitical endeavors rooted in genuine human concern;
- to make possible creative, nontraditional, high-risk new programs;

- to retain some independence from government policies and to reduce the threat of government controls attached to government grants.

The categories of private sources of funds are fairly obvious. Foundations, profit-making corporations, churches, wealthy individuals, and the general public of small givers all play significant roles in providing the needed financing. All their gifts taken together, however, fall far short of what is needed to sustain the private programs of relief and development abroad.

It can be argued, of course, that such private endeavors, however worthy, should be sensibly restricted to a scale that can realistically be funded from private means. Such caution seems to run against human nature and public pressures. Individuals, churches, and volunteer organizations that get caught up in the problems and dire needs of hungry, sick, and uprooted people in impoverished areas of the globe experience constant inner compulsions to do more, to take greater risks, to act on faith and hope that the money will be found somehow. There are enough spectacular success stories of the services accomplished by courageous men and women who took such leaps of faith in reaching out to suffering humanity that realistic financial calculations will be decisive only now and then. Highly motivated individuals committed to these humanitarian causes will continue to reach further than available funds would seem to allow, but there are almost always some generous people around who will come up with at least part of the needed extra money.

Moreover, the managers and policymakers for government aid programs are now thoroughly convinced that it is clearly in the national interest that private voluntary groups be encouraged to carry out an increasing portion of U.S. assistance activities abroad. That is a judgment that has not been weakened by the drastic changes related to the Reagan administration. Within both the public and the private sectors thoughtful concerned people are trying to devise strategies to get private agencies still more deeply involved in overseas relief and development. Whatever else that means, it certainly means increasing pressures for private givers to give.

3

Churches and Individuals

Historically, the private givers of foreign aid were individuals – those who contributed money and those who volunteered their working lives. Most of them made their contributions through religious institutions, either individual churches or organized missionary societies. The traditional overseas evangelizing missions have undergone considerable transformation over the past century, and particularly since the decolonization movement brought independence to scores of developing regions around the globe. Yet individuals and church bodies in the United States still play wide-ranging and significant roles in private foreign aid.

Church Giving

The church-related agencies that work abroad have natural grass-roots constituencies both in the United States and abroad, and, in most cases, a long tradition of denominational support for overseas projects to draw upon. Most of them operate within formal church structures: Baptists, Methodists, Episcopalians, Presbyterians, Catholics, Seventh Day Adventists, Salvation Army, Mormons, Pentecostalists, Lutherans, and many others. They have central administrative offices (once generally called missionary boards), church publications, and local women's societies that carry on activities to inform their fellow church members about programs overseas and to solicit funds. Their programs of relief, education, hospital services, and training in agricultural and industrial skills are usually related to those areas and peoples identified with the churches' missionary projects, some of which go back more than one hundred years.

The potential for volunteer labor and cash contributions from church groups to support foreign assistance programs is enormous. Success in developing that support, of course, varies with the nature of local, regional, and national church leadership and with the extent and quality of personal interaction between field workers sent abroad and the congregations at home. The people who have "been out there" and "served among the native peoples" usually make the most effective spokesmen for these programs when they return for home assignments or, as is increasingly the case, when they complete relatively short-term periods of work abroad on leave from their regular stateside jobs. (It should also be pointed out that local people who can be brought to the United States as "success story" exhibits of programs that have worked effectively are particularly compelling spokesmen with church audiences, and often are highly successful fundraisers.)

In addition to the many denominational missionary programs, two major church-based organizations established since World War II are directly committed to overseas relief and development work: Catholic Relief Services and the Protestants' Church World Service. They do not attempt to carry on the usual activities associated with religious evangelizing, and they are not subsidiaries of traditional missionary boards. That they have many links to church groups in the United States and to emerging local churches in the developing world is obvious. But their mandate is to perform humanitarian services comparable to those undertaken by secular agencies. Both Catholic Relief Services and Church World Service have become the instruments for distributing substantial amounts of the U.S. government's foreign assistance funds and, in particular, large quantities of surplus food stocks. Both organizations also draw considerable support from nonchurch private sources, but it is clear that core funding from the respective networks of church bodies is essential for these programs to exist.

The roles of churches and other religious bodies in providing funds for development programs have always been enormously important. Their true significance, however, can not be measured adequately by the foreign aid moneys they raise. More important is their contribution to the shaping of public opinion on foreign assistance issues. The vast attention given by the media in recent years to the problems of hunger, disease, social unrest, and refugee calamities in foreign lands has helped sensitize the American people as never before to the plight of the less fortunate in the developing world. The "conquest" of world hunger has been raised high as a political goal by important government officials, and it has been energetically promoted by numerous independent volunteer organizations. This cause has been aided by children's house-to-house solicitations, by "telethons," and by sponsored endurance marches. The continuing church activities on behalf of needy people overseas helped to create the climate in which these public demonstrations of support could come forth. Heightened public awareness, in turn, helps the churches carry on their fundraising endeavors for overseas programs under more favorable circumstances, thanks in part to purely secular initiatives. Moreover, there is growing evidence that churches are now willing to give to projects beyond their own parochial organizations and denominational missions.

A few random examples of spontaneous church involvement in overseas assistance programs suggest something of the unpredictable, almost open-ended, nature of the potential for expanding church-related giving.

In 1951, the Reverend John Peters preached a Sunday morning sermon in St. Luke's Methodist Church in Oklahoma City. His subject was world hunger, and he told his congregation that Christians have a duty to do something about it. When the final hymn was sung and the service ended, the congregation refused to go home. A member of the congregation stood up and said, in effect: "We can't leave this matter here. If what our minister has told us about world hunger is true, we have to find a way to act." Others spoke up in agreement. On the spot, they raised five thousand dollars to send a team, including the pastor, to find out what they could do about world hunger and to come back with a plan of action. They went first to Washington, D.C., to confer with government experts, then made an exploratory trip abroad. The result: World Neighbors, Inc., an independent, nonprofit service organization that today has a staff of 43 Americans and 405 foreign nationals abroad. It conducts community development programs in nineteen countries, and in 1980 was operating with a budget of $2.3 million. Every cent of its funds was raised from private contributors, foundations, and corporations, most of it in the form of small donations sent in by mail.

Another illustration: In the mid-1970s, severe drought in the Sahel region of West Africa caused extensive hunger and human suffering in that remote desert area, which came to the attention of a group of church members, many of them farmers, affiliated with a Methodist conference in Kansas. At the same time they heard of an experimental farm irrigation project being developed under private auspices on the banks of the Niger River in a onetime French colony, now the independent Republic of Niger. Already drawing upon funds raised by Africare, based in Washington, D.C., and by World Vision, based in Monrovia, California, the irrigation program was in no way related to any church denomination, and certainly not to the rural Methodists of Kansas. Yet these Kansas Methodists sent a delegation to visit the Niger experimental farm and, when the group came back with a favorable report, they promptly raised $250,000 to help.

A third illustration: The Church of the Savior, which calls itself an ecumenical church and is unaffiliated with any denomination, has long been involved in a variety of humanitarian works, reaching out beyond its central base in an old brownstone mansion set among the embassies of Washington's Massachusetts Avenue. Better housing for the slum-dwelling poor, job programs for unemployed youth, better care of small children and the elderly—these are a few of the projects this remarkable religious fellowship has undertaken in the thirty-five years of its existence. Now it reaches out through international service, giving fresh witness to its Christian faith and principles. In part, that means a study and advocacy role on problems of arms control and international conflict resolution. In early 1980, it also came to mean sending a team of more than a dozen men and women to set up camp on the shoreline of Thailand to offer direct emergency assistance to the frightened, pirate-harassed "boat people" who were refugees from Cambodia. Through money collected from its members and others, and through volunteer labor freely given, this small church sought to deal with human need in a land far removed from its home congregation.

These, admittedly, are unusual happenings. They are not predictable; they cannot be programmed. Yet among the tens of millions of U.S. citizens actively or passively involved in religious organizations, there are vast reservoirs of social concern and financial resources that can be tapped for private overseas assistance endeavors.

Church groups and individual donors that demonstrate interest in international affairs and in the problems of the developing world are inclined to give their funds in direct support of projects that help people, either to assist with immediate emergency relief or to encourage grass-roots self-help projects intended to improve local health, education, and economic conditions. They are not likely to involve themselves in major research endeavors designed to analyze the socioeconomic conditions and related human problems in a developing country or region. Nor are they likely to launch such programs as new universities or schools of management, agriculture research stations, tropical disease control programs, or national population planning campaigns—all of which a few of the larger foundations have done, sometimes with joint funding from the local governments and official U.S. agencies.

Church givers and most individual donors tend to channel their gifts through American-based church bodies or interdenominational or independent agencies, and sometimes give directly to an individual church, hospital, or school overseas with which they have had some contact. They rarely make donations to a project under direct governmental supervision. However, they are increasingly responsive to appeals for support of non-church-related programs of relief and development assistance operated by private agencies that may obtain part of their funding from government sources. The age of narrow parochialism in church work abroad, if not dead, is surely fading.

Believable statistics about the expenditures of churches and church-related organizations for international service programs are hard to come by. There is no central agency to which all such bodies report. The government's records are far from complete, and those that exist are likely to be at least a couple of years out of date. Moreover, most of the church boards concerned with overseas missions are not sure of the exact totals of their own denomination's giving because many individual congregations conduct special collections for a particular project or an individual missionary and never report such gifts to anybody.

Yet over the years, some figures have been made available. Incomplete as many of them are, they do suggest the impressive overall scale of the involvement of religious groups in foreign assistance of various kinds. For example:

- *Catholic Relief Service* reported that in 1978 it distributed foodstuffs, relief supplies, and various forms of development assistance totalling $286,800,000. Of that amount, about $43.5 million came from private gifts and church collections; the remainder consisted chiefly of surplus foods provided by the U.S. government.
- *Church World Service*, a branch of the Division of Overseas Ministries of the National Council of Churches, made overseas expenditures in 1978 of $37.3 million; part of that consisted of surplus "Food for Peace" supplies.
- In his book *American Philanthropy Abroad*, Merle Curti recorded an accounting of private giving from 1919 through 1960. His "rounded-off" figures for that 41-year period

reported contributions through religious groups as follows: Protestant — $1,961,500,000; Jewish — $1,473,000,000; Catholic — $523,400,000.

- The American Friends Service Committee, between its founding in April 1917 and the end of 1978, calculated its contributions of cash and goods shipped abroad for foreign aid to be $97,142,409.
- According to the publication "North American Protestant Ministries Overseas," edited by Edward R. Dayton, the budgets for 579 Protestant missionary groups in 1975 totalled $632 million, with an additional $41 million worth of gifts in kind shipped abroad that year. He noted that another 260 Protestant groups provided no statistics.
- The 1978 edition of the "U.S. Non-profit Organizations in Development Assistance Abroad," a directory published by the Technical Assistance Information Clearing House (TAICH), reported that 189 organizations, self-described as having a "Christian dimension" to their work, showed expenditures for the previous year of $562,043,204 to support relief and development programs abroad.

Clearly, these samplings of financial reports give a very incomplete picture of church support for relief and development. Moreover, it must be stated that there is no way an accurate and comprehensive accounting of such giving can be put together without an extraordinary amount of research — more than any organization or government agency has, up to now, been willing to undertake. A number of church groups that have not supplied figures on the costs of their activities abroad explain that they are not able to separate the expenses for their evangelization work from the costs of their relief and development programs. Among Catholic groups, some simply say that they forward their money for missionary activities to Rome and really don't know how the central authorities divide the funds. Despite these impediments to an accurate accounting of church support for private foreign aid, it is clear that the total of these contributions is substantial and that they are the result of the interest and concern of millions of individual U.S. citizens.

Individual Giving

Most people give because somebody asks them; few experience a self-generated impulse to hunt up an agency that is doing good work and press money upon it. Motivating people to give and organizing the solicitation effort is a major enterprise in American society; it is both a capricious art form and an arcane science.

Fundraising among the general public offers enormous challenges and problems for churches and PVOs. Among them are high costs, competition, public apathy, hostility and ignorance, and neverending uncertainty about what methods of fundraising succeed best. Workers in the field have observations on all of these points. But, once again, a word about the distinction between church-related and non-church-related organizations is in order.

Among church-related groups are the built-in "constituencies"—churches where people are brought together regularly, through which publications are distributed, and where fundraising for any church-blessed project is as taken for granted as the passing of the Sunday morning collection plate.

This is not so with secular groups. Their publics are much less well-defined and they generally lack large organized groups of supporting members. They are "competing," as it were, with all the churches and all other volunteer agencies that are seeking funds. The public fundraising problems the two groups face are similar, but are not identical.

The least expensive way to reach a mass audience, many fundraisers now believe, is solicitation through direct mail, though this is not necessarily the most cost-effective. Millions of pieces of literature are sent each year to "prospects," good ones and remote ones. For some organizations it is a strategy that works well, and at costs that are clearly justifiable. For others, direct mail solicitation, as they do it, has not worked well, and sometimes the cost is absurdly high.

The best known organizations, religious or not, obviously have the best opportunity for successful outreach to many prospects. The national "recognition factor" is crucial. CARE, for instance, spent more than $5 million for fundraising in 1978. It received more than $21 million that year in contributions, thanks in large part to the careful building of its mailing list over many years—and to its now well-established name. It guards that list carefully and does not make it available to any other organization. The average gift size, according to comptroller Richard Vogler, is $15 to $20. CARE has worked long and hard to build up its prospect list and currently has close to one million names and addresses.

Many smaller secular organizations do not take in as much money in total as CARE spends on its direct mail program, and they usually don't have any such targeted prospect lists. Nor do most of them have much access to the church pulpits or newsletters. With costs and inflation exerting a pincerlike effect on direct mail income, many groups are finding mail solicitation less and less economical and only marginally dependable.

For example, the International Rescue Committee (IRC) raised about $1.9 million in private contributions in 1978. Ira Sternberg, IRC's head, indicated that about $500,000 of that came from direct mail. But he also said, "Direct mail costs probably can't be kept below 25 percent, which means that for every dollar contributed, we can only use 75 cents. . . . Moreover, we have never been terribly successful in getting foundation money and we have even less success in getting corporate money." Such is the situation with one of the most highly respected private agencies that works with refugees.

While costs rise, competition among the PVOs gets tougher. Agencies are cautious about paying out money to "rent" a mailing list that they can't be sure will provide a reasonable return. The sophisticated giver is not likely to make a contribution to any organization he or she doesn't know something about. Even if the giver increases contributions to the favorite charity, it may not provide the extra amount needed to offset inflation and to allow program expansion. Many PVOs are not doing very well in adding new prospects to what are generally quite modest contributor lists.

Although there are many approaches to gift motivation, many PVO staff members are uneasy about one that is widely used and often highly successful: photographs of the obviously malnourished human being, adult or child, living in squalor—a picture so often seen in direct mail brochures and magazine advertisements. Uneasy or not, some of those engaged in this hard-sell solicitation ask, "What else is there that is so effective in getting people to open their pocketbooks?"

"I don't think anyone has come up with a terribly good answer," says Sister Marilyn Norris, past president of Coordination in Development, Inc., (CODEL). "It's a matter of changing people's mentality from giving to the sickly, bloated child, using that image as a kind of motivating force. That's degrading for the people we work with and we cannot, in conscience, use that kind of sell anymore."

However, another PVO person could say, when receipts for a recent year seemed to be down, "The only thing that's saving us is Cambodia. It's good that's still in the news." The highly publicized suffering of the Cambodians greatly boosted contributions.

Americans do become concerned and will give when they are shocked into awareness of the suffering of other people, but not without some such dramatic motivation.

On the other hand, Americans often are turned off by violence, revolution, and corruption in developing countries. The chaos in Iran and the seizure of American hostages there undoubtedly had a negative effect on American attitudes toward helping people in that region of the world. Yet there is no way to know for sure what effects the Ayatollah Khomeini may have had on the long-term thinking of American contributors to Middle East charities. Father Andrew M. Greeley, head of the National Opinion Research Center in Chicago, has written, "Minimally, the era of Third World worship is over. . . . The question is not whether the new president of the United States is going to have to follow a hard-line policy against the Third World. The question rather is how hard-line the policy will have to be."

Thus, if PVOs have faced considerable apathy as they sought funds from individual contributors, that condition may be replaced by hostility. PVOs generally argue that politics doesn't enter into their decisions to help people. Yet those that take government money often have no choice; foreign-policy decisions preclude operating with government funds in some countries. Other PVOs that accept only nongovernmental contributions are free to work in those same countries as long as the host governments let them. Now another hazard may arise: the giving public may simply retaliate against unpopular Third World countries by closing its wallet.

What concerns PVOs is backlash repercussions from other Irans, Nicaraguas, and Pakistans. They are afraid the American giving public won't see the important distinction between the behavior of governments and the needs of poor people. In the Third World there is also a backlash directed at U.S. policies that could spill over into opposition to genuine people-to-people efforts to engender self-help and development in those countries. Nonetheless, it is not uncommon for church-related groups working through indigenous churches to maintain assistance programs even in Third World countries where particular governments may have taken a hard-line position toward the United States.

As Paul McCleary of Church World Service points out, the World Council of Churches and the Vatican operate networks that have existed for many years and have continued to function through all kinds of turmoil in some very chaotic countries. He notes, also, that some of the rising political leaders in Africa, even in some unstable areas, are leaders in Christian churches:

> Bishop Muserewa, who was Rhodesia's interim Black prime minister, is a Methodist minister. The leadership of the revolutionary movement in Angola has included Christian ministers. In Latin America, the Catholic Church has been giving unusual leadership to social ferment. Throughout Latin America, the church has been a major factor in making social change acceptable. In Vietnam, the Catholic Church is alive, with 1.3 million adherents and a Cardinal and Archbishop in Saigon. Governments can come and go, but these church networks are still there.

The difficulties PVOs face in raising funds from individuals are complex and persistent. Costs mount. Inflation soars. Revolts turn people off. But Third and Fourth World people continue to need help, and the PVOs continue to search for ways to raise money to provide the assistance. Some are turning to television "telethons," "walk-a-thons," and weekend fasts for world hunger. Ingenuity and energy are still available for private fundraising.

But the overall impression of the fundraising efforts on behalf of private foreign aid is that they are random in nature, sometimes competitive, and poorly coordinated. Continually, PVO leaders speak of the need for some sort of "concerted" effort—not necessarily for a new form of United Way for international programs, but for at least some coherently orchestrated effort to educate the public. The people who are asked to give need to understand better what the issues are and what the churches and the private voluntary agencies, alone or in conjunction with others, are doing—and could do with more private funds.

4

Foundations

- The larger and older foundations in the United States have given major attention to international issues and programs from their beginning.
- Most U.S. foundations have never given a cent to international projects of any kind.
- Foundation grants in support of international activities have always been limited and now are even declining in size and number.
- There are evidences of new interest by private grantmakers in programs and projects of assistance to people in need in foreign lands.

All of the above statements are true. They simply have to be said together.

Among the long-established foundations, Rockefeller, Carnegie, Ford, and Kellogg have had continuing interests in overseas programs for many years. Rockefeller and Ford have had, and still have, what can be described as major global commitments. Carnegie, by direction of its founder, the Scottish-born Andrew Carnegie, has concentrated its international involvements on the United Kingdom, the British Commonwealth, and present or former British colonies. The Kellogg Foundation has traditionally directed its overseas activities primarily to Latin America, but operates on four continents. The Tinker Foundation has special interests in Latin America. A number of foundations created by Jewish families allocate their overseas giving exclusively to Israel. Other foundations whose founders have had strong Christian church ties have tended to assign their grants abroad to projects and countries identified with missionary or other church-related service activities in developing countries. A few foundations, such as Kettering, Compton, and Stanley, have strong interests in projects related to international conflict resolution and problems of maintaining peace. Lilly

Endowment, the Public Welfare Foundation, the International Foundation, and the Rockefeller Brothers Fund have given substantial support to private American voluntary agencies working in a variety of developing countries.

Overall, there is no grand strategy of foundation involvement in international affairs, no agreement on the importance of private support for international activities, and no broadly shared sense of priorities for American philanthropic giving related to international interests. Many foundations, for clear and understandable reasons, limit their giving to a home state or a home city. Of the more than 21,000 foundations in existence in the United States, perhaps no more than 150, in a given year, make grants that are readily identifiable as supporting some international program or foreign institution. However, these and other foundations sometimes assist projects abroad indirectly, through grants to domestic organizations with primary program interests in this country but with certain involvements overseas. Other foundations assist PVOs that spend the bulk of their funds outside the United States. In times of great disasters abroad, a considerable number of foundations and corporations come forward with emergency contributions quite outside their normal grantmaking guidelines.

The Rockefeller Foundation

The Rockefeller Foundation probably has had a more profound effect upon the lives of more people in the emerging lands of Asia, Africa, and Latin America than any other single private American institution. Before the term "Third World" had been coined or anyone spoke of "developing countries," representatives of the Rockefeller Foundation and its financial resources were moving into many areas of the globe where the problems of disease, poverty and illiteracy cried out for attention. Formally launched in 1913, the foundation proclaimed the simple, if visionary, purpose of serving "the well-being of mankind throughout the world." Yet foreign aid, as we think of it today, was not its explicit or primary function.

Health and Medical Programs

The Conquest of Specific Diseases

Although the Rockefeller Foundation did not set out on a path of "foreign assistance" as such, it did seek to "eradicate" certain diseases. Its founder and his advisers came to the judgment at the very beginning of their endeavors that one of the surest, quickest ways to promote the "well-being of mankind" was to do something about a few specific health problems that, year after year, took enormous tolls in lives and in the health and physical energies of people, particularly in the less advanced regions of the world. Yellow fever, malaria, hookworm, and tuberculosis were chronic, deadly, and crippling plagues. Yet the scientific knowledge was already available, and if widely and properly applied, it was then believed, these human afflictions could be wiped out. So reasoned the man whom John D. Rockefeller selected to help organize his substantial private giving into "scientific philanthropy." Frederick T. Gates, in a memorandum entitled "Philanthropy and Civilization," wrote: "Disease is the supreme ill of human life, and it is the main source of almost all other human ills — poverty, crime, ignorance, vice, inefficiency, hereditary taint, and many other evils."

Even before the Rockefeller Foundation was established, Mr. Rockefeller had already made a major commitment to the cause of preventive health. In 1901 he provided funds to create the Rockefeller Institute for Medical Research. In 1903 he launched the General Education Board, which gave serious attention to Negro education in the southern states. That work, in turn, led in an unexpected way to an awareness of the problem of hookworm and to the establishment of the Rockefeller Sanitary Commission in 1909. The commission members, given initially one million dollars to be spent within five years, undertook to "eradicate" hookworm. They rather quickly realized that total elimination of that parasite was not likely, but they had remarkable success in bringing it under control.

Thanks to the Rockefeller initiative, state health departments were stirred into decisive action in eleven southern states. Meanwhile, the Rockefeller health team took account of the fact that the hookworm affliction also caused chronic suffering in millions of other people in warm climate countries around the globe. In 1913 the Sanitary Commission was renamed the International Health Board, made an integral part of the newly chartered Rockefeller Foundation, and directed to "extend to other countries and people the work of controlling the hookworm disease."

Cooperating with all the local governments involved, and acting on their invitation, Dr. Wickliffe Rose, director of the program, developed a global strategy and carried the antihookworm campaign into fifty-two countries on six continents and to some twenty-nine islands scattered across the tropical seas. In the process, the

Rockefeller scientists and administrators learned some crucial and still relevant lessons about the dynamics of development. "Demonstrations in which the (local) authorities do not participate to a substantial degree," Dr. Rose once wrote, "are not likely to be successful. The country must be sufficiently interested to risk something, to follow the plan critically, to take over the cost of the work gradually but steadily, and within a reasonable period to assume the entire burden of direction and expense."

In the end, the Rockefeller efforts did not completely "wipe out" hookworm, but they did demonstrate how to bring it under control and helped to restore to health millions of sufferers in such widely scattered places as China, Brazil, Australia, British Guiana, India, and the Fiji Islands.

While the battle against hookworm was still in full course, Dr. Rose and his colleagues began to investigate ways of attacking other endemic diseases. Their conclusion, as summarized by Raymond B. Fosdick, president of the foundation from 1936 to 1948 and author of *The Rockefeller Foundation—Nineteen Thirteen to Nineteen Fifty*, was that "malaria was responsible for more sickness and death than all other diseases combined . . . perhaps the greatest handicap to the welfare and economic efficiency of the human race. . . . " On the basis of that judgment, the Rockefeller Foundation launched a long-term global campaign against malaria and the mosquitoes that spread it.

Beginning, as in the hookworm program, with research, mass education and control demonstration projects in the southern United States, the Rockefeller Foundation extended its antimalaria efforts to Central America, then Brazil, and finally to malarial regions on all continents and many islands. Along the way, it took on whatever relevant tasks had to be undertaken: operating research laboratories in New York and training stations in Athens and Karachi; providing physicians and scientific researchers with fellowships for advanced study; publishing "primers" on the subject in a score of languages; helping various governments to set up malaria control divisions in their health departments; and, endlessly, studying the despised mosquito in its many habitats—from the rain forests of Trinidad to the marshlands of Egypt to the hill streams of the Philippines.

Similarly wide-spread, sustained, and intensive Rockefeller Foundation programs were undertaken against typhus, tuberculosis, rabies, yaws, and schistosomiasis, all of which have been particularly burdensome to people in various developing, primarily tropical, countries.

Of all the diseases the Rockefeller Foundation attacked, none received more concentrated attention and financial investment than yellow fever. Another mosquito-borne disease, it produced some of the most frightening and hazardous epidemics mankind experienced over many centuries. Building on the antimosquito techniques developed by Major Walter Reed and other U.S. Army Sanitary officers during the Spanish-American War in Cuba, and further applied on an intensive basis by General W. C. Gorgas in the jungles of Panama during the digging of the Canal, the foundation created in 1915 a special yellow fever commission, headed by General Gorgas. Over the next thirty years it waged intensive campaigns to eliminate the offending mosquito, *aedes aegypti*, in Ecuador, Peru, Colombia, Venezuela, Brazil, and the countries of Central America. Later it undertook the same kind of crusade against other yellow fever mosquitoes in various parts of Africa.

According to Fosdick, "In all this work in yellow fever carried on by the Rockefeller Foundation, the high point was the development of a vaccine by which people can now be protected against the disease as successfully as they are protected against smallpox or typhoid." That vaccine came out of the research laboratories of the foundation in New York, the result of work by Dr. Max Theiler, for which he received the Nobel Prize.

The contribution of the Rockefeller Foundation's health programs to the social and economic advancement of the peoples of the developing world is an enormously important aspect of development assistance. That would be true even if the foundation had done nothing more for them than lead a series of crusades to bring under control hookworm, yellow fever, and malaria. Yet the conquest of particular diseases has been only one part of the total Rockefeller efforts to serve the health needs of the developing nations and of all mankind.

Medical Assistance for China

As a devout Baptist, Mr. Rockefeller began early in his business career to contribute substantially to the church and to various of its activities, including numerous foreign missionary projects. As his advisor Frederick T. Gates once wrote of Mr. Rockefeller's charitable activities prior to creation of the foundation, "He had conducted a small foreign mission society . . . of his own. . . . He was in daily receipt of appeals from individual Baptist missionaries in every region of Baptist missionary endeavor."

As with most Christians interested in missionary activities at that time, Mr. Rockefeller was fascinated with China. At one period he gave serious thought to financing the establishment of a great university in China, but by 1911 he and his advisors had dropped the idea. Instead, the Rockefeller group turned to the more limited but still formidable ambition of "developing modern medicine on a significant scale in China." The result was the China Medical Board, from 1914 to 1928 an integral division of the Rockefeller Foundation. Its principal project, Peking Union Medical College (PUMC), was designed, equipped, and staffed to be the "Johns Hopkins of China." The main concern was to create an institution of such unquestioned excellence that it would bring to China the highest quality of research, medical care, and medical education available anywhere, and thus to prepare the leaders in Chinese health services for generations to come.

The project began with land and a few buildings in Peking, purchased from the London Missionary Society in 1915. There, by 1921, the China Medical Board had created an impressive campus of fifty-nine buildings on twenty-five acres, with laboratories, classrooms, dormitories, staff houses, a 225-bed teaching hospital, an animal house, and all the other medical school facilities that could be thought of in that day. In 1928 the foundation gave the China Medical Board independent status and a substantial endowment, and set it free to operate on its own. (It still functions as one of the ten largest foundation sources of funds for programs outside the United States and has contributed to a variety of health and medical endeavors in various parts of Asia, not only in China.)

By 1947, Peking Union Medical College had become one of the most highly respected medical institutions in Asia. Meanwhile, with the intervening years of Japanese conquest and occupation, and amid the postwar rise of Chairman Mao's communism, it had also become a completely indigenous institution. In 1947, despite great uncertainty about China's future and abusive communist propaganda against "greedy capitalists," the foundation trustees made a final gift of $10 million for medicine in China and expressed the belief that the distinguished medical institution it had founded and nurtured "will not be allowed to die out." In its new incarnation, it still lives.

Medical Education Around the World

The Rockefeller Foundation's interest in medical education found expression in many different ways, through many grants, and, in time, in many lands. It was an interest that began in the United States out of a considered desire to improve the quality of preparation of medical doctors in this country. Influenced by the famous Flexner Report of 1910, financed by the Carnegie Foundation for the Advancement of Teaching, the Rockefeller Foundation and its partner, the General Education Board, began a major effort to assist the improvement of U.S. medical schools, a cause in which it ultimately invested more than $100 million.

In 1916 the officers of the foundation decided to take a look at medical education abroad and began with a study of medicine in Brazil. In 1919 the foundation set up a Division of Medical Education and embarked on an ambitious plan to help "strategically placed medical schools in various parts of the world." Initially, it did not seek out the weaker institutions in need of help, nor did it put money into the underdeveloped regions of the world, except for its work in China. Rockefeller grants went in the beginning to Oxford, Cambridge, Edinburgh, and University College Hospital School in London, all of which were then judged to be superior to virtually all medical schools in the United States.

In time, after careful study, the Rockefeller Foundation began to channel medical education grants to less well-developed regions: the American University of Beirut, serving a vast area of the Middle East, and the Hong Kong Medical School, the King Edward VII Medical School of Singapore, and the Royal Medical School of Bangkok, serving peoples scattered over a large expanse of Southeast Asia. In all of these medical schools the aim was to reproduce first-rate institutions on the American or European model, with training no less rigorous than that required to practice in the United States.

That kind of "meet the U.S. standards" resolve, it should be noted, has characterized the approach of many U.S. foreign assistance endeavors in many fields. The American and European models for this or that activity or institution, it has been reasoned, are the best available, so, naturally, everyone else will want to duplicate them. Every effort should be made to transfer to the less fortunate peoples of the earth what is already known as the best.

There is, obviously, much to recommend the support of high standards everywhere. The continued eminence of the American University of Beirut Medical School throughout the Middle East, as well as the long-time superior position of PUMC in China, can be taken as strong endorsement of the judgment of the Rockefeller Foundation officers who wanted to concentrate their funds in developing elite institutions. Yet in time another approach to medical education came to the fore, pushed by at least two of the Rockefeller medical men in the field: Dr. John Grant, professor of public health at PUMC, and Dr. Sylvester M. Lambert, who directed the foundation's public health work in the South Pacific.

John Grant was a maverick. Brought up in China, the son of Canadian missionaries, he knew the country and its people well and spoke fluent Chinese. He also held an M.D. degree from the University of Michigan, and received training in public health at Johns Hopkins. More importantly, as a young doctor he had two powerfully formative field work assignments for the foundation: one in Pitt County, North Carolina, and the other in the coal mining district of China's Hunan Province. From these direct exposures to the public health problems of poor people he developed a passionate conviction about the need to link preventive and curative medicine, and to take health services to the masses of people who were unlikely to visit a physician or a hospital, if they could find one, until it was too late. In numerous ways he pressed PUMC to expand its preventive medicine courses and guided the Chinese authorities in the development of public health and sanitation services. Eventually, in 1925, he was able to develop a Health Demonstration Station in an inner city ward of Peking. Along the way, he acquired a great and sometimes discouraging understanding of how Chinese bureaucracy worked. He also became increasingly aware of the profound social changes that were overtaking China.

Dr. Grant grew more and more disenchanted with what he regarded as the failure of both the Medical College and the Chinese government to deal with the problems pressing upon an increasingly turbulent society. However, he saw great hope in the rural reconstruction work of James Y. C. Yen. Strongly rooted though he was in PUMC, he felt that something like Yen's comprehensive approach to transforming rural village life, through linking efforts to improve health, education, and economic development, was essential for China. It was that broad vision he communicated to Rockefeller Foundation officers, and particularly to Selskar M. Gunn, whom he influenced strongly in the development of the foundation's new China program, launched in 1935. He was a prime force in the move to integrate health work with community development and to produce health workers, including "retrained" Chinese midwives and other paramedics who could deliver elementary health care to the millions of ordinary Chinese who would never be touched directly by an elite medical college.

Dr. Sylvester M. Lambert, who spent twenty-one years doing public health work in the South Pacific, argued that the health needs of millions of people in the most backward regions would never be adequately met by Western doctors or by local physicians trained to Western standards; there just couldn't be enough of them. He argued for support of short-term intensive training of native "practitioners." In his own Rockefeller assignment to conduct campaigns against hookworm, yaws, and malaria throughout Southeast Asia and the far-flung islands of the South Seas, he had had to rely on countless native helpers, many of whom he trained himself despite their inadequate educational backgrounds. He urged the foundation to put money into "a school of sorts" already operating at Suva in the British Fiji Islands in order to help it train more nurses and "practitioners." The very thought of such a thing horrified the able, high-standards men who then ran the foundation's Division of Medical Education; they would not allow their funds to be used for such a low-level purpose. However, Dr. Lambert was a determined fighter and he convinced other Rockefeller officials to allocate the funds from another division of the foundation. In time, the foundation came to believe, as Dr. Fosdick put it, "that institutions for lower-level training frequently deserve as much help as the old 'centers of excellence.' . . . " This meant moving away from so much emphasis on "raising standards at the top in the belief that benefits will seep down automatically to the less educated or privileged. It made available a medical and health service to native people at low cost and in a form that was most assimilable by their society. More than that, it provided a pattern which is perhaps applicable under similar circumstances to other areas."

Many years later, Chairman Mao's People's Republic of China gained world attention for its supposedly "innovative pioneering" health services provided by the so-called barefoot doctors working in the most backward regions of China. Professor John Grant at PUMC, and Dr. Sylvester Lambert, in his public health work on the islands of the South Seas, had anticipated those services years earlier, and with Rockefeller Foundation support they had already established the precedents.

Public Health Services

One common theme of all the varied health and medical programs undertaken by the Rockefeller Foundation was the necessity everywhere to develop local public health services staffed by competent professionals, and to bring practical application of the scientific knowledge available to the health conditions of the local areas. In their campaigns against specific endemic diseases, Rockefeller health specialists emphasized the importance of enlisting local professionals and paraprofessionals—or training them if they did not exist.

In many places, public health work was given a new dignity because of centers or postgraduate schools of hygiene that the foundation helped establish or strengthen. Public health nurses were trained, thanks to Rockefeller grants, at major institutions in more than twenty-five countries around the globe. In sixty-eight countries national and local health departments were helped to improve their facilities, their programs, and the competence of their personnel.

Preventive medicine in all its ramifications was a long-term commitment of the foundation; over the decades that commitment led it into an enormous range of activities.

In the forty years following the establishment of the Rockefeller Sanitary Commission, and continuing through the programs of the International Health Division of the foundation, at least $94 million was spent by Rockefeller sources on the development of public health services around the world. The widespread attention by all governments and by intergovernmental agencies to public health matters—and the quality of the institutions and services now in place—must be considered, in some measure, a tribute to the Rockefeller public health endeavors that began prior to World War I.

Food and Agriculture

In the post–World War II period, the Rockefeller Foundation has become best known for its research and development work improving strains of rice, corn, wheat and other staple crops, thus expanding food supplies for a hungry world. However, its work in agriculture goes back to earlier times and objectives.

Agricultural Education

Between 1906 and 1914 the General Education Board expended approximately one million dollars, in partnership with the U.S. Department of Agriculture, in developing more than 100,000 demonstration farms in the southern states and in New England, thus carrying scientific agriculture to the average dirt farmer, an education endeavor then in its infancy. These Rockefeller/USDA demonstration farms, it has been said, "paved the way" for the U.S. Agricultural Extension Service.

In the mid-1920s the foundation investigated the state of

agricultural education in countries as varied as Denmark, Hungary, Bulgaria and China. Grants were made for a number of university agriculture programs. More than 200 fellowships were awarded young people from thirty-one countries to do graduate study in preparation for careers in agricultural teaching and research.

Rural Reconstruction in China

In 1931 a Rockefeller Foundation officer, associate director for social services Selskar M. Gunn, spent seven weeks in China visiting hospitals, academic institutions and community development projects. He examined carefully the work the foundation had supported in China over the previous two decades and attempted to assess the most critical needs of the country. Although long associated with the Rockfeller public health programs, he concluded that the large investments made in PUMC and in the other medical programs and academic institutions were not having a very significant impact on the lives of the great masses of the people and were not likely to affect substantially the future of China. He saw the country in a turmoil of social and economic change, and rural reconstruction was the dominant issue.

During his tour he encountered a remarkable Chinese educator, James Y. C. (Jimmy) Yen, who had been trained at Princeton University for a role among the academic and administrative elite, but had gone back to China to work at improving the life of the rural poor. Gunn visited Yen's rural reconstruction center at Tinghsien and studied his Mass Education Movement. He also gave particular attention to what a few universities were doing in rural sociology, agricultural economics, and in various branches of the agricultural sciences.

A return visit in 1932 strengthened Gunn's convictions about the primacy of rural development on the China agenda. In early 1934 he submitted a major document, "China and the Rockefeller Foundation," in which he declared that the foundation's heavily health-oriented program was not adequate for the times, that great opportunities existed for Rockefeller to make a real difference in China, and that a radically revised program emphasizing rural life improvement should be undertaken.

In December 1934, the foundation board approved the Gunn recommendations and voted to appropriate one million dollars for a three-year period. The largest allocation went to Yen's Mass Education Movement, which, in addition to carrying on its demonstration centers, was to train rural community workers to tackle village problems in the fields of education, agriculture, health, local government, and economics. Eventually the program was to be spread nationwide, although in the early stages there would be a concentration on certain provinces in North China. Allocations were also made for related programs in agriculture, economics, and preventive health at several universities. By April 1936, there had emerged a North China Council for Rural Reconstruction, and the Rockefeller Foundation was being praised by government officials, educators, and missionaries for its support of what was seen as a peaceful revolution to benefit the rural masses.

However, the dedicated and toughened communist followers of Mao Tse-tung and the Japanese military had different ideas. Despite impressive results in the first two years of its operation, the foundation's new China Program was dealt a near fatal blow in July 1937 when the Japanese overran North China. Nankai University, one of the principal academic participants in the China Program, was destroyed. The North China Council, the Mass Education Movement, and some of the cooperating universities became refugee institutions, moving from place to place until they wound up in Chungking, the base of Chiang Kai-shek's government in the last years of World War II. By 1942 the foundation had invested almost two million dollars in China's rural reconstruction, but in 1943, with war, rampant inflation, and the growing power of the communists, Rockefeller suspended its support.

Eventually the communists took over the whole country. Chiang Kai-shek fled to Taiwan. Dr. Yen eventually established his base at a "college" for rural development workers in the Philippines. Rural reconstruction by way of violent change and the communist commune triumphed over the hoped-for dream for a peaceful rural village revolution, sponsored in part by an American foundation.

Crop Improvement: The Green Revolution

For all the importance of the extraordinary Rockefeller contributions to public health and other fields over more than half of the past century, Rockefeller Foundation officials came to see that other threats to the welfare of mankind urgently demanded attention; chief among them was world hunger. The Rockefeller Foundation decided to do something about this problem, too, especially after the early days of World War II.

In February 1941, Mr. Fosdick, president of the foundation, had a conversation with Vice President (and former secretary of agriculture) Henry A. Wallace. In a "casual comment" Mr. Wallace, just back from a trip to Mexico, remarked that "if anyone could increase the yield per acre of corn and beans in Mexico, it would contribute more effectively to the welfare of the country and the happiness of its people than any other plan that could be devised."

Subsequently, U.S. specialists representing the foundation and Mexican agricultural officials negotiated an extraordinary research and development agreement. The foundation became a full partner with the Mexican government in a long-term agricultural improvement program. The government agreed to provide land, a portion of construction costs, and considerable local labor. The foundation promised to put up most of the annual operating costs and to bring in professionals in such fields as entomology, soil science, and plant genetics. The first member of the Rockefeller team was Dr. George Harrar, a plant pathologist from Washington State University, who later became president of the foundation. The Mexican government gave the project extraordinary official standing by creating the Office of Special Studies as the base for the program, with Dr. Harrar as its director.

The primary purpose was to improve food crop production. Although predominantly an agricultural country, Mexico was chronically short of food and had to import much of its wheat and corn. Wide variations in topography, soil conditions, temperature, and precipitation, plus the prevalence of plant pests and diseases, made crops highly unreliable from season to season. Yields were often disastrously low.

One of the first tasks was to determine which of the many strains of corn, wheat, and beans were most productive, most resistant to fungus diseases, and most tolerant of drought or excessive rainfall. Similar studies were made on potatoes, barley, sorghums, legumes, and a variety of vegetables. More than two thousand different varieties of corn were tested, and plant breeders crossed the more promising strains. After five years, eight especially good corn hybrids were produced. Several million acres of corn were planted with the new seed, and per-acre yield soared. Even more spectacular results came from the new varieties of rust-resistant, high-quality, high-yield wheat that the program's plant experts developed. The Mexican wheat harvest doubled in ten years. From having to import 50 percent of its annual wheat consumption, Mexico became, for a time, self-sufficient. By 1963 Dr. Harrar was able to report also that "bean production has doubled, broiler production has tripled, eggs have increased two and a half times." Overall, Mexico's annual rate of increase in food production became one of the highest in the world.

The success of the whole enterprise ultimately depended on getting the new seeds and new farming techniques to the farmers, and getting them used. Research and demonstration centers were set up in various parts of the country. "Field days" were held, at which experts showed the initially skeptical farmers how to increase production with the new seeds and methods. Various approaches were devised to spread the information in practical terms. The farmers learned — and changed their ways of farming.

The spectacular achievements in Mexico, of course, attracted attention in other food-deficient countries. Agriculturists from Brazil, Colombia, and other Latin American countries came to Mexico to learn how to increase food supplies in their own countries. What had started as a modest Office of Special Studies within the Ministry of Agriculture grew into a multifaceted complex of research and demonstration centers for the benefit of local Mexican farmers, and also an inspiration for the improvement of agriculture in many lands.

Despite the success of the Mexican experience, the Rockefeller Foundation resisted the temptation to try to duplicate that pattern in the scores of other developing countries that would have liked the foundation's help with similar intensive agricultural improvement programs. Instead, in the late 1950s, the Rockefeller and Ford foundations decided to work jointly on another approach. They would set up a new kind of assistance organization: an international agricultural research institute devoted to the improvement of a particular type of crop. The first one they picked was rice, the "principal food of more than half of mankind." The International Rice Research Institute (IRRI), established in the Philippines, was devoted to learning everything possible about how to increase the production of rice and how to teach the farmers to use the new information. Such a comprehensive and intensive "systems approach" paid off — handsomely. The IRRI scientists learned how to breed rice plants that were shorter and sturdier, more responsive to fertilizers, and better able to withstand insects, diseases, and adverse weather. The institute also was able to determine the most effective techniques of rice farming for a variety of soils and weather conditions. All across the rice-raising regions of Asia production rose significantly.

In 1966, Ford and Rockefeller turned their attention to another kind of crop, the bread grains. Building upon the successes of the earlier Mexican national program, the International Maize and Wheat Improvement Center (known by the Spanish acronym

CIMMYT) was established. The Rockefeller Foundation, the Mexican government, and the Ford Foundation provided the initial support. Later, substantial funding came from the U.S. Agency for International Development, the Canadian International Development Agency, the Inter-American Development Bank, the World Bank, and the United Nations Development Progamme. Although its headquarters are located in Mexico, the center operates projects and programs in various parts of Latin America, Asia, and Africa. It participates in cooperative research activities in more than fifty countries. Its work in improving the yields of corn and wheat was at the heart of the Green Revolution. Rockefeller staff member Norman Borlaug, stationed at the Mexican center for a number of years, was awarded the Nobel Peace Prize in 1970 for his contribution to that peaceful, life-supporting "revolution."

In 1967 the foundation assisted in the establishment of two additional institutes to serve the food needs of the developing world. One was the International Institute of Tropical Agriculture based in Ibadan, Nigeria. The other was the International Center of Tropical Agriculture, with headquarters in Colombia. Both of these institutes were designed to work for comprehensive improvement of agriculture throughout the lowland tropics.

The results of the work of the various institutes have been spectacular, even in such chronically food-short countries as India. The Green Revolution has succeeded beyond the forecasts of its sponsors. At the same time, it has been attacked by some critics as having made the rich farmers richer and the poor ones poorer and having speeded up the migration of rural people to the cities. The local government leaders and agricultural experts in the countries that have become involved in the Green Revolution have generally answered in emphatic terms. They point out that total food supplies are increasing, that they are locally produced, and that they are overcoming the threat of famine. They see rising income for the farm population; they see spreading benefits of development finally reaching the masses. The argument over the Green Revolution and land policies, however, continues.

In 1975 the Rockefeller Foundation was instrumental in the creation of the International Agricultural Development Service (IADS), an autonomous, nonpolitical and nonprofit organization to "help developing nations expand production of crops and livestock and raise rural income." The service was led by the late Dr. Sterling Wortman, long-time agricultural scientist for the foundation and later its acting president. Building on the experience of the various crop research institutes, IADS undertook its missions through extending and strengthening agricultural research, training agricultural specialists, and implementing certain experimental production projects and programs in the developing world. These services have been provided under contract with the governments of such countries as Bangladesh, Botswana, Ecuador, Indonesia, Nepal, Panama, Nigeria, Senegal, Somalia, Thailand, and Western Samoa.

Well over half of the costs of these services is borne by the governments involved. (The two major purchasers of such services in 1979 were Nepal and Indonesia.) The two principal private foundation funders were Rockefeller and Lilly. Some support (about $100,000) came from U.S. AID, with lesser amounts from the Asian Development Bank, the World Bank, and the International Fund for Agricultural Development. IADS, however, has been primarily a Rockefeller Foundation initiative to provide long-term institutionalization and local rootage for the Green Revolution.

The effects of that revolution, regardless of how they ultimately may be assessed, have helped both in the production of the world's food and in calling attention to some of the other problems of the developing lands. The threat of mass starvation has been pushed back, but other challenges have remained and in some cases have intensified. Chief among these is the threat of overpopulation. Even the great success story of expanding food production in Mexico has been clouded by the ever-increasing population.

Problems of Population

In 1948 the Rockefeller Foundation sent an interdisciplinary team of scientists to survey the human welfare issues facing five Asian countries. They concluded that "the reduction of human fertility" was one of the most important problems, yet one of the most difficult.

The Foundation's initial response to this analysis was cautious. Assistance was provided for a variety of medical and basic science research projects on reproductive biology and human genetics. The field of demography was strengthened through grants to Princeton University's Office of Population Research, which undertook major fertility studies in Africa, Asia, and Europe. The foundation also gave support to the Population Council, an information and advocacy service that has had considerable influence in expanding public awareness of population problems in the United States and worldwide.

By 1963 the Rockefeller Foundation determined that "Problems of Population" would become one of its five major programs, and it launched into a comprehensive effort to promote "restraints on human fertility." In 1970 it spent $15 million, roughly one-third of all its grant expenditures, on population programs in the United States and around the world. During most of the 1960s and 1970s Rockefeller expenditures on population issues ranged from $5 million to $6 million per year. Over the past two decades the foundation has assisted university medical schools in Colombia, Indonesia, Thailand, Turkey, and other countries, educating doctors and nurses with the latest knowledge on contraception. Family planning clinics have been supported in their work with the urban and rural poor in a number of developing countries. Extensive research has been encouraged through U.S. and foreign universities, United Nations agencies and a number of private organizations.

One of the major forms of investment in the population field has been in the development of contraceptive devices, drugs, and techniques, guided by the International Committee for Contraceptive Development. Along the way, the foundation has gathered impressive evidence of the importance of improving the administration of family planning and other health services and of adapting the information dissemination activities to the local cultural traditions.

University Development/Education for Development

In 1963, when the Rockefeller Foundation began its large-scale assistance in the population field, it also initiated a major new program called University Development, with the intention of helping create a group of strong universities in a few of the strategically located and potentially important developing countries. Over the following decade substantial Rockefeller grants were directed to universities in Brazil, Colombia, Kenya, Indonesia, Nigeria, Philippines, Tanzania, Thailand, Uganda, and Zaire. The hope was that these investments could help bring about such a critical mass of scholars and teachers that they could be the instruments for broad national development in each of the countries. As was expressed in the *President's Ten-Year Review* in 1971, "if The Rockefeller Foundation can be said to have a single preeminent interest historically, it is the development of institutions to train professional people, scientists and scholars in the applied disciplines, who in turn will train succeeding generations of students, advance the state of knowledge in their fields, and respond to their countries' needs." It was a concept that had seemed to work with remarkable success in the establishment of public health services and in the improvement of agriculture. Would it work equally well in coping with the overall problems of nation building and social and economic development?

By 1974, when the foundation trustees reviewed the program of assistance to the universities, some doubts, or at least impulses toward modification, were beginning to surface. The evidence was clear that there was "a serious maladjustment between educational systems and the aspirations of the societies they are designed to serve all over the world." Critics felt that although there were good reasons to build strong, professionally elite universities, the "trickle down" benefits to the whole society were not sure enough or fast enough to satisfy the rising expectations and demands of the people. As a result of the questioning of the original pattern, the foundation renamed the program Education for Development and directed its emphasis in this field increasingly into enabling universities to contribute more directly to the particular development needs of their societies.

The foundation also became more fully aware of the all-pervading problem of management in delivering many kinds of needed services to the peoples of the developing world. It wasn't enough to devise a vaccine against yellow fever, develop a new strain of hybrid corn, and train competent doctors and agriculture specialists. Effective systems of management in public health, in education, in agriculture—in all fields—were required. Political and business structures, administrative competencies, and orderly patterns of management were, in country after country, found to be woefully inadequate for coping with the problems to be faced—including the problem of making good use of the financial resources available and of the newly trained specialists.

These were matters that could not suddenly be set right just by transferring Western knowledge and skills in administration. The developing countries had their own ancient cultural traditions about authority, family responsibilities, the status of women and older brothers, the influences of religion and tribe—all of which helped to shape the local style of management. Moreover, most of them had inherited a Western colonial system of administration that defined many of the operational norms, processes, and regulations. New technologies and new programs for development were often handicapped by overly complex administrative patterns. The local leaders, however, were themselves often very much aware of the need for improvements in management.

The Rockefeller and Ford foundations have been particularly sensitive in recent years to these management training problems and have undertaken to help in assorted ways through universities and management institutes. Elaboration of this subject may be found in the discussion of Ford Foundation programs.

It is obvious to the able men and women who serve the noble ambitions of the Rockefeller Foundation that there remain a great many frustrating problems to be dealt with—even after many successes in trying to promote "the well-being of mankind throughout the world." Yet the record of achievement is truly exraordinary. Life in the developing world, for all its continuing difficulties, is significantly better; the chances for human survival and human fulfillment are greater because of the work of this one American foundation under the grandiose mandate set forth by its founders just before World War I. As Dr. Richard Lyman became Rockefeller's tenth president in mid-1980, it was clear that while its programs and policies would change, the commitment to mankind's welfare, abroad as well as at home, would continue.

The Ford Foundation

Beginning in the 1950s, the Ford Foundation became involved in a series of ambitious international programs. They came about by deliberate design and as the result of an extended and comprehensive study of overall long-term foundation purposes. Ford did not move into overseas projects as a gradual extension of activities begun earlier in the United States, as the Rockefeller Foundation had done with its southern states campaigns against hookworm and malaria that it eventually extended around the earth. Moreover, unlike Rockefeller, Ford did not focus on a search for specific solutions to a few particular problems through its own teams of experts. Nor was there need or occasion to show great deference to the original charitable interests of the donor family. Following the death of Edsel Ford in 1943 and of his father, Henry Ford, in 1947, and after the settlement of their estates, the Ford Foundation trustees were faced with the necessity for prompt action to dispose of large sums of money—and that required serious attention to long-range philanthropic policies.

Founded in 1936 through an initial gift of $25,000 from Henry Ford, the foundation enlarged gradually, concerning itself primarily for the first two decades with rather traditional charities, chiefly in the state of Michigan. In 1948 the trustees chose a committee of consultants to propose a plan for transforming the foundation into a national organization capable of distributing many millions of dollars each year for major societal needs. Their recommendations, couched in very broad terms, proposed that the Ford Foundation organize its work around five "areas of action":

1. Activities that promise significant contribution to world peace and to the establishment of a world order of law and justice.
2. Activities designed to secure greater allegiance to the basic principles of freedom and democracy in the solution of the insistent problems of an ever-changing society.
3. Activities designed to advance the economic well-being of people everywhere and to improve economic institutions for the better realization of democratic goals.
4. Activities to strengthen, expand, and improve educational facilities and methods to enable individuals more fully to realize their intellectual, civic, and spiritual potentialities; to promote greater equality of educational opportunity; and to conserve and increase knowledge and enrich our culture.
5. Activities designed to increase knowledge of factors that influence or determine human conduct and to extend such knowledge for the maximum benefit of individuals and of society.

Many years later an officer of the foundation, Richard Magat, wrote that the purposes stated in that 1950 document "were so broad and comprehensive that virtually everything the Foundation has done in the intervening years can be rationalized as flowing from the original blueprint." However, no strained rationalization was ever needed to justify Ford's work in a variety of international endeavors. It committed itself from the outset to "world peace," to "the economic well-being of people everywhere," and to "freedom and democracy," presumably even in countries that had neither. It should never have been a surprise to anyone that in some years Ford expenditures for international programs would exceed forty percent of its total budget.

Running through all the original policy recommendations was the implicit assumption that whatever good purposes were to be served, they might be applied not only to the United States but to every other country to which the Ford staff and board might be drawn. The scale of resources available to them and the freedom of the mandate given them encouraged the trustees to think big and think globally.

For administrative and budgetary convenience the Ford Foundation organized its international activities around three functional divisions: an Overseas Development Program, an International Affairs Program, and an International Training and Research Program. For each of these separate but interrelated enterprises generous funding was provided and well-qualified professional staffs were assembled in New York and overseas. In all of these areas major attention was given to the building of institutions and the training of professionals, in the United States or in some foreign country, and often in both.

International Training and Research

The Ford Foundation's interests in international training and research found expression through a series of large grants to a number of the most distinguished American universities to establish centers of excellence in international studies, especially centers organized around particular regions and cultures. Within one short period (1960–1962) the foundation made grants of $45 million to encourage the expansion of non-Western studies at major universities in the United States. It already had helped develop African studies programs at Boston, Northwestern, and Harvard universities. Harvard, Yale, Michigan, Stanford, and Cornell were among the universities assisted in creating centers of Asian studies. Princeton, the University of Chicago, and Harvard received support for work on Middle Eastern peoples and their problems.

Ford supported these university centers of regional studies on the principle that if the United States was to handle effectively its growing relationships with the developing world it would have to acquire more knowledge and do more research about those areas. Consequently, the foundation began to train an army of experts who would acquire skills in foreign languages, detailed knowledge, and informed understanding of the diverse cultural, political, and economic conditions in the emerging new nations — such competencies would be needed by anyone who would become an effective participant in those relationships. The results have been mixed.

The story of those international studies centers is a long, fascinating, but not altogether happy one. Such centers are costly, and they have never had enough money. Moreover, some argue that too many universities tried to get into the act; more centers were established than could be sustained on a level of quality. Eventually, Ford had to cut back drastically on its support, and other donors did not come forward to pick up the slack. U.S. government funding has been erratic and never reached the level hoped for and needed. A tantalizing promise of large-scale assistance was offered in the International Education Act, passed in the Johnson administration, but it was never funded.

Some critics argue that adequate attention was never given to the development of the undergraduate dimensions of international studies. Others have charged that the graduate centers tended to focus too much on training additional Ph.D. academicians, for most of whom there were not appropriate academic posts. Others have complained that of all the people being sent abroad to work for government or business in the developing world, far too few have had suitable preparation for understanding and adjusting to the alien cultures into which they were being sent. Not enough of the "training" available at the university centers had been reaching the people who needed it most. Other critics have deplored the lack of linkage between the centers and the outgoing or returning Peace Corps volunteers and field people from AID and other government and private agencies.

Not all of these centers for regional studies may survive, and changes in program may be required of those that do, but the fact is that if they did not exist, they would have to be invented. Ford's role in inventing them was part of its long-term investment to enable the United States to prepare itself to deal more intelligently and responsibly with the developing world. Two big questions remain, however: How are such valuable research and training centers to be sustained financially? How are their information resources and their training opportunities to be made more widely available to the individuals and institutions that need them? The United States' capabilities for significant participation in the continuing development process abroad and the soundness of U.S. policies toward the developing world may well be shaped by the extent, form, and quality of the research and training done at these centers.

International Affairs Program

First on the list of recommended "areas of action" proposed by the consultant team that reported to the Ford Foundation's board in 1950 was "world peace and the establishment of a world order of law and justice." Under that rubric, extraordinary groupings of institutions, programs, and projects have been supported, most of them based in the United States; overseas grants commonly have concentrated on activities in the "developed countries."

In order to increase public understanding and participation by Americans in world affairs, the Ford Foundation has given significant funding to a number of nonacademic organizations involved in research, publication, and public discussion on matters of foreign affairs. The Council on Foreign Relations and the Foreign Policy Association, both based in New York, have been two of the chief beneficiaries of these kinds of grants. World affairs councils, scattered from coast to coast, also have been assisted with their broad public education endeavors. The American Assembly of Columbia University, the Carnegie Endowment for International Peace, the business-oriented Committee for Economic Development, the Brookings Institution, the National Academy of Sciences, and other private organizations in the United States have shared funds from Ford's international affairs division. Similar organizations abroad that have had Ford grants include the Atlantic Institute, the Congress for Cultural Freedom, the European Center of Sociology, the Center of Human Sciences, and the French National Foundation of Political Science, all based in Paris; the Institute for Strategic Studies and the Royal Institute of International Affairs in London; the Institute of Research and Publications, Madrid; the Royal Hellenic Research Institute, Athens; the International Institute for Social History, Amsterdam; and the Society for the Advancement of Economic and Socio-Economic Education, Frankfurt.

Among the foreign academic institutions assisted by Ford have been the Free University of Berlin, Oxford University, Cambridge University, the University of Naples, the University of Paris, the University of Bologna, and the Institute for Advanced Studies of Vienna. Moreover, many scholars and professors from all across Europe and other parts of the world have received Ford grants to pursue their studies in the United States and elsewhere.

There are several concerns behind the International Affairs programs of the Ford Foundation:

- to strengthen the economic, political, and cultural relationships between the United States and Western Europe;
- to promote deeper knowledge of the Soviet Union and of its challenge to the noncommunist world;
- to alleviate suffering among people who have fled from oppressive authoritarian countries;

- to encourage closer cooperation between the United States and Japan;
- to foster understanding and appreciation of the United States in foreign countries;
- to advance, both within and outside the United Nations, efforts to build more effective international processes for arms control and conflict resolution.

To these ends the foundation has distributed its funds to many different kinds of American, foreign national, and multinational institutions and organizations. It has made grants directly to the United Nations, to various U.S. and foreign governmental agencies, and to myriad nonprofit private voluntary organizations. Over the years, many of the international initiatives once funded by Ford have ceased to receive its support—some were never intended to be other than objects of short-term, special project assistance; others now have an established existence quite independent of any American foundation backing; some have disappeared with scarcely a trace. The foundation itself, meanwhile, has made a number of shifts in its program interests and priorities. Yet, standing out in both scale of giving and persistence of purpose has been the Ford Foundation commitment to overseas relief and development assistance for the so-called Third World countries.

Overseas Development Programs

More than any other foundation—more than any other private institution—the Ford Foundation has made worldwide comprehensive assistance for the advancement of the less developed countries a major objective. That interest has been expressed in countless ways, through grants to great numbers of institutions, organizations, and governmental agencies, and by an assortment of projects directly administered by Ford staff members.

Development Projects through Developed Countries' Institutions

Even in Ford's support for many of its European grantees there have been strong elements of developmental assistance to Asia, Africa, and Latin America. For example:

- *Overseas Development Institute*, London, to stimulate public discussion of the British role in development assistance and to encourage the work of development specialists at Oxford and Cambridge.

- *Royal Institute of International Affairs*, London, to conduct research on economic development problems in Latin America.
- *London School of Economics and University of Manchester*, to provide specially designed graduate and service training courses for students from Africa and Asia.
- *The German Institute for Developing Countries*, West Berlin, to promote discussions between officials of West Germany and the developing countries on "all phases of the development process," and to train German technical experts to serve overseas.
- *Carl Duisberg Society* of Cologne, to prepare written materials on economic and industrial problems of less developed countries.
- *Friedrich Ebert Foundation*, West Germany, to promote support for development programs by German trade unions and cooperatives.
- *Institute of Social Studies*, The Hague, to study and report on church-sponsored education and medicine programs in Asia, Africa, and Latin America.
- *Graduate Institute of International Studies*, Geneva, to produce written papers on constitutional government problems of emerging new nations.
- *Organization for Economic Cooperation and Development*, Paris, to develop policy studies, training programs, and technology transfer plans to bring western assistance to various countries in the developing world.
- *Centre for Educational Television Overseas*, London, to assist developing countries in making use of television in their school programs.
- *Kyoto University Center of Southeast Asia Studies*, Japan, to prepare information materials and trained specialists to help with development needs in Southeast Asia.
- *Committee for Economic Development*, Australia, to promote research and discussion on Australian participation in assistance programs in Asia.

Assistance to National Governments

The Ford Foundation is one of very few private philanthropic organizations in America that have provided financial assistance directly to many foreign governments and their development agencies and programs. This giving has been natural, and perhaps inevitable, in view of the shortage of effective private indigenous organizations in most of these countries and the dominant roles the governments play in planning and carrying out development strategies. The purposes of such grants to governments have been varied but have related to planning, to the strengthening of administrative capabilities, to research, and to the establishment of pilot development projects.

For example, among the projects Ford supported in Bangladesh during the period 1975–1980 were these grants to the national government: $138,000 for population studies, $50,000 for development planning, and $220,000 for agricultural and rural development. During that period there were many other Ford grants to specific developmental organizations and other institutions that are essentially agencies of the government or primarily supported by it: the Bangladesh Bank, the Bangladesh Agricultural Development Corporation, the Cholera Research Laboratory, and the Bangladesh Academy for Rural Development.

During the same five-year period the Ford Foundation made similar development grants in India, not only to the national government but to the Indian state governments of Madya Pradesh, Gujarat, Bihar, and Rajasthan, and to the Municipal Corporation of Greater Bombay. Other national governments that received Ford grants for development programs included Egypt, Botswana, Tanzania, Kenya, Colombia, Peru, Zambia, and Upper Volta.

Most universities in the developing countries are government financed and administered, and many of the Ford development program grants have been channeled to them: the Bangladesh University of Engineering and Technology, the University of Indonesia, Delhi University, the University of the West Indies, and the University of Dar es Salaam, to name only a few of many that Ford has assisted.

Institution and Profession Building

A major thrust of Ford philanthropy abroad for many years was toward the creation of new or expanded public service institutions, in partnership with the governments concerned, to serve national needs. These include the Indian Institute of Management, the Indian Institute of Public Administration, the Indian Family Planning Foundation, the Management Foundation of East Java, the Pakistan Institute of Development Economics, the Philippine Institute for Development Studies, and many others. Parallel to the stimulation and support of these special institutions, the foundation has undertaken to encourage the training and professional advancement of specialists in a variety of fields, particularly in the social sciences. According to Francis X. Sutton, long one of the key officials in the international programs of Ford, one of the major contributions the foundation has made to Latin America has been the development of social scientists.

"In Brazil, when we began working there in 1958–1959," he recalled, "the number of really competent Brazilian economists was small. They now have a powerful array of them. It wasn't all our doing, but we had a big hand in it; and if you went around Latin America and looked at the principal research organizations, you would see that almost all of them have had significant Ford Foundation support and almost all of the leading people in them, at one time or another, have been Ford Foundation Fellows."

In line with concern for the advancement of local professionals as one of the keys to development, the foundation has made grants to encourage professional societies: the Social Science Association of Thailand, the Latin American Social Science Council, the Brazilian Society of Agricultural Economics, the Brazilian Society for Instruction, the Central American Higher Education Council, the Language Association of Eastern Africa, the African Association for Public Administration and Management, and others.

Research for Development

To an extent unmatched by any other private funding source— and at times, in some fields, to a greater extent than by any government— the Ford Foundation has poured resources into research activities related to development problems. Often this has been through grants to major universities in the United States or other developed countries, and at times through grants to the emerging universities in the less developed countries. On occasion, the Ford-sponsored research programs have been carried on through special institutes: the Indian Council of Social Science Research, the Birla Institute of Technology and Science, the National Council of Applied Economic Research, and the Sandhar Patel Institute of Economic and Social Research, all in India; the Social Service Foundation in Indonesia; the Center for Studies of the State and Society in Argentina; the Brazilian Association for Population Studies. Many of the programs have been conducted at U.S. universities and research organizations: Social Science Research Council, International Council for Education Development, the Brookings Institution, the Overseas Development Council, International Food Policy Research Institute, and many others.

Two long-term concerns of the Ford Foundation relating to development-oriented research have been (a) the training of competent American specialists in the problems of development, and, increasingly, (b) the training of indigenous specialists in agriculture, economics, administration, education, and population to serve the needs of their native developing lands.

Year after year, in the detailed annual report recordings of Ford Foundation expenditures, there are numerous entries that begin, "Foundation-managed project: . . . " The sums listed have been substantial and have covered a wide range of activities. In large part, such expenditures have been concerned with fellowships, training grants, and research awards for individuals. For example: "research and consultants" in rural development in Colombia; "training and research" for specialists in nutrition in Brazil; "research awards" in agriculture in Mexico; "consultants and training of agricultural scientists in Eastern and Southern Africa," "research and training in the role of women" in West Africa; "consultants and training in agricultural economics, education, the environment, population and management" in the Middle East; "postdoctoral fellowship" and "research awards" for population studies in Brazil, West Africa, East Africa, and the Middle East.

Agricultural and Rural Development

Although Ford became involved in world food problems somewhat later than the Rockefeller Foundation, it has been a full partner with Rockefeller in some of the most significant, sustained efforts to increase agricultural production that have been attempted by any institution: the various international crop research centers set up in Mexico, the Philippines, Colombia, Nigeria and other countries—projects it still supports. Ford has also moved ahead on its own to fund a considerable number of other programs directed toward the expansion of food supplies and the improvement of rural life. A sampling of the grants made or continued in 1979 indicates the range of approaches to these vital problems Ford has been supporting in recent years:

- *Algeria:* further stimulation of farmers to increase vital grain production through still broader use of the new high-yield varieties of wheat and barley introduced earlier with help from Ford grants.

- *Nigeria:* assistance to the Department of Agricultural Economics to redesign certain agricultural development projects "aimed at making Nigeria self-sufficient in most major food crops."
- *Egypt:* a grant to Catholic Relief Services to "assist the development of simple farm machines—a multi-crop thresher, a seed cleaner, a water pump, and an insecticide sprayer—that can be manufactured locally."
- *India:* assistance for the National Dairy Development Board to expand the cooperative movement for milk distribution and increase income opportunities for small farmers and landless laborers.
- *Bangladesh:* support for the Institute of Nutrition and Food Science at the University of Dacca to study the worsening malnutrition problems among rural villagers and to conduct a pilot project aimed at improving diets.
- *Thailand:* grants for two northern Thailand universities to help farmers move away from the single-crop cultivation of rice pattern to "year-round multiple cropping (rice, corn, tomatoes, peanuts)."
- *Peru:* funds for the National Agrarian University to conduct research on "the impact of agrarian reform on poor rural families."

There are many grants to other organizations over a number of years that testify to Ford's long-term and extensive commitment to the expansion of agricultural production in the food-short countries of the developing world. Considerable achievements have come from those programs. But the race between expanding food supply and expanding population is still on.

Population Programs

Ford was an outstanding pioneer in encouraging research in the developing countries on matters of demography, population policies, and techniques of birth control. In a field that is culturally highly sensitive and politically explosive, the foundation made funds available for a number of countries to explore their population trends and the nature of related problems—and to examine the options.

"Ford was in the population area much ahead of a lot of other donors," Frank Sutton explained. "We made major contributions of at least two sorts. We helped to get countries around the world to see that they needed to have a population policy. This was done in various ways, often through economic planners, sometimes through special missions of population specialists, sometimes through demographic studies. But the emergence of population policies at a time when a lot of people were still inhibited about being active was significant, we think. Also, we gave a lot of early support to the growth of scientific studies on reproduction, much more than the U.S. government was putting in."

Ford's initiatives in the population field undoubtedly helped to spur comparable activities by a number of governments, promoted expanded funding by U.S. AID, and encouraged several founda-tions—Rockefeller, Hewlett, and others—to make grants for popula-tion programs.

Of all the forces affecting the course of development among the less advanced peoples of the world, few are likely to be more in-fluential than population growth between now and the year 2000. Neither the Ford Foundation officers nor the recipients of Ford population grants would claim that certain or generally acceptable answers have been found. Yet Ford, as much as any single private in-stitution anywhere, deserves the credit for bringing this question to its high priority place on the work schedule for world develop-ment—and survival.

Understandably, the Ford Foundation, by the beginning of 1981, had concluded that it could "phase out" large-scale support for population control programs. In an interview with *The New York Times*, Ford Foundation president Franklin A. Thomas observed that this issue has now been firmly placed on the "world agenda," and that national governments and the UN are now investing large sums of money in population planning; hence, Ford could reason-ably reduce its involvement.

Other International Ford Foundation Interests

Although this book focuses on private foreign aid for relief and development, any discussion of the Ford Foundation's international programs should mention two areas of activities that are inevitably related to the fate of developing countries—and the whole world. One is *arms control*, the other is *human rights*. How much atten-tion the foundation will give these issues in the future is unclear, as it moves toward implementing new plans for its international ac-tivities. Nevertheless, the issues remain urgently important and no quick solutions to them seem to be in the offing. The Ford Foundation is one of the few nongovernmental organizations to have attempted serious sustained explorations in these fields.

Some governments in developing countries and elsewhere have, of course, repudiated criticisms of any of their actions as human rights violations. Moreover, in conditions of civil war or prolonged terrorist activity aimed at producing changes in government, accusations of human rights violations can often be lodged against both leftist and rightist factions. It is a tricky area for intervention from abroad. Nevertheless, certain responsible private voluntary organizations have undertaken to monitor a number of the human rights cases at issue. Ford has provided partial funding for such projects through grants to Helsinki Watch, Inc.; the International League for Human Rights; the International Commission of Jurists; the American Council for Emigrees in the Professions; Freedom House; and the Anti-Slavery Society for the Protection of Human Rights.

Toward arms control and international security, the Ford Foundation has directed its grants primarily to support specialist training and research programs at a few major universities — Massachusetts Institute of Technology, Harvard, Stanford, California, and Cornell — and for technical studies by such research bodies as the Rand Corporation, Brookings, and the International Institute for Strategic Studies (London).

It used to be said that the United States could not sneeze without Europe catching cold. It is hard for the Ford Foundation to modify, change, or reduce its international activities without causing considerable concern, if not alarm, among many foreign institutions, U.S. institutions with international interests, and even governments. The range and scale of Ford involvement overseas and its grants in support of international activities by U.S. institutions have given it an unwanted impact upon a great number and variety of overseas institutions and programs. Yet it could never respond favorably to more than a very small fraction of the requests that flow into Ford offices from all over the world. As the foundation has curtailed its overall grantmaking in recent years in an attempt to live more nearly within its income (which it did not do for many years), the grants to international programs have shrunk considerably.

In 1965, with the dollar worth far more than it would be a decade and a half later, Ford made expenditures for international activities totalling $123.3 million. In 1979 total Ford expenditures for grants

and programs in *all* fields, domestic and international, amounted to
$109,633,289. Of that sum, $43,159,146 went to activities sponsored by the foundation's International Division. Although the
dollar amounts have dropped, international activities, over the
years, have tended to claim 35 to 40 percent of Ford's annual grants
budget. In the period 1950–1980, the grand total of Ford Foundation
expenditures for international programs came to approximately
$1.75 billion.

As Franklin Thomas moved toward the completion of his second
year as president of the foundation, there were indications that the
scale of Ford's investment in foreign projects would remain substantial and that the emphasis would change. There were signs that
there would be further reductions in investment in institutions and
in the support of academic and professional research activities, with
perhaps some increase in direct support for development projects.
There were also indications that Ford would seek to draw transnational corporations into partnership arrangements with Ford in programs to improve the quality of life for the poor in the less developed countries.

Whatever the exact nature of the Ford Foundation's international
activities, they seemed certain to remain among the major factors in
private U.S. foreign aid.

The Other Foundations

Over the years, all the other American foundations combined have
hardly matched the total investments of Rockefeller and Ford in international programs, and no other foundation has come close to
them in the breadth of their contributions for relief, development,
and other global purposes. Yet it must be made clear that at least
another one hundred foundations play useful roles in international
programs each year. Relatively modest grants for overseas projects
can be highly significant; even small, unstaffed foundations discover ways to help worthwhile international activities, particularly
in relief and development.

The reasons for giving abroad vary enormously among private
donors, and the range of program interests among them is extraordinary. Much of the motivation for international grantmaking by
U.S. foundations to this day is rooted in the religious, ethnic, economic, or cultural interests of the original donors. Operating from

these special kinds of interests, responsible and worthy grant-making takes place for a variety of programs in many lands.

Carnegie Corporation

When Professor Merle Curti wrote his landmark work on private American giving for international purposes in the 1950s and early 1960s, the full effect of the Ford Foundation's grantmaking overseas had not been felt. The joint Rockefeller-Ford endeavors to improve agricultural production around the world had not begun. In 1963, Curti's study *American Philanthropy Abroad* was published; in that work, he stated his considered judgment that "in truth, the philanthropies initiated abroad by Andrew Carnegie overshadowed all others in magnitude and impact."

In the sheer numbers of private dollars given away for charitable purposes outside the United States, that statement is no longer correct. But the impact of Carnegie philanthropies overseas has been enormous. The Carnegie Endowment for International Peace, an operating foundation, is still one of the principal independent institutions working on international conflicts and their resolution. The Carnegie Corporation is one of the handful of major American grantmaking foundations that conducts an ongoing program of giving to institutions outside the United States. All of this is one more reflection of the interests of the remarkable Andrew Carnegie, the creator of U.S. Steel, of Carnegie libraries, of teachers' pensions, and of a philosophy of giving that revolved around his often-expressed conviction that a rich man should "be ashamed to die rich."

Carnegie was still a boy when brought to the United States by his parents in 1848. He never forgot the grimy Scottish town of Dunfermline, where he was born and spent his childhood. At the end of the century, as a prosperous businessman, he made his first publicly noticed gift abroad: public baths for his birthplace. That gift was followed by other donations for a public library, organs for three churches, a park and recreation center, and finally a $2.5 million Carnegie Dunfermline Trust Fund "to bring into the monotonous lives of the toiling masses of Dunfermline more of 'sweetness and light' . . . some charm, some happiness. . . ."

Education and other cultural activities were of great importance to Mr. Carnegie, and he gave away many millions of dollars of his fortune to build hundreds of public libraries in the United States, Great Britain, Ireland, Australia, and various British colonies.

The Carnegie Corporation of New York, the general grantmaking organization (one of the half-dozen foundations that bear the Carnegie name), has operated significant international programs since the 1920s. It began making grants for activities in Africa under its Commonwealth Program in 1926. No other major American foundation goes back that far in relationship to Africa, although the Phelps-Stokes Fund did a study there in 1922.

Since 1911 the foundation has spent 7.5 percent of its income in certain British Overseas Commonwealth areas. Alan Pifer, Carnegie Corporation president, puts these recent expenditures at about $1 million a year. In the two decades from 1953 to 1973, total costs of the Commonwealth Program were about $25 million.

Normally, the foundation records its grants in terms of those made in the U.S. and those under the Commonwealth Program. But it also has had a continuing interest in supporting U.S.-based institutions and organizations to help underwrite international activities. (In 1979 the name of the program was changed to the International Program to "emphasize that present Commonwealth membership is not a prerequisite to funding eligibility," according to the 1978 annual report. The corporation's charter, however, requires that overseas grants be limited to countries that were British colonies, protectorates, or protected states as of April 1948. An excellent accounting of the Corporation's African program is given in the book *Creative Philanthropy: Carnegie Corporation in Africa, 1953–1973,* by E. Jefferson Murphy, Teachers College Press, 1976).

Alan Pifer has reported that after 1953, most of the foundation's Commonwealth Program expenditures were made in tropical Africa and in the West Indies, with a small number of grants going to Southeast Asia. Of the African expenditures, Pifer says, "a great deal of the money went into the development of institutes of education in the universities so that they, in turn, could assist other levels of education."

The corporation, according to Pifer, "put a lot of money into an association for teacher education in Africa," and it supports some curriculum projects, particularly in the social studies fields. However, a decision was made a few years ago to discontinue large "developmental" grants in favor of smaller ones, including those that facilitate communication between the United States and Africa within education and other professional fields.

Relations with South Africa is a sensitive issue for almost every American nonprofit or profit-making organization. Yet, for years, the list of recipients of Carnegie grants has included organizations in South Africa. At one time, much earlier, the foundation had "operated heavily" in that controversial country, according to Pifer. From 1953 to the 1960s, he recalls, "we did nothing there except give travel grants to individuals. There was even a period when we made no grants at all in South Africa."

Now, however, the foundation has a specific and continuing thrust for its programs in South Africa. It is supporting a "careers development project" that operates under the U.S./South African Leadership Exchange Program. Through it, people beyond student age who are classified as one of the three nonwhite races in South Africa are given grants for studies of a few months, a year, or even longer. Aimed at upgrading careers for nonwhites, the grants apply in all sorts of fields, and for studies either in South Africa or outside the country.

Additionally, Carnegie is supporting the Institute for Legal Studies at the University of Witwatersrand in Johannesburg, and a legal resources center, both of which "have to do with the legal rights of non-whites in South Africa."

Among the corporation's most successful Commonwealth Programs, Pifer names the Ashby Commission on Higher Education in Nigeria. Organized as a Nigerian government commission in 1959, it planned the future of higher educational development in that country. Pifer also cites two major studies of Africa by Lord Hailey—one in 1938 and another in 1956—as significant scholarly and public policy contributions, comparable to Myrdal's "The American Dream," an outstanding analysis of Black/White relations that was done with Carnegie assistance. The corporation also has a Women in Development program that operates largely in Kenya and the West Indies.

Among Carnegie research projects that Pifer believes have been highly significant was one he calls "the poor white study," done in South Africa around 1930. "At the time it was the biggest piece of social science research that had ever been done there," he says, "and it was extremely important." At that time the Afrikaner "was sort of an outcast in his own country. He was extremely poor, largely rural, and outside the mainstream. The premise of the study was that until the economic position of the Afrikaner improved there was nothing that could be done about the political and economic conditions of non-whites. It was a famous and important piece of work."

Because many of the expressions of American interests in the British colonial areas of Africa initially aroused resentment among the white settlers and British colonial officials, the Carnegie Corporation undertook a mediating role in the years before the colonial controls were dissolved. "We saw to it that people met each other," Pifer explains. "We saw to it that people from this country went to England and there met people involved in African issues. We had representatives from the Colonial Office and the Commonwealth Relations Office and the universities come to this country to meet people here. We sponsored special conferences, and a lot of good projects came out of them. In the long run, much prejudice was overcome, especially in higher education."

Asked why more American private foundations haven't been involved in international programs, Pifer cites the lack of internationally knowledgeable staff. "With the great welter of problems all over the world, when you have $25,000 to spend it is difficult to relate that sum to India, for example. Why pick that country over Latin America or Africa?" Moreover, he points out, in most cases it "probably wasn't the intent of the donor to be involved internationally."

Pifer also expresses the opinion that most foundations would have to work through existing organizations that "know what they are doing. Foundations want to do something distinctive, and just contributing to the general funds of an organization isn't very appealing."

Nevertheless, Pifer believes that foundations, corporate givers, and individuals should involve themselves in more philanthropic activity abroad. Recognizing that foundation resources are finite, he agrees that "The more that is given overseas, the less will be given here. . . . Nonetheless, the real problem is part of a larger one . . . Americans' lack of interest in international affairs." To deal with that broader issue, he feels, will require "new and expanded initiatives for affecting our educational system and the media."

W. K. Kellogg Foundation

Since 1937, just seven years after its founding, the W. K. Kellogg Foundation has been making international grants. The first assistance was in the form of fellowships to two Montreal physicians for a year's experience in the U.S. public health field. At roughly the same time, Kellogg subsidized a couple of postgraduate medical courses for doctors at McGill University in Montreal. In the next twenty years, Canadians received 160 fellowships and the foundation financed sixty-one projects involving people abroad at a cost in excess of $2 million.

That, of course, represents only an early part of the foundation's international story. During its first fifty years, Kellogg expended $15.6 million in Canada, nearly $14.2 million in Europe, more than $4.8 million in Australia and Pacifica, and almost $51.8 million in Latin America and the Caribbean. The foundation's total international program expenditures, through 1980, stood at $86.4 million, roughly 17 percent of its overall program expenditures of more than $495.8 million.

Kellogg began making grants in Latin America in 1941. Again, fellowships played a significant part in the relationship: Nine Chilean doctors came to the U.S. that year for "a brief educational experience."

The foundation's fiftieth anniversary book reports that "The success of that modest activity drew the attention of the U.S. State Department. After World War II began, when there was concern about maintaining good relationships with the rest of the Western Hemisphere, the State Department suggested that the foundation could aid the war effort by continuing and expanding its assistance in the field of Latin American health." As a result, the foundation made more than 200 fellowship awards between 1941 and 1945.

The foundation's policy governing its Latin American grants has been rooted in a concern for the training of leaders in the health professions for that region's developing countries. In medicine, dentistry, and nursing it has supported extensive post-graduate training. On occasion it provided the resources to train several members of a single hospital department. The foundation points out with great satisfaction that "many former Kellogg Fellows have risen to top positions in their countries and within their professions. In Latin America, especially, the list is staggering: several became national ministers of health; others have held the post of secretary of health in their state governments. At least five have been rector (president) of a university and more than fifty achieved the rank of dean or assistant dean. Dozens of others have gone on to head hospitals, nursing schools and dental clinics. And many have become prominent in international or intra-national organizations. Several have gone on to other top government positions. For example, one former Fellow became president of El Salvador and another was governor in a state in Brazil."

Beyond the fellowship programs for outstanding health professionals, Kellogg underwrote the establishment of the first department of preventive dentistry in Latin America, encouraged the development of "progressive patient care" in a number of the principal teaching hospitals in the region, and supported the expansion of family health care programs in several countries. Symbolic of Kellogg's strong commitment to health services in Latin America is the largest grant the foundation made during its first fifty years: $5 million to assist in the construction of the Pan American Health Organization headquarters building in Washington, D.C.

In recent years Kellogg has moved increasingly into the activities related to nutrition and the improvement of agriculture. Established with funds earned in the breakfast cereal business, Kellogg began assisting other countries with food production problems in 1953, when it initiated efforts to share with Western Europe food production technology developed in the United States. Young agricultural leaders in England, Norway, Ireland, Denmark, Finland, Sweden, and West Germany received fellowships and scholarships. Other project grants were aimed at helping European institutions and organizations develop and improve food production programs. Lately the foundation has been concerned with problems associated with the marketing and distribution of food domestically and internationally; the management problems and the preparation of farm leaders; the structure of European agriculture; low incomes from small farms; and the development of national agricultural policies. It also has helped set up training programs for agricultural specialists in Ireland, England, and Denmark.

Kellogg has been a partner with the Ford and Rockefeller foundations in founding and supporting the Center for Tropical Agriculture (CIAT) in Colombia. Its grants have helped fund the construction of conference facilities in Cali, Colombia, and disseminate information about tropical food production and the improvement of diets for people who live in tropical lowlands.

Having been involved in international grantmaking for many years and in substantial measure, Kellogg attracts numerous requests for funding for overseas projects, yet a high percentage of them must be turned down as outside its policy guidelines. The foundation does review these policies from time to time, but it seems likely to continue to give primary attention to programs related to health and agriculture in Latin America and in a few other selected countries such as Canada and Australia.

Lilly Endowment

By the early 1970s, Lilly Endowment of Indianapolis, founded in 1937, had grown into one of the half-dozen largest foundations in the country, with assets of more than one billion dollars. Throughout its history it had been oriented primarily toward educational, cultural, and social service programs in Indiana and the Midwest. With the great increase in its capital assets, the board of the endowment decided in 1973 to expand into a number of new national and international program areas. Already, for some years, its religion division had been involved in grantmaking activities abroad.

As with Rockefeller and other foundations, the interests of the original donor had crucial influence. Mr. and Mrs. Eli Lilly were devoted members of the Episcopal Church and, according to denomination officials, they personally contributed more money to their church during their lives and through their wills than any other couple in the history of American Episcopalians. It is small wonder, then, that Lilly Endowment designated the support of religion as one of its principal purposes. Although Eli's father, Josiah K. Lilly, and his brother, Josiah K. Lilly, Jr., joined him in the contribution of stock in the family pharmaceutical business to provide the initial capital for the foundation, it was "Mr. Eli," long-time president and board chairman of the endowment, who primarily shaped its purposes. Several of the key staff administrators over a period of several decades have been ordained ministers or deeply involved laymen. Lilly grants in religion have gone to many different denominations and many kinds of activities—from Protestant theological seminaries to Catholic retreat centers to Jewish youth groups to Black church social service programs. Some grants were directed to the support of overseas missionary projects and for relief and development programs sponsored by church-related or interdenominational service organizations. These set the precedents for the substantially enlarged international grantmaking endeavors in which Lilly was involved in the period 1973–1978, and which have continued to influence the limited international involvements of the endowment since then.

During the five-year peak period of its support for international programs, Lilly chose to allocate the major part of its international grants to American-based private voluntary agencies working in developing countries in Asia, Africa, and Latin America: World Neighbors, World Vision, and Accion, International; the Heifer Project, Volunteers in Technical Assistance, Technoserve, Partners of the Americas; the Asia Foundation, the International Institute for Rural Reconstruction, Partners for Productivity, the American Friends Service Committee, and others. It was the first foundation to give significant assistance to Africare, the Black-run PVO through which more than a million dollars of Lilly money was channelled for water resource development and experimental farm programs in Niger and other famine-afflicted, arid areas of West Africa. Through Cornell University, it helped underwrite a novel wild game ranching project in Kenya. It helped the World Rehabilitation Fund, based in New York, to develop physical rehabilitation centers in Egypt and in West and East Africa. Through the Catholic diocese of New Ulm, Minnesota, the endowment directed funds to an imaginative rural economic improvement program among Indian communities in the mountains of Guatemala. Other church groups it assisted included the Caribbean Conference of Churches, the International Congress on World Evangelism, the Holy Cross Foreign Mission Society, the All Africa Conference of Churches, and numerous overseas relief and development projects associated with the Episcopalians, the Mennonites, the Quakers, and the Church of God. One grant assisted a group of refugee Tibetan lamas.

In addition to the Kenya wild game ranching project, which began as a research undertaking related to the Cornell University College of Agriculture, Lilly Endowment made grants for international research, peace studies, and education programs to Columbia, Harvard, Indiana, Pennsylvania, Notre Dame, Georgetown, Yale, Wellesley, Texas, Stanford, and Pittsburgh universities, the Great Lakes Colleges Association, and, abroad, to American University in Beirut, Haifa University (Israel), the University of the Americas (Mexico), and the University of London.

In support of student and other people-to-people exchanges, the endowment made grants to Youth for Understanding, Executive Council on Foreign Diplomats (formerly Travel Program for Diplomats), and Council on International Education Exchange. It also made grants for expanding public understanding of international affairs through such organizations as the New York and Chicago Councils on Foreign Relations.

The drastic reduction of Lilly involvement in international programs since 1977 has produced much disappointment among grantees and regret among the all-too-limited community of international-minded foundations.

"We had to make some agonizing choices," Executive Vice President Richard O. Ristine has explained in discussing the drastic shift in Lilly's funding pattern. "The Board wanted the endowment to continue in business, but we had been paying out much more than our income, thanks to the requirements of the Tax Reform Act of 1969. Moreover, market conditions had brought about a drastic decline in our capital assets — from a peak of $1.3 billion to less than $700 million. Our payout dropped from about $55 million in our highest year to less than $25 million."

Ristine points out that other Lilly programs besides the international one were greatly reduced or phased out: rural community development in the United States, adult criminal justice programs, and parent/early childhood programs. "We tried to narrow our focus to a few areas," Ristine says. "We were guilty of scatteration."

Ristine says the foundation has continued modest support of some internationally oriented organizations, such as Freedom House, the Overseas Development Council and World Neighbors. He emphasizes that the foundation wasn't dissatisfied with the international projects, but "there was some feeling that some of the things Lilly had funded, appropriate technology, for example, AID was beginning to understand and to support."

Regarding the role of government money in the funding of PVOs, Ristine feels "that foundations believe that as long as government moneys come in the organizations are apt to lose at least some of their independence. Moreover, at least some of the organizations don't make an appropriate effort to broaden their base of support. That's one reason why we have on our staff a senior advisor to help groups develop broader-based fundraising efforts."

As far as funding patterns are concerned, Ristine believes foundation funding can be more valuable if the grantmaker stays with one agency over an extended period to see that it succeeds in providing a service needed in a particular area, rather than scattering "seed money" for a lot of different projects. He also stresses the importance of knowing as much as possible about the PVO to be funded and its chances for effective continuity after the orginator of the project, often an idealistic, energetic, and charismatic figure, disappears from the scene.

Despite the fact that it has had to cut back its international grantmaking severely, the Lilly Endowment is still spoken of by the PVO community as a foundation that knew what development assistance was, knew the problems PVOs had and what they were attempting to do, and was willing to be supportive without being overly restrictive.

Rockefeller Brothers Fund

Founded in 1940 by the five Rockefeller grandsons of John D. Rockefeller, Sr., the Rockefeller Brothers Fund (RBF) has had diversified interests ranging from local art, welfare, and health projects in

New York City to educational and rural development programs in Africa, Asia, and Latin America. In varying ways its grants over the years have reflected cultural interests and social concerns of the family members. John D. Rockefeller III was strongly drawn to the cultures and problems of Asia; he was also seriously committed to the cause of family planning. Winthrop Rockefeller was very much interested in agriculture and in rural development. Nelson A. Rockefeller had extensive involvements with the economic, social, and political problems of Latin America, both as a high U.S. government official and as a businessman. David Rockefeller, as trained economist and banker, has had a long-standing concern for development issues and the problems of international trade and diplomacy. Laurance S. Rockefeller has given sustained attention to environmental issues, both at home and overseas. Both he and his brother David have been interested for many years in the problems and needs of the Caribbean.

RBF has been one of the few U.S. foundations ever to assign a professional staff person to concentrate on international grantmaking for developing countries. For several years that person has been William S. Moody. Under his guidance, RBF interests in Central America and the Caribbean have been related to a number of grassroots development projects.

Since its founding in 1969, the Overseas Development Council has received substantial support from RBF for research studies, publications, and conferences on development issues and public policies and programs that deal with the needs of the Third World. The fund has also supported such internationally involved institutions and programs as the Center for Inter-American Relations, the Woodrow Wilson International Center for Scholars of the Smithsonian Institution, the Asia Foundation, the International League for Human Rights, the Trilateral Commission, the Asia Society, the Japan Society, the Council on Foreign Relations, and others.

In the early 1970s the fund concentrated substantial attention on Africa, with grants to the African-American Institute, the South African Institute of Race Relations, the National Council of Churches Emergency Fund for Southern Africa, and to a number of education and community development programs in Botswana.

More recently, Central America and the Caribbean have had top priority for RBF overseas development grants. Beginning in 1976, it provided funds to support planning, training, and pilot demonstrations in wildland management in each of the Central American republics through the Tropical Agriculture Center for Research and

Training (CATIE), based at Turrialba, Costa Rica. Substantial support for similar wildland management projects in the eastern Caribbean was given through the Caribbean Conservation Association, with headquarters in Barbados. Other Barbados-based regional organizations funded by RBF include the Association for Caribbean Transformation, which is concerned with training and technical assistance for agricultural cooperatives and low income worker groups, and Christian Action for Development in the Caribbean, which supplies advisory services for small businesses.

To an extent unmatched by any other private American foundation, RBF has sought out and funded indigenous Caribbean private voluntary groups working on grass-roots community development projects. It has funded them for such endeavors as a self-help youth employment program on the island of Dominica, improvement of agriculture and nutrition on St. Vincent, encouragement of small business ventures in Trinidad and Tobago, and expansion of local food processing in Antigua.

Particular attention has been given by RBF to the Windward and Leeward Islands of the Eastern Caribbean, where per capita income is low and unemployment high and where deforestation, soil erosion, and water pollution have become major problems. The fund correctly identified this as an area of acute social tensions and urgent needs some years ago. Recently the U.S. government, belatedly, has become sufficiently alarmed about the chronic agonies of the region to try seriously to address them.

After a Cuban-style group of armed leftists staged a coup on the island of Grenada during the Carter administration, the White House sent out directives through the foreign policy and defense establishments that attention had to be given to the Caribbean immediately. Not much happened. At the beginning of the Reagan administration these same concerns came to the fore again, and there was earnest talk of a "Marshall Plan" for the Caribbean. The White House expressed the hope that private U.S. financial institutions and the governments of Mexico and Venezuela would join in a large-scale and sustained effort to deal with the problems and needs of the region. The Rockefeller Brothers Fund may, at last, have found some partners.

Reflecting on the RBF experience with development programs, William Moody concludes that consultation among U.S. foundations on these issues should be encouraged and a greater measure of cofunding should be attempted. Strongly committed to the kind of work the fund is supporting abroad, he has been trying quietly to recruit corporate and foundation partners. His advocacy efforts, so far, have not produced conspicuous results, but he has not given up.

"Whenever I get to one of our major cities I try to find out what is going on among foundations of the area, which ones are active, whether any of them might be considering some international work. . . . I have been disappointed that so few foundations have taken an interest in international affairs when there are so many opportunities and the needs are so clear. The challenges are really pretty interesting for a foundation, big or small, to get involved."

In his efforts to enlist other foundations as cofunders, Moody says he finds himself, again and again, falling back on Ford, Carnegie and the Rockefeller Foundation as his most likely prospects for some partnership arrangements. "So, I turn to the Canadian Government or . . . some branch of the United Nations system . . . or . . . some foreign church organization . . . because I don't see much growth among American foundations . . . with their existing budgets."

While deploring the limited interest of foundations in international programs, Moody says that U.S. PVOs need to define more sharply their "individual missions for the next decade"; need to "blend their resources, their staffs, their experiences" more fully with each other, with government development assistance agencies, and with the emerging PVOs in foreign countries; and they need to work more effectively at communicating their case to prospective donors. In the long run, he says, the likelihood is that there will be fewer PVOs in the field, and he hopes they will be stronger, more flexible, and less paternalistic.

Charles F. Kettering Foundation

One of the most internationally minded of the private foundations has for a number of years been the Charles F. Kettering Foundation of Dayton, Ohio. This is a reflection of the interest of its long-term president, Robert G. Chollar, and several of its board members. Kettering, moreover, has been one of the few grantmaking organizations to have among its senior officers a vice president charged with responsibilities for international programs. The expression of its international interests has taken some unusual forms.

Primarily an operating foundation, administering many of its projects through its own staff, the Kettering Foundation from its beginning has had a major commitment to a natural science research program in the field of photosynthesis. This was a concern of the infinitely curious inventor/engineer and General Motors Vice

President, Charles F. Kettering. "Boss Ket," as he was known, liked to say that one of the really big questions that still had to be answered was "What makes grass green?" If scientists could probe the mysteries of photosynthesis, they would find out how and why carbohydrates are formed in the chlorophyll-containing tissues of plants exposed to light, and would then be able to find surer ways to feed the whole world. Not waiting for others to do the job, Mr. Kettering established a special laboratory on the edge of the Antioch College campus at Yellow Springs, Ohio, less than twenty-five miles from his home, and assembled a staff of scientists to work on the photosynthesis project. He frequently dropped in to putter around the laboratory and to speculate about where this research might go.

Since his death, the Kettering Foundation board has continued the research on photosynthesis and nitrogen fixation and has established links with other scientists at home and abroad, looking for breakthroughs that could make a major contribution to the expansion and improvement of world food supply.

The chemical nitrogen fixation studies are intended to find ways to synthesize the nitrogen-fixing catalyst *nitrogenase*. This in turn, it is hoped, will lead to the production of better plant nutrients and, hence, expanded crop production. Parallel to the chemical synthesizing project, the Kettering scientists are probing further into the mysteries of nitrogen fixation via the biological route, learning all they can about the symbiotic associations between nitrogen-fixing bacteria and certain legumes such as soybeans. The central purpose of its "Science and Technology" program, say the Kettering mission statements, is to gain knowledge that "will lead to increasing world food supplies."

Building on these scientific research activities, the "International Affairs" program of the foundation has fostered nongovernmental communications in a variety of fields. It has sponsored conferences, in cooperation with the Overseas Development Council, that have brought together citizen leaders of Latin American, African, and Asian countries to exchange information and viewpoints about food and development. It has also helped bring together from a number of developing countries science policy leaders to plan collaborative research projects involving their scientists and the U.S. scientific community. Understandably, Kettering has given particular attention to international communication about nitrogen fixation research and its implications for development.

A theme of public policy development runs through many of the programs sponsored by Kettering, so it was natural that it should join the Ford and Rockefeller foundations and the Overseas Development Council in sponsoring the creation of the Congressional Staff Forum on Food and International Development. In 1980 this nonpartisan educational forum attracted the participation of 250 congressional staff members who attended at least one session.

Collaborating with the International Center for Law in Development, the Kettering Foundation has sponsored three Asian workshops in transnational economic relations. These, in turn, have led the foundation into the planning, with representatives of the People's Republic of China, of a workshop "directed toward China's emerging needs in the area of international investment and development."

Among the activities related to development that Kettering has sponsored through grants to outside organizations are the following:

- studies of the effect of climate on global food production by Case Western Reserve University;
- studies of the effect of climate on the production of rice and wheat in India by the University of Missouri;
- an examination of the processes for unofficial consultation between developing countries and multinational corporations by the Policy Sciences Center;
- dialogue on Inter-American policy questions conducted in Latin America under the auspices of the International Center for Tropical Agriculture.

An overarching major concern of the international programs has been to foster nonofficial communications on critical world issues. To that end Kettering has for a decade played a leading role in organizing and carrying through a series of high-level (though nongovernmental) talks, called the Dartmouth Conference, between Soviet and American representatives. Arms control, trade relations, scientific exchanges, and conflicts in the developing world have been among the chief topics of these far-ranging and often very blunt dialogues.

Tinker Foundation

This New York foundation, established in 1959, has a unique mission as a private grantmaker: It focuses on the Spanish-speaking and Portuguese-speaking peoples of the Western Hemisphere—"Ibero-America." Within that framework it supports a great variety of programs in such fields as demography, communication, history, political science, and a number of technical areas.

About 20 percent of its grants go to projects related to "natural resource development." It supports programs concerned with marine biology, climate and agriculture, pollution of the seas, the transfer of intermediate technology, and regional economic and social development.

For the most part, it makes its grants to organizations and institutions that are rooted in Latin America or to universities in the United States that have strong ties with that region. It rarely gives to U.S. PVOs, but has supported a few on projects related to community economic development.

Public policy issues affecting relations between the United States and the countries of Ibero-America are of great concern to Tinker. It provides support for conferences, seminars, and educational programs that deal with a broad range of topics. It has promoted a limited amount of people-to-people exchange, particularly for journalists.

De Rance, Inc.

This Milwaukee, Wisconsin, foundation, with assets of more than $125 million, reflects the deep concerns and religious interests of its founder, Harry G. John. The largest share of its grants, totalling in a typical year more than $14 million, go to religious, educational, and charitable activities related to the Roman Catholic Church, many of them in foreign countries. Hospitals, social service organizations, the poor, the handicapped, schools, colleges and universities, plus churches, convents, monasteries, and religious orders comprise the list of its grant recipients.

While the foundation restricts itself to single-year grants only, and does not provide endowment funds or support research-related programs, it is willing to give to a great variety of projects: a water system, conferences, film production, debt retirement, building renovation, scholarships, publications, and general operational expenses. Recent grants, in sums ranging from less than $10,000 to more than $200,000, went to such projects as these:

- a new dormitory at Saint Mbaaga's Seminary in the Archdiocese of Kampala, Uganda;
- an educational building complex attached to Sacred Heart Church in the Accra Diocese of Ghana;

- homes for poor families related to the Gopalapetta Mission in the state of Kerala, India;
- emergency relief for the work of the Verona Fathers Mission in Uganda;
- five school buses and a new telephone system for the College of the Holy Family in Cairo, Egypt;
- reconstruction of a church in the village of Allamata, Ethiopia;
- $60,000 for shipping costs for medical supplies sent to various overseas missions.

Besser Foundation

This locally oriented midwestern foundation with no professional staff, managed by a small board of businessmen in Alpena, Michigan, was an unlikely prospect for the funding of any international programs. But then, offhandedly, it became involved in the problems of Africa. This is what happened, as told by Carl F. Reitz, a trustee of the foundation:

> Besser Foundation's statement of policy includes a phrase, "programs and projects related to the welfare of the citizens of northeastern Michigan are of primary concern to the Foundation." However, a session at the 1978 meeting of the Council on Foundations in Washington, D.C., entitled "Economic and Human Resource Development: the U.S.A. role" . . . convinced us that philanthropy, although it may begin at home, should not stop there. A single question—"What can a small northern Michigan foundation accomplish in big faraway Africa?"—brought a quick response from C. Payne Lucas, executive director of Africare and one of the speakers. He proposed a $15,000 package of health care for the Sahel, a region barely beginning to recover from the drought of the early 1970s. (You might agree, it's safer to wave a red flag in front of a bull than to ask such a question as I did.) The Besser trustees approved and sent their check to Africare. It was that simple to become involved.

A year later Reitz and a fellow trustee made a trip to West Africa and visited the "two projects funded by the Besser Foundation: a dispensary building at Bitagoungou and furnishings for one at Dovekene," two villages "near ancient Timbuktu, in Mali." There they found that "our first investment in Africa now provides previously unavailable health care for several thousand people."

In talking with "ministry officials, village chiefs and villagers," these two businessmen from Alpena, Michigan, became convinced that "the answer to Africa's future lies in water for drinking and irrigation." Their response to that conclusion was another Besser Foundation grant, this one for "$12,000 for four diesel-operated pumps to provide water for irrigation projects in four villages in the Goundam Region of Mali. . . . Our second investment will help them develop an adequate food supply."

Besser will continue to support primarily the local community service projects in northeastern Michigan that are its central mission, but the concern and imagination of its officers have been stirred by what they have learned about the "incredible impact" that can be made on human lives by small sums of money invested in poor people in the developing world.

China Medical Board of New York, Inc.

China Medical Board of New York is an independent grantmaking foundation. It was originally a division of the Rockefeller Foundation, and since 1923 has been a separate corporate entity. With assets near the $50 million level, and with annual grants in excess of $2 million, it is one of the top ten foundations of the country in expenditures for international programs. Virtually all of its grants go to projects in developing countries.

The original primary purpose of China Medical Board was to give continuing support to Peking Union Medical College, created in 1915 by the Rockefeller Foundation. Most of its funds were, indeed, directed to that purpose until, in 1951, PUMC was nationalized by Chairman Mao's new People's Republic of China. After that time, the board distributed its grants among a variety of medical educational institutions for medical libraries, the purchase of equipment and supplies, and fellowships for study in the United States. More recently it has shifted its interests toward support of medical research, and medical education and postgraduate study within several Asian countries.

Most China Medical Board grants in recent years have been for both endowment and operating purposes at medical colleges and schools of nursing and public health in Hong Kong, Indonesia, Korea, Malaysia, Philippines, Singapore, Taiwan, and Thailand. The stated objective of the board's work is to help these eight countries "to attain self-sufficiency in medical, nursing and public health education as related to national needs; specifically to help institutions to improve the health levels and services and to increase the numbers and quality of health practitioners in these societies."

An unusual feature of the board's grantmaking in recent years has been the substantial proportion—in some years more than half of its grant expenditures—that has gone to help build endowment funds at the several medical colleges. Earmarked for either "staff development" or "medical research," these contributions have generally been made on the basis of a requirement of matching funds to be raised from other sources.

The board has been concerned with more than just strengthening the facilities and programs of those institutions; it has helped them broaden their base of support and extend their services within each nation.

The International Foundation

One of the few foundations in the United States—if not the only one—concerned exclusively with grantmaking for international programs is a "low-profile" organization called the International Foundation. Managed without paid professional staff by a small board of men who live in the New York metropolitan area—two of whom are medical school professors—the foundation concentrates on the support of relief and development work in Asia, Africa, and Latin America. About one-third of its grant funds in a typical year go for health projects.

Private voluntary organizations constitute a considerable percentage of the grant recipients, and include U.S.-based human service groups that provide direct assistance to needy people overseas, e.g., International Rescue Committee, Technoserve, World Neighbors, Meals for Millions, and International Voluntary Services (IVS). It also works with other private organizations and institutions in the United States that train volunteers for overseas work, hold conferences, conduct studies, or provide support to selected indigenous agencies abroad. The American Red Cross, the Asia Foundation, the National Academy of Sciences, Columbia University, and the World Rehabilitation Fund are among the recent grantees that have performed these intermediary and supervisory functions related to the foundation's purposes. Several church-related groups have also received support, including the Maryknoll Sisters, the Divine Word Missionaries, The Mustard Seed, Inc., and the Oblate Philippine Missions.

Refugees and war victims have obviously been of concern to the board members of the International Foundation, as reflected in grants for the benefit of POWs in Africa and Lebanon and Angolan refugees in Zaire.

Development projects supported by the foundation have included homecraft training for women in the South Pacific, boats for fishermen in the Philippines, assistance for a cooperative cotton gin in Nicaragua, and training for agricultural and health workers in Yemen.

Only rarely is an International Foundation grant made for as much as $50,000; annual disbursements generally do not exceed $500,000. Yet within the philanthropic community, its commitment to relief and development programs abroad is highly respected. The PVOs wish that there were a lot more foundations like it.

Foundations with Limited but Specific International Interest

There are several foundations with well-defined and overwhelmingly domestic programs that have, nevertheless, involved themselves in certain specific concerns that are at times expressed through international grants. This may be the case with foundations that have interests in such fields as the environment, health, family planning, archaeology, and religion. Moreover, a considerable number of foundations, on rare occasions, will make special "out of program" grants for some emergency need abroad such as assistance to earthquake or war victims. Following is a very abbreviated sampling of this type of international grantmaking.

The Edna McConnell Clark Foundation

This New York foundation concentrates on domestic programs of assistance to the poor and handicapped. Its own international activity is also directed at helping the needy, but in lands far away. This is the basis of its Tropical Disease Research program, which seeks to control and cure the major health problem of schistosomiasis (snail fever) that "debilitates many of the 200 million infected people in the developing world."

Scientists working on this problem at American universities are assisted in their laboratory analyses and in their field work. Other grants go to foreign institutions and health agencies operating in the infected countries. This has been a stubbornly baffling puzzle to medical science for many years. Its solution would be a great boon to some of the poorest people in the developing world.

The William and Flora Hewlett Foundation

This California foundation has expanded its grantmaking considerably beyond the educational, cultural, and human service organizations it has traditionally supported in the San Francisco Bay area. One of its program commitments is now to the difficult global problem of population planning.

It currently supports projects related to the training of population experts, the carrying out of policy-related research in population issues, development of comprehensive family planning services, and education on human sexuality.

Recognizing the worldwide significance of this issue, Hewlett has stated that "the Foundation is particularly interested in projects involving the less developed countries, where most of the unsustainable population growth occurs." With equal straightforwardness, it says it will not fund "the development of contraceptives . . . [or] . . . population-education programs directed toward the general public."

The Pew Memorial Trust

The various foundations created by the late J. Howard Pew and linked together for management under the umbrella of the Glenmede Trust of Philadelphia have a strong orientation toward education, health care, and community services programs in the Pennsylvania region. They also tend to reflect the staunchly conservative philosophy of the founder. Pew interests in international programs have been expressed almost entirely through an assortment of grants to churches and PVOs.

An active Presbyterian, Mr. Pew gave to the missionary enterprises of his denomination. By extension, Pew contributions have been made since his death to such groups as the American Leprosy Mission, Food for the Hungry, Meals for Millions, the Christian Service Corps, and The Mustard Seed. Concern for refugees and the victims of man-made and natural calamities is reflected in grants for disaster relief in Bangladesh and Uganda and in general support for such organizations as the American Red Cross, CARE, the World Rehabilitation Fund, the International Rescue Committee, Project HOPE, and other PVOs.

The West Foundation

A small family philanthropy located in Indianapolis, the West Foundation gives perhaps half of its grants each year for international projects. This is a direct reflection of the social service concerns and international interests of members of the family. The late Harold West, head of a strong regional bakery, was a supporter of missionary programs and got interested in World Neighbors soon after it was established; the foundation he created has continued to support that PVO for more than two decades. His widow, Hilda West, and their son, Richard, have concerned themselves with a variety of projects for relief and development abroad year after year. They are always alert to disasters that create relief needs, and budget about 20 percent of their giving for such emergency appeals—for example, in India, Guatemala, Nicaragua, and Somalia.

Committed to participating in development programs, the Wests keep a wary eye on these activities and have acquired a rather detached sophistication about the appeals that come to them. They prefer projects that exhibit a strong self-help component and skillful management able to "squeeze the dollar." They tend to shun programs that are deeply involved in government funding, for their conviction is that government projects are often conducted on a grandiose scale and are wasteful. They like to support small grass-roots projects that show signs of helping people, as through the application of appropriate technology, to help themselves.

Behind their modest giving, about $25,000 a year, is their belief that "the world is going to be won or lost in the developing areas." They want to do what they can to help the people of those regions— one of the best ways of trying to build a sane and peaceful world.

The Henry Luce Foundation

The founder and long-time editor-in-chief of Time, Inc., Henry Luce was the son of Dr. Henry W. Luce, a Christian missionary/teacher who helped establish Yenching University in Peking. The foundation he created in 1936, predictably, has taken a strong and continuing interest in higher educational institutions and, particularly, in the study of Asian cultures and relations between the United States and Asian countries.

Among the research topics supported by Luce in recent years are U.S. relations with Southeast Asia after the Vietnam War, U.S. relations with China, Korean-American relations 1945–1950, American and Japanese security policies since World War II, U.S. interactions with the Philippines, past experiences and future alternatives in American-Chinese relations, and Malaysian attitudes toward multinational corporations. Most of these research projects have been undertaken as part of a long-term program of competitive grants to major university centers on Asian Studies, including Princeton, Yale, Michigan, Chicago, Cornell, Columbia, Stanford, Washington, California, and Harvard.

In addition, Luce provides grants for individual scholars, and has endowed a number of Henry R. Luce university professorships. In general, the foundation shies away from grants to PVOs. However, it has provided substantial funding for the Asia Foundation to further the work of its field representatives in their developmental programs related to provincial educational institutions in various parts of Asia.

5

U.S. Corporations

The relationship between U.S. corporations and relief and development activities abroad is difficult to document, and unpredictable. Yet for some companies in some countries the involvement of U.S. profit-making corporations in nonprofit service programs is substantial and of considerable social and economic significance. There are also signs that these philanthropy activities are being enlarged and extended. More crucially, the normal business activities of U.S. firms are themselves of enormous importance for the development endeavors of many countries.

The Varied Development Activities of
U.S. Business Abroad

Despite extensive suspicion and hostility toward U.S. multinational corporations operating in the developing world, and in spite of persistent efforts by anti-American propagandists to make "whipping boys" of American businesses, most of the less developed countries still find it advantageous to maintain good working relations with U.S. corporations. In the performance of major engineering and construction projects, in the operation of mines, in the exploration for oil and other minerals, in the development of certain types of industries, even in the management of major agricultural enterprises involved in export crops for needed foreign currency, many Third World leaders see U.S. business firms as important to their national economies and to the realization of their development dreams.

The extent to which that kind of perception of self-interest can overcome political and ideological hostilities is, at times, almost unbelievable. For example, at the height of anti-American anger in Egypt during and following the Six Day War with Israel in 1967, President Nasser accused the United States of having participated in the Israeli destruction of the Egyptian Air Force. He broke off official relations and expelled virtually all American diplomats and private

99

citizens in the country—including teachers and retired professionals long associated with Egyptian endeavors. Yet, throughout that period of hostility and ruptured relations, the American employees of certain U.S. petroleum concerns continued their oil exploration work in the Egyptian desert and along the Red Sea, undisturbed and fully supported by Egyptian authorities.

Despite strong Soviet and Cuban involvement in the affairs of Angola and the obviously strained relations with the U.S. government, the Marxist-leaning leaders of Angola have chosen to go forward with Gulf Oil in the development and marketing of their substantial oil resources.

All of this, of course, demonstrates two basic facts: (a) how high a value Third World countries place upon their own development, and (b) how much respect they have for American technical competence and reliability. It also may be inferred here that even leftist, pro-Soviet governments (as both Angola is and as Nasser's Egypt was) are not automatically disposed to turn to and trust the Soviet Union for development assistance. In the handling of sensitive, economically crucial projects, even if the Soviets have the technological capabilities and willingness to take on such responsibilities, as they frequently do, the Americans may be preferred.

The simple fact is that U.S. firms, doing their regular business for profit, can be significant agents of development in the developing world. Moreover, from the U.S. viewpoint, business conducted with the developing world in recent years has become increasingly important to American farmers, manufacturers, and merchants. Recent estimates indicate that business with the developing world now accounts for about 40 percent of U.S. export trade, considerably more than the total U.S. trade with Europe. Many U.S. business firms derive a high percentage of their profits from their operations abroad, particularly from their overseas subsidiaries. They are dependent upon various kinds of foreign raw materials and other imports, and, in some cases, are substantial beneficiaries of expenditures for foreign assistance.

Some U.S. firms, of course, understand well the many and varied implications of their assorted roles in the developing world, and they go beyond a strictly "business-as-usual" approach to their overseas activities. Some of them increasingly involve themselves or their foreign subsidiaries in endeavors of a philanthropic nature. Some, for a variety of reasons, choose to confine their operations abroad to as narrow a set of objectives as possible. In any case, U.S. corporate participation through philanthropic activity in certain social and educational goals of the foreign countries where they function has become an increasing reality. However, the extent of these activities in terms of dollar expenditures is virtually impossible to establish. Most U.S. corporations remain highly secretive about the nature and extent of their philanthropic involvement abroad. Indeed, many of those activities can be hidden as legitimate "business expenses."

Corporate Attitudes Toward Giving Abroad

Corporations have long been reluctant to publicize their charitable contributions programs. They don't want to encourage unwanted applications for grants; they feel high-level apprehension toward the public relations problems they might create by controversial charitable projects; they fear criticism from their stockholders. In the case of overseas projects they are also concerned about the possibility of annoying the government of the host country in which they do business, their foreign trading partners, as well as their stockholders back home.

Wherever possible, most corporations prefer to follow the lead of their local managers and direct their charitable contributions to the interests of the communities in which their employees live. This rule is applied quite broadly, both to American plant locations and to the sites of overseas operations. With an eye for public relations and for the contentment of their stockholders, they generally wish to gain some legitimate benefit from their philanthropies and, at the very least, to avoid controversies.

In any case, corporate philanthropic activity is not, for most business firms, a high priority concern. Normally they do not devote enough top-level managerial attention to the issue or assign enough professional personnel to the task to establish a capability for sophisticated decision making about broad and sometimes complex development issues. They tend to focus on projects of interest to their own local employees and to the communities in which they live. This is not a formula for general assistance for development or for direct aid to the grass-roots poor, yet it does provide substantial social benefits. And it would be a mistake to assume that U.S. corporations operating overseas are indifferent to a wide range of social needs in the countries where they do business.

Ray Pagon of the San Francisco firm of Castle and Cooke, with shipping and agribusiness interests worldwide, rejects the idea that multinational corporations are unconcerned with development needs in the Third World. "The problem," he says, "is not lack of action, but lack of publicity; we've been lousy communicators about a story that has been there all the time." He points out that his company has been involved for more than a hundred years all over the world, but that it, like many other firms, had been guided by the belief that it was "bad taste" for a business to publicize its charitable work.

Through its Standard Fruit Division, Castle and Cooke has had extensive involvement in the improvement of life in a number of Third World communities—supporting hospitals and schools, training paramedics, and providing relief programs following natural disasters. Pagon cites in particular the achievement of Guanchias Cooperative, a group of banana farmers in Honduras who, backed by their U.S. marketing partner, have become "a major force in the agricultural community both of the Sula Valley and of the country at large. . . . While actively pursuing a goal of self-interest, the company has paved the way for a meaningful improvement in the standard of living of the co-op members and their families in an atmosphere of mutual respect."

Pagon expresses a caution, shared by other corporate representatives, against excessive expectations about what could be accomplished by the charitable activities of multinational corporations working abroad. "There are those who contend," he says, "that a profit-making organization in a developing country should take responsibility for the entire country—or, at least, the community in its area. That is not possible. Our efforts are aimed at the development of a partnership designed for the mutual benefit of both partners. We each must, and we each can, receive benefits. If this were not so, the partnership would undoubtedly cease. But the synergism of the partnership itself causes it to grow, to change, to be dynamic, and to mature. Our goal is that these communities, which yesterday did not exist, tomorrow will be . . . self-sufficient."

The Conference Board Study of Corporate Guidelines

These concepts of "enlightened self-interest" and of the desirability of focusing on the life of those communities in which American corporations have operations and employees are ideas that run through much of the discussion of principles for corporate grantmaking abroad, and that are embodied in prevailing practices. The Conference Board, generally considered the best source of information on the foreign philanthropies of American corporations, conducted research studies of a significant sampling of U.S. multinational enterprises in 1973 and 1976, under the direction of James R. Basche, Jr. Among the findings that still appear to be relevant:

1. "Most U.S. companies . . . do not have formal written policy guidelines . . . [but] rely on informal understandings" between U.S. headquarters and field managements.

2. "Most U.S. companies do not initiate public service projects" either at home or abroad. "The initiative lies with the foreign or American-based international organization."

3. "The three most common criteria for corporate support of public service activities and organizations are (a) that they be "related to the company's principal business interests"; (b) that they be located in "the countries' regions and communities in which the company has facilities"; and (c) that they "provide benefits to the company's employees and their families."

4. Constraints generally applied against "the use of company charitable funds" prohibit contributions for "support of political organizations and candidates" or "to assist religious organizations in their religious programs."

5. "Decision making in foreign public service activities is generally delegated to the management of the company's foreign affiliates for their respective countries."

6. The program interests of the corporate givers cover the same wide spectrum abroad as they do at home: hospitals, schools, cultural programs, management training, scholarships. However, a number of them also include projects particularly related to the Third World: nutrition, adult literacy, and rural community development.

7. Some corporations encourage their foreign subsidiaries or affiliates to provide opportunities for their employees to participate in local public service activities, with varying degrees of company backing, as is the case at their company locations in the United States; and some make gifts of company products for local social service purposes.

PVO Relations With Corporate Giving Practices

The U.S. private voluntary agencies that function in the developing world receive limited support from U.S. corporations operating abroad. Although grateful for corporate funding when they can get it, the PVOs are generally quite frustrated in their dealings with American businesses from whom they seek grants.

They are forever hoping that the multinational corporations will provide them with substantial support, but they have endless problems in winning their case. All too often they are told that their development assistance projects just don't fit the traditional corporate contributions guidelines. The corporations, in turn, sometimes say that they do not have enough knowledge about the PVOs and their programs, and about the nature of the needs they propose to serve, to make a responsible judgment. They do not know how to evaluate competing appeals, and fear that if they choose to support one PVO they will offend others. Moreover, they sometimes claim that PVOs appear to be naïvely idealistic and at times express overtly religious purposes with which the business corporation cannot identify. Some corporations also have been put off by what they have perceived as "moral superiority" attitudes of some PVOs and by fundraising tactics that seem to be based on trying to shame the corporations into giving. No doubt, these are two quite different groups, not well acquainted with each other—even if they work in the same foreign countries—and not communicating very effectively.

The PVOs, focused as they are on the problems of the poor—often on the poorest of the poor—have goals and motivations different from those of U.S. corporations working overseas. They want to think of the business representatives as fellow Americans who should be natural partners in their works of charity. They may say they realize that corporations exist "primarily to make profits for their shareholders, not to alleviate poverty," but they resist that idea, even when saying they accept it. They clearly want the American corporations to do much more to aid relief and development programs abroad, and to do it differently. Among their specific criticisms:

- the corporate philanthropic contributions tend to flow into the more advanced, industrialized, and affluent communities and neighborhoods where their employees live—not into the rural villages or the slums, where the needs are greatest;
- they tend to support only "safe projects," i.e., hospitals and scholarships;
- they are too insistent on some "benefit-for-the-company" aspect to the project, along with serving the good of the community;
- they prefer to give a lot of small grants to many agencies rather than occasional large grants that could make a significant difference to some major problem;
- the corporate grantmakers tend to be "unapproachable" and provide little information to guide grantseekers in preparing their requests;

- at times they give PVOs the "run-around"; U.S. home offices say the decisions are made at the field locations, and the field representatives say that the headquarters people decide;
- the "enlightened self-interest" approach to corporate giving tends to make them vulnerable to political pressures.

Despite these expressions of PVO disappointments toward the multinationals and their corporate philanthropy practices, it would be a mistake to assume generally unpleasant relationships between PVOs and U.S. corporations working overseas. On the contrary, many corporate representatives are deeply involved in the work of PVOs; some serve on PVO boards. A Xerox vice president has headed fundraising activities of CODEL (a consortium of church-related agencies interested in development). Another consortium of PVOs, PACT (Private Agencies Cooperating Together), has had long-term backing from IBM, and a number of the organizations in the PACT group are heavily supported, through both cash contributions and volunteer work, by corporate executives. YMCA programs abroad, many of which are of a social service nature, have had unusual success in enlisting the participation of American corporate employees overseas. The Overseas Education Fund of the League of Women Voters, after much effort, has been able to draw increasing corporate backing.

Accion International and Partners of the Americas, both operating in a number of Latin American countries, have secured substantial financial assistance from U.S. corporations. The reason: steady work for many years at a deliberate strategy of corporate fundraising; and telling the story again and again to the officers of U.S. corporations, making careful efforts to get to "know the right person who knows the other right person." A spokesman for Accion says that raising financial support from corporations for overseas projects is not impossible—it just requires persistence and the "cultivation of the right contacts." Alan Rubin, the head of Partners, agrees.

Social Service Programs by Individual Corporations

There is only one way to indicate the sweep and variety of corporate giving programs abroad, and that is through a sampling of U.S. corporations that operate abroad and descriptions of some of the programs they support. Interviews by the authors of this book and a series of case studies prepared by Business International have been drawn upon to provide the material for this sampling.

Ford Motor Company—Mexico

Since 1967 the Ford Motor Company, through its local dealers, has undertaken an extensive program of education, agricultural development, and disaster relief in various states of Mexico.

Its most visible and expensive program has been the construction of elementary schools in isolated villages. Designed by Ford architects and Mexican officials, scores of these schools are now in use, attended by more than 80,000 pupils. Built of simple materials, usually at a cost of less than $50,000, each school has been sponsored by an area Ford dealer who initially raised half the cash needed. The other half was contributed from Ford public relations funds provided by the company and the 120 Mexican dealers. The government or an individual donor gave the land.

Ford zone managers make regular maintenance inspections of these schools as they go about the country conferring with the various dealers, who in turn have organized local committees of businessmen to bear the costs of keeping the schools in good repair.

A second Ford social service activity in Mexico, operated from 1967 to 1977, was a rural training program. Its purpose was to teach the small or marginal farmers basic principles of soil conservation, correct techniques for applying insecticides and herbicides, the use of hybrid seed corn, and even how to build their own improved farming tools. Ford paid for some of the first of the agriculture teachers/engineers who were sent on these extension service missions and provided them with pickup trucks equipped with campers. The Mexican government added a number of agriculturalists to the project. Some 40,000 small farmers in twenty-three states took part in the program, with substantial improvement in their farm production and in their standard of living.

Emergency relief is a third Ford service program that has proved highly beneficial in Mexico, which seems to have more than its share of hurricanes, earthquakes, fires, and floods. The company and its dealers have set up an emergency reserve fund that can be drawn upon immediately when a disaster strikes. Each Ford dealer has been given the responsibility to notify the company promptly when emergency needs arise, to receive relief supplies, and to oversee, with other community volunteers, their distribution.

A program that Ford has initiated recently provides funds for dormitories to house school children who live too far away from school to make the round trip every day.

In all of these activities there are, of course, public relations benefits for the Ford Motor Company and its dealers. Some of the farmers who took part in the rural training program were eventually able to buy Ford trucks. Moreover, in all these activities, government agencies, other business firms, and a variety of local volunteers have participated.

Caltex Petroleum Corporation – Indonesia

A chance visit in 1971 by the Caltex board chairman to the Research Institute for Estate Crops at Jember, eastern Java, has led to a series of small but highly significant gifts for scientific equipment, including a $5,580 spectrophotometer. With this equipment, the laboratory, operated by the Indonesian Ministry of Agriculture, was able to multiply more than tenfold the annual rate of accurate soil analyses. This enabled the experts to make much more rapid recommendations on the use of fertilizers, with significant improvement in crop production throughout the region.

A longer-term program of corporate assistance to rural development is represented by Caltex involvement in the establishment of an agricultural research center on the island of Sumatra. Engaged in oil production in Riau Province, where the soil is poor and most foodstuffs had to be imported, Caltex entered into partnership in 1973 with the provincial government to find out how to expand rice production. The government provided the land and the company committed itself to two-thirds of the operating budget for five years. The first company contribution was a diesel-powered pump to irrigate the paddy fields, and another early donation made it possible to send four Indonesian agronomists to study for six months at the International Rice Research Institute in the Philippines (a program initiated by the Rockefeller and Ford foundations).

Another contribution by Caltex to Indonesia's rural development has been in health services, including family planning. Its two company hospitals and several field clinics in Sumatra have been made available to provide emergency and continuing care for local people, in addition to corporate employees, in a region where public health facilities had not yet been installed. At the request of the Indonesian government, which has made population control a major policy objective, Caltex medical staff members have agreed to operate family planning clinics and to carry on a broad educational program on nutrition, sanitation, and general health issues.

These activities by Caltex, it is clear, came about not through some general company policy to "support development in the Third World," nor through the urging of some U.S. PVO, but out of awareness and concern for immediate local problems confronted by company officials on the scene. That the company had the resources, the imagination, and the flexibility to respond quickly was, of course, crucial.

Carnation Company—The Philippines

For years the Philippines imported about 95 percent of its commercial dairy goods, and obviously needed to expand local milk production, including technical expertise.

The California-based Carnation Company had had a modest manufacturing operation in the Philippines for some time, but was bothered by a severely limited supply of raw milk. The Filipino government was troubled by the drain of foreign exchange to pay for milk product imports and by the nutritional deficiencies in the diets of many children. Both problems, of course, were related to the low level of Philippine milk production. Expensive experiments trying to duplicate large-scale, technically sophisticated American-style dairy operations had generally not worked out; the small inefficient backyard dairy farmer was still the main supplier. What could be done for him?

In 1976 the Carnation Company was asked by the Filipino government to help develop a plan. It set out to upgrade local cattle through scientific breeding, and to improve the quality of cattle feed. The resources of Carnation Genetics, a branch of the company's activities in the United States, were pressed into service for the breeding project. A comprehensive program of crop diversification was initiated to improve cattle feeds. Farmers were shown how to plant leguminous grasses for fodder and still improve the quality and productivity of the soil. They were taught to combine coconut farming and dairy farming in one complementary operation, and even how to get additional cash crops by planting market vegetables in place of underbrush between the rows of trees. The animal manure would, of course, further enrich the soil. The purpose was not to replace coconut farming with dairy farming, but to show how both types of farming could be done together—and better.

Carnation helped recruit a team of Filipino agriculturists and sent them on observation and training assignments to the company's operations in the United States, to a Carnation demonstration dairy farm in the Tabasco region of Mexico, and to tropical dairy farming projects in Sri Lanka. At three villages in the Sariaya district of Quezon, about 120 km. from Manila, Carnation undertook a pilot program, utilizing a network of small, readily reproducible demonstration farms—to enlarge and improve milk supplies, to raise farm incomes, to enrich rural life in many ways. The self-interest of

Carnation should be served in time, but the development ambitions of rural Filipinos are already being furthered.

Gulf Oil Corporation — Nigeria

The overall development plans of Nigeria are being advanced more directly by its booming oil industry than by any other single factor. With substantial hard currency earnings, the Nigerians can buy a lot of economic and social development every year — an approach not so readily available to many other poorer developing countries. Gulf Oil is one element in the growth in Nigeria today, but not only as an operator of oil wells and shipping facilities. It has become involved in trying to find solutions to the acute housing problem, which is now of critical social concern to the Nigerian government.

The capital city of Lagos has become severely congested, as have so many cities in the developing world, with streams of people pouring in from rural areas and finding only unsanitary hovels to live in. On land donated by the Nigerian government, Gulf has set out to build several hundred houses in a satellite city west of Lagos near the oil export terminal of Warri on the coast. Although intended primarily to house Gulf employees, these will not be traditional company towns. The houses are of ample size and of high-quality construction. They are being sold to the occupants on convenient rental terms, and the decisions as to allocation are being made *not* by company officers but by committees of employees.

The success of the Gulf housing program has been cited by the Nigerian government as an example that should be followed by other concerns, domestic and foreign, in finding satisfactory answers to at least some of the acute housing problems of the country. That reputation also got Gulf involved in a purely public service project to assist the people in the fishing village of Ugborado in getting a dependable supply of safe water and in coping with a silting problem in the neighboring river that had curtailed the supply of fish. Gulf laid water pipes to the village from wells at the company's terminal facilities. It also used its equipment and personnel to dredge the river. For this "good neighbor" gesture Gulf spent approximately $150,000.

Levi Strauss — Various Countries

Since "blue jeans" and "Levis" have become an ongoing international rage, it is not surprising that their originator moved out across the world with subsidiary plants and distribution facilities in many lands. It is also no surprise, given the strong tradition of corporate philanthropy and imaginative "social responsibility" activities carried on by Levi Strauss at its home base in San Francisco, that this company's officials encourage participation in social service activities wherever they have operations abroad.

At the heart of the company's program in each location is a "community involvement team." This is a committee of ten to fifteen employees, primarily from the "factory floor," who come together as volunteers (with company encouragement) to explore the social needs of their communities. They can hold their meetings in the plant on company time. If they identify a project or program for which they are willing to contribute some of their own spare time, or for which they want to raise money, the company will help. It will allow an amazing range of fundraising efforts to be carried on within the company walls and often during working hours: bake sales, bingo games, disco dances, etc. All of the activities are for the purpose of establishing a broadly based involvement in and support for some public service enterprise. From that point on, the company is willing to entertain requests for financial contributions from either the company foundation or from funds assigned to the contributions committee.

Levi Strauss is open to applications for support of an exceedingly broad range of projects: e.g., a home for battered women, a youth camp, programs for handicapped and retarded children. In the Philippines, a community involvement team became interested in promoting the construction of nutrition center annexes at a number of high schools, and went as volunteer workers to assist in the bricklaying. The company agreed to provide financing for certain needed equipment.

According to Fred Kirschstein, coordinator of these philanthropic programs, "the concept behind these teams was that local people knew best what problems affected their community. We wanted to give our employees a way in which they could materially affect their environment."

Beyond that concept, however, was a corporate determination to try to be "good citizens" and not just "visitors in the country." "As citizens in that country," Kirschstein explains, "and with all the responsibilities that are charged to us . . . we have to become involved in trying to solve some of the social problems that directly affect that country."

If that philosophy were activated by top-down management decisions and implemented as company projects, there might be charges of paternalism or outside interference. The local involvement committees, however, provide down-to-earth guidance as to what is needed and will be acceptable. It is a pattern that apparently works as well in Australia as in Mexico, as well in Belgium as in Canada, as well in the Philippines as in California.

Dow Chemical Corporation — Brazil

Chagas' disease is a chronic, incurable plague that afflicts or threatens many millions of people in various parts of Latin America. It is a special hazard for poor rural Brazilians who live in mud-and-wattle homes, for the disease is transmitted by an insect called barbeira, which thrives in the walls and floors of such houses. For a number of years the Brazilian government has carried on an extensive campaign to eradicate the insect by chemical spraying. The big difficulty has been the limited effectiveness of the insecticides that have been available, the continuous reinfestation of houses that have been sprayed, and the toxic hazards to the people and their animals.

Scientists at the Federal University of Rio de Janeiro were asked to tackle this problem. They in turn approached Dow Chemical, which has a substantial chemical manufacturing complex in the state of Bahia, for samples of one of the company's insecticides known as Dursban. Dow donated supplies of the chemical, and its own research and development team became involved in the study directed by the Rio University scientists. Together they have tested ways of controlling the dangerous insect; together they have been able to agree on the characteristics of the chemical needed — long staying power and low toxicity — and to experiment with various new formulations of the sought-for improved insecticide.

In addition to contributions of chemicals and the services of the company's technical personnel, Dow has also provided limited funds for administrative costs and travel expenses for the field work. Moreover, the active involvement of its local communications manager, who was also the corporate contributions officer, led to extensive press coverage of the project and re-awakened public concern about the disease. As a result, additional funds for the university's research efforts have come from other sources.

Dow, of course, stands to benefit eventually from this philanthropic activity. To the Brazilian government the whole enterprise is seen as a hopeful step toward reducing a major health problem for Brazil and other countries in Latin America — and toward eliminating another significant impediment to development.

Another Dow involvement in development has been its multifaceted participation in the furthering of Brazilian scientific and technical education. Here again, it has been a case of enlightened self-interest. In the early 1970s, when Dow established extensive manufacturing facilities near the city of Salvador in a developing region of Bahia, there were few people available with scientific and technical skills. Qualified people, initially, had to be recruited from the outside. Yet from the beginning the company undertook an active role, working with the schools, to help people develop various technical skills. Dow chemists, geologists, and engineers regularly gave lectures at the Federal Technical School of Bahia. Student groups were invited to the company installations for tours and scientific demonstrations. Cooperative work-study arrangements were set up with a number of promising young people while they completed their education. In addition, Dow made contributions of equipment, books, and cash for the work of the technical school. The result is that Dow and other industrial firms in the region now have a growing supply of locally trained scientific and technical personnel to draw from, and local people now have career opportunities that were once beyond their reach.

Syntex Corporation – Mexico

This pharmaceutical manufacturing company, based in Palo Alto, California, has a major subsidiary that has been operating in Mexico for more than thirty years. Thus, it has developed considerable staff familiarity with the interests and needs of that country. Its foreign assistance activities reflect this familiarity through substantial funding for two human service programs in Mexico. That support from Syntex, in large measure, is channeled through Mexican-oriented private voluntary organizations based in California.

One of these PVOs which Syntex began working with in the late 1960s is Chiapas Relief and Encouragement Organization (CREO). Organized by a group of Stanford University doctors, nurses, medical school students, and other technicians who participated in a traveling summer clinic, it undertook to serve a number of isolated Mexican Indian villages. Along the way, it developed considerable local backing from individuals and groups in the Palo Alto area. Syntex was impressed by the strong public interest in its home-base community. When company staff members involved with the Mexican subsidiary looked into the work of CREO, a most encouraging report came back. Syntex not only assisted the summer traveling clinic with money and in-kind supplies, it continued and expanded its support when CREO branched out into projects to help the Indians from villages around the city of San Cristobal to design and construct low-cost safe water systems.

Believing in the value of the sponsoring U.S. PVO, Syntex has provided funds and counseling to assist CREO in its broad fundraising efforts, including assistance in the preparation and publication of its annual report. Not glamorous philanthropy perhaps, but an important contribution enabling a U.S.-based PVO to expand its development assistance program abroad.

Another San Francisco Bay area PVO that Syntex has supported for several years is the Hesperian Foundation. Operating a primary medical care service, Project Piaxtla, in a remote mountainous region of the Mexican state of Sinaloa, this organization has set up a paramedical training center and a dozen clinics in and around the town of Ajoya, reaching out into rugged country where there are virtually no roads and life is extremely hard. It has also initiated agricultural demonstration projects to help expand local food production and improve the quality of the people's diet.

A major characteristic of Project Piaxtla that obviously appeals to Syntex and other backers is the emphasis on local self-help. Residents of the area have been trained as paramedics, dentists, and lab and x-ray technicians. Although some American volunteers still take short-term assignments to help with training, it is the local resident health workers who now provide this vital care.

An example of how a small amount of money, used imaginatively, can accomplish something significant is a particular Syntex contribution of $4,000, which paid for the first printing of a simple rural health handbook called *Donde No Hay Doctor* (Where There is No Doctor). It tells in elementary Spanish, with numerous graphic illustrations, how to stay well, how to maintain essential standards of sanitation, what foods to eat for good nutrition, and how to use correctly the many medicines sold over the counter in Mexican pharmacies. It also deals with prenatal and postnatal care, midwifery, and family planning. In addition, it gives basic information about injections, vaccinations, and a number of common diseases. It has been translated into at least one Indian language and English. Today it is being used in fourteen Latin American countries.

Xerox Corporation — Various Countries

In official policy statements the Xerox Corporation, based in Rochester, New York, has declared its commitment to foreign service activities. Its chairman and chief executive officer has said "We regard Xerox as a social institution as well as a business institution. We believe that Xerox companies throughout the world should contribute to their societies. It's a responsibility, and unless we accept it we will not succeed in the long run." The head of the chief subsidiary, Rank Xerox, which supervises more than twenty-five companies outside the United States, has endorsed that philosophy on behalf of the international operations of the corporation: "The company can survive and flourish only in a world that is peaceful, civilized, prosperous, healthy, educated, nourished and unpolluted. A better world is better for Rank Zerox and its employees as well as for society at large."

Xerox has attempted to help build that better world by an unusual program of encouraging its employees to take "social service leave"—from one month to a full year—to work on projects of their own choosing. Xerox pays full salaries and provides for all company benefits during the leave periods. Travel costs and local expenses are the responsibility of the individual leavetakers or the organizations for which they work. Xerox does not attempt to direct the choice of projects, and they need not be related in any way to the person's regular job. However, they must be nonprofit, nonsectarian, and nonpolitical.

Because most Xerox employees live in the United States, Canada, or Western Europe, most social service leave projects are in these developed countries. However, in recent years leavetakers have engaged in such far-ranging activities as helping to establish a clinic on an Israeli Kibbutz, working on the development of appropriate technology for India, and assisting with long-term famine relief in Ethiopia.

Decisions about who gets to take a social service leave are made by committees of employees, not by management. Applications must include detailed descriptions of the proposed project and background information on the sponsoring organizations. Recently, about 20 percent of the applicants have been granted leave, with the company now contributing to these social service programs each year the equivalent of more than twenty years of employee time and salaries.

In addition to the social service leaves, Xerox also has been developing a "community involvement program" under which employee committees are encouraged to identify worthy local service projects that deserve support, in which employees are involved, and for which company grants of money may be proposed.

Employee interest, commitment and involvement are the key to the Xerox formula for philanthropic giving, at home and abroad.

Employee Training—Many Companies, Various Countries

On-the-job training and company-supported education of employees is a basic and accepted pattern in personnel relations in many companies around the world. In developing countries, straining to expand their supply of skilled and productive manpower and woman-power, such programs are doubly important. Some illustrations:

• In Mexico, *Gerber Products* set up a center for basic education in its plant at Queretaro. With the approval of the local educational authorities, Gerber provides a director, six licensed teachers, and the use of company office facilities. Instruction is given at the primary school, intermediate, and high school levels, and students may proceed at their own pace. There is no cost to the individual except for some of the textbooks. Classes are offered before and after plant shifts, not on company time. Worker participation in the program, originally very limited and skeptical, has become extensive and enthusiastic, with about one-fourth of the employees enrolled. Skills have improved. Work errors have decreased. Productivity has improved, as has plant morale. The company has benefited by its investment in the education of its employees. The workers, many of whom have stuck with the program until they received their government-validated diplomas, have reached levels of personal achievement and opportunities for advancement, within and outside the company, that they had not previously believed they could ever attain.

• In Costa Rica, *Kativo Chemical Industries*, a subsidiary of *H.B. Fuller*, provides financial support for its employees to take courses in educational institutions of their choice. Courses may be, and often are, related to the individual's work assignment. They may be at a professional level or for simple trades training. But the company is also willing to underwrite their personnel in the pursuit of studies for cultural enlightenment and sheer personal enjoyment—music, literature, or karate.

• *General Motors*, which has had many years of experience in training engineering and technical personnel through its GM Institute in Michigan, has set up and finances similar and highly ambitious vocational training programs for its workers in South Africa. Open to all races on an equal basis, it has provided educational opportunities and job advancement for black South Africans that they might well not have had otherwise.

• U.S. corporate support for education of employees sometimes extends to the children of employees. *S.C. Johnson and Son* offers college scholarship assistance to the children of its personnel in the United States and in the countries where it operates abroad. These scholarships sometimes go to children of retired or widowed employees.

This particular program, incidentally, is only one part of an overall public service policy the company arrived at in its "global management conference" in 1976. At that time it formulated a commitment to "contribute to the social development of every country and community where we conduct business by involving ourselves in social, cultural and educational projects which enhance the quality of life."

Chase Manhattan Bank – Korea

The International Department of the Chase Bank supervises branches in many countries around the world. All of them are encouraged to undertake at least one "corporate responsibility project" each year and more than fifteen of the major branches, including the one in Seoul, Korea, are required to do so. Under guidelines laid down in New York, the bank wishes these social programs to be related to one of three areas:

- Community and economic development;
- Human resource development;
- Consumer and personal financial services.

Although cash contributions may be made for a variety of public service organizations that solicit support, the branch bank's own "corporate responsibility project" must involve bank personnel or bank facilities in addition to grants of money. Representative of such projects are these activities in Korea:

• In 1977 a night school for working youth in Seoul, sponsored by the police department, approached the local Chase branch for a financial contribution. The bank gave relatively modest funding for classroom equipment and materials. More importantly, it contributed several members of the bank staff to teach courses related to their fields three nights a week. The program of this privately supported academy for about 200 drop-outs, 80 percent of whom are young women employed in nearby factories, leads to an equivalency diploma that, in turn, opens the way to a secretarial or advanced technical school. More than half of the students, once back on the learning track, go on for further study.

• Chase involvement with rural problems is manifested in an unusual "calf-a-month" project, worked out in collaboration with a government-sponsored "New Community Movement." A self-help approach to improving life in rural Korea, major responsibility for the program falls upon local village councils. Chase invests in this grass-roots approach by providing a high quality New Zealand calf to some rural family each month. That family agrees not to slaughter the calf or sell it, but to breed it and give its first offspring to another village family. The local village council sees to it that this self-perpetuating mutual assistance continues to help more and more people. Meanwhile, the bank can shift its giving to more and more villages.

Singer Company—Mexico

One corporation that has focused a significant part of its philanthropy on helping the poorest of the poor is *Singer Mexicana*, a subsidiary of the long-established U.S. manufacturer of sewing machines. It donates commercial models of its sewing and knitting machines to a variety of organizations around Mexico to benefit needy people.

Going far beyond the donation of some of its products, the company sets up fully equipped sewing rooms and sends its own staff of teachers to train people to use them. Schools, hospitals, community centers, and prisons are sites for these workshops. Special attention is given to prisoners and the urban poor.

The prison program has been unusually successful for both men and women, a significant step in gaining self-esteem and skills to aid their reentry into the labor market. Some of them even save money earned in the prison workshop, buy their own machines when they are released, and go into business for themselves.

The community center sewing rooms provide opportunities for poor people to make or repair their own clothes. Sometimes groups of local women attached to these centers have received government contracts to take on special production orders for hospital sheets and blankets.

The Mexican government has been so impressed by the sewing room projects paid for by Singer in urban areas that it has decided to establish a number of them in rural areas.

By concentrating on this particular form of philanthropy, doing something in which it has complete competence, Singer officials feel they can get the maximum effect from their charitable giving. They assign thoroughly professional people to the task, give them encouragement to plan each center carefully, and follow through to see that each center functions as it should. The appreciation of those who benefit from the program, the praise of public officials, and the pride of the 3,000 Singer employees in Mexico, indicate that the company has hit upon a real philanthropic "winner."

Union Carbide—Puerto Rico

Business firms the world over, particularly those engaged in extractive industries and chemicals, have been increasingly under attack for despoiling the land and polluting the air and water. Many of these companies are working hard at trying to clean up their operations in a variety of ways. Some of them now have become virtual activist educators on environmental issues. Such a concern has prompted Union Carbide to undertake its Ecology Education Project in Puerto Rico.

With extensive counsel from the local schools and environmental agencies, Union Carbide developed an "ecology kit," which it donated to Puerto Rican elementary schools. Consisting of a teacher's guide, a miniature greenhouse, seed tapes, posters, puzzles, litter bags, and even a phonograph record of catchy ecology jingles, each kit was intended to help teachers instruct up to forty students in the basic issues related to air, water, and land conservation. The Secretariat of Education approved the distribution of the kit to the schools, and it was an overnight success. Teachers and students were delighted with its "fun approach" to learning about a serious subject. The media gave it extensive coverage, and environmental organizations commended the whole effort. It was, in fact, a quite serious project that took eighteen months to develop and cost Union Carbide $50,000.

Company Services Available on a Good Neighbor Basis

The facilities and specialized personnel assembled by U.S. corporations in many developing regions of the world constitute unusual resources. Access to them can be of great value to the local people. Many firms, often in the most casual and unpublicized way, provide services, through their facilities and with their own staff people, that simply are not otherwise available:

• In Daharki, Pakistan, an affiliate of *Exxon* operates a company clinic for its employees. Because the nearest hospital is sixty miles away and the local people have severe needs for various kinds of health care, the company has opened its clinic to nearby villagers for treatment of eye disease, a common affliction there, and other ailments. Perhaps the most dramatic recurring service is treatment for snakebite. With many poisonous snakes in the area, this is a constant problem. Over the last few years, it is estimated, the oil company's clinic has saved more than 1,000 lives by prompt treatment of snakebite.

• In Mexico and other countries, *IBM* offers computer time on its equipment for graduate students to pursue their research at the company's science center.

• *G. D. Searle & Company*, a pharmaceutical firm, operates a manufacturing plant at Naucalpan de Juarez in Mexico. There it maintains a substantial library in medicine and chemistry for its scientists and technicians. Qualified local college and university students are invited to use this collection. Moreover, company specialists often give time to discuss with the students their research projects.

In Mexico City the company maintains an attractive conference center for the medical profession to use for meetings, seminars, and advanced courses. Thirty-three medical societies now regularly hold their meetings at Casa Searle, and its facilities are often booked for two years or more in advance. A library of reference books and international medical journals is available for physicians working on research or individual study projects.

• *Dow Chemical* has a subsidiary in Quito, Ecuador, which must maintain a well-equipped scientific laboratory and an extensive collection of technical books and scientific periodicals for its own staff. Professors and qualified students at the local university are welcome to use the company laboratory and library.

Some Reflections on Corporate Assistance Programs Abroad

The involvement of American business firms in activities that relate to the relief and development needs of the developing countries is vast, varied, complex, and difficult to appraise. Much of it is unknown to the public. Most of it has evolved casually over time. It has, however, become a significant factor in foreign assistance. With some diffidence, we set down these random reflections:

1. The facilities and staffs assembled in developing countries by U.S. business firms are important resources that often assist in providing certain human services and in dealing with many problems of social and economic development. Such assistance is often of practical, direct importance to people and communities assisted, but it is virtually impossible to quantify.

2. The normal business operations of these companies contribute significantly to the development process, particularly in the training of skilled workers, technicians, and managers.

3. U.S. corporations tend to concentrate their overt charitable activities in the communities in which they have plants or other centers of business operations.

4. Some give special attention in their philanthropic endeavors to those groups likely to be customers for their products or services.

5. Increasingly, U.S. corporations are encouraging their workers in foreign countries, through employee committees, to identify appropriate social causes to be given company support and to draw their fellow employees into directly related community service activities. Fear that this will be viewed by local people as something of American culture being imposed from abroad seems not to have been justified.

6. U.S. corporate support of either American or indigenous PVOs for human service programs where both the PVOs and the companies operate has been limited and erratic. There have been and still are communications problems. However, long-term persistent efforts by PVOs to inform corporations about their work have increasingly paid off in direct corporate support through cash contributions, gifts and services in kind, and assistance with fundraising and public relations.

7. A promising possibility for corporate foreign aid is in the policies some companies have adopted of allowing their staff members to take paid leave for humanitarian service endeavors.

8. There is still a widespread tendency of U.S. corporations to try to avoid attention to their philanthropic endeavors abroad. Rarely are such activities mentioned in company annual reports. Media coverage is often discouraged. The idea that multinational corporations should "keep a low profile" is widely accepted, despite much evidence to the contrary. An increasing number of corporate spokesmen seem to feel that American business firms operating abroad need to accept the fact that they are highly visible and vulnerable and, in their own self-interest, need to "allow this positive story to be more fully covered."

9. There is often inadequate communication within the complex structures of the multinational corporation about philanthropic activities abroad, with confusion, at times, as to what the policies followed by a company and its subsidiaries actually are.

10. There is inadequate attention to the interrelationships of U.S. government assistance policies and programs to the profit-making and philanthropic activities of the U.S. business firms. Closer consultation and cooperation are desirable.

11. There is little consultation or cooperation of American foundations and other private donors with the business concerns operating abroad. The possibility for greater direct collaboration ought to be seriously explored.

Photographs

The photographs in this section were provided by the various organizations represented. Where the photographer is known, his or her name appears below the picture.

Care

A Kenyan mother and her children draw disease-free water from the water-tap system CARE helped build in their village. Polluted rural water sources have caused serious health problems, and CARE's partnership program with the government of Kenya provides funding for such projects, which are built with the aid of the people in the communities. CARE's programs are aimed at guiding millions of impoverished people toward self-support through food, development, disaster, and medical aid projects.

Millet stalks are planted in a sand dune in Niger (above) to halt wind erosion. Still another CARE project in Niger is reforestation and the planting of thousands of seedlings. Below, a rural Lesotho woman, using an inexpensive bicycle-wheel spinning wheel, learns to spin mohair yarn from Angora goat fleece. This small-industry CARE project produces many thousands of pounds of yarn for sale.

Schools in the Philippines have set aside one or more acres for vegetable gardens (above) worked by the students, who plant CARE seeds and use CARE hand tools. The vegetables are added to the school lunches, and the children learn the basics of modern agriculture in the process. Below, a group of young Dominican Republic students show off the fruits of their labors—rabbits. Animal husbandry is part of the CARE school gardens project on their area, for which CARE provides seeds, fruit trees, tools, rabbits, and training for school garden directors.

THIS PROJECT SUPPORTED BY THE WEST-VIRGINIA GARDEN CLUBS. U.S.A.

Pupils at the Grammar School in the village of Palewahun, Sierra Leone, are nourished by the CARE meal served to them at noon each day. The meal increases school attendance, reduces sickness, and improves the children's scholastic performance.

Ford Foundation

The marketplace in Karnal, a small town in the Punjab, the wheat granary of India, about 80 miles from New Delhi. The Ford Foundation has provided more than $13 million since 1959 to support India's efforts to increase food production under the Intensive Agricultural District Program.

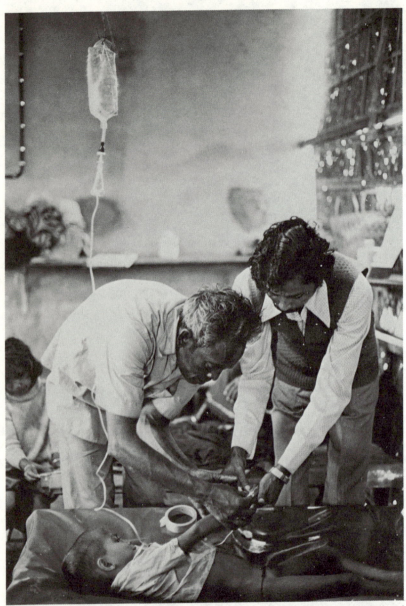

The Matlab treatment center is one of two field stations operating outside of Dacca as part of the International Centre for Diarrheal Disease Research, headquartered in Bangladesh. It was begun in 1963 during a cholera epidemic that required the innoculation of some 30,000 people in the area. Today a staff of 130 do work in diarrheal control, nutrition, and family planning. The center maintains four ambulance speedboat stations and one regular ambulance.

Sheldon M. Machlin

As part of its overseas development program, the Ford Foundation under-took to strengthen existing educational institutions, including the University College of Beirut, formerly Beirut Women's College, shown above. Below is a Behera thresher, which is being tested on a government farm near Tanta, Egypt. Through Catholic Relief Services, the foundation has funded a small-scale farm mechanization program in Egypt for several years to help produce higher yields. It has introduced here a seed cleaner, a water pump, and an insecticide sprayer in addition to the thresher.

The scene above was photographed for "That Our Children Will Not Die," a film produced by Joyce Chopra for the Ford Foundation. These mothers have taken their babies for one of the regular checkups offered by the Institute of Child Health in Katsina, Nigeria. The children pictured below are part of an experimental program in Colombia, in which regular meals are provided to help prevent physical deficiencies and permanent retardation often caused by malnutrition.

Red Cross

The Red Cross uses many means of transportation to deliver its packages, no matter how far or how difficult the trip. Back in 1944 American Red Cross supplies were delivered in China by sampan, as well as by truck and cart.

In 1946, as a long train of boxcars carrying repatriated Poles pulled into the Lublin, Poland, station, Polish Red Cross workers were there to give medical aid and to pass out vitamins and clothing provided by the American Red Cross. Such exchanges provided care for over two million people caught up in the relocation effort.

Today the Red Cross is no less active throughout the world. Here in Guatemala, after the 1976 earthquake, the Red Cross sent in supplies and medical teams to help Peace Corps personnel and U.S. AID officials provide emergency assistance to the injured and homeless. Many villages were almost totally destroyed, and some were completely cut off from the outside world until rescue helicopters began bringing in aid from central staging areas.

W. K. Kellogg Foundation

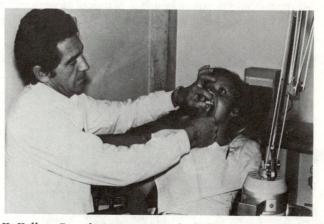

The W. K. Kellogg Foundation's strategy for bolstering access to health care services in Latin America is based on a close union of teaching and services. For example, a project is being funded at the Catholic University of Minas Gerais to improve the teaching of community dentistry. The project enables university faculty members to visit innovative treatment centers like the Dental School of the University of Sinaloa, shown above. Sinaloa's dental school is paving the way for reforms in dental health care delivery and in the education of health professionals and their assistants in Mexico.

Rockefeller Foundation

One of the Rockefeller Foundation's early projects was a campaign to eliminate hookworm in the southern United States. Clinics like the one pictured above attempted to treat and educate the local citizens. Barefoot children (front row) were almost certainly infected. Using patterns of health improvement developed in that and other domestic campaigns, the foundation carried the concepts of public health to practically every country of the world. Below, a public health nurse in Brazil explains the rules of prophylaxis to two women.

Because some billion people lived in lands hospitable to hookworm, the foundation carried its sanitation programs into fifty-two countries on six continents and to twenty-nine groups of islands, including the Fijis, site of the clinic shown here. Dr. Sylvester Lambert, twenty-one years a foundation public health physician in the South Sea Islands, believed that 94 percent of the islanders suffered from the parasite.

Over 95,000 hybrid seedling lines of potatoes were planted in Mexico during a single year—many of them at experiment stations in the Toluca valley (above) in a great, systematic effort to find disease-resistant varieties. The results of this program will have benefits around the world as others learn from the experiments carried out in Mexican soil. Other programs have focused on improving the yield and quality of the corn crop in Mexico. Below, a farmer takes seed samples from a common variety of corn for use in a local corn improvement project.

Rice is the staple in the diet of half the world's population, and efforts to increase the yields of this vital crop have been supported by the Rockefeller Foundation since 1953. In 1960, following large grants by the Ford Foundation to cover capital costs and operational and equipment grants by the Rockefeller Foundation, the International Rice Research Institute (IRRI) was incorporated. By 1962 it was in operation. Above is an aerial view of the 88 hectares of land devoted to experimental crop projects in the institute's fields near Los Banos, Laguna, in the Philippines, next to the College of Agriculture of the University of the Philippines. Below, workers at the institute use carabaos to comb-harrow plots to be planted with a world collection of rice varieties.

Pupils and teachers at the Peking Union Medical College, 1921–22.

Partners of the Alliance

For centuries, people in the village of Yaxachen on Mexico's arid Yucatan Peninsula had to rely on a 300-foot well for all their water. Above, a young man starts the engine that now pumps water to a new reservoir. The pump is the result of one of many projects sponsored by the Iowa-Yucatan Partners of the Americas in the village. Below, a chicken-raising project, another of the Partners' activities in Yaxachen.

Dale Harding, a member of the Utah team of Partners of the Alliance and an agricultural specialist, gives a field lesson on potato raising to a teaching nun associated with a community development project in the high country of Bolivia.

World Neighbors

World Neighbors founder, John Peters (right), listens intently to a member of a 4-K club in Kenya as she talks about her dreams and problems. Peters believes that only by asking questions and listening to the answers local people give about their own priorities can programs be designed that will outlast the financial input of outside agencies.

Above, Felimon Blancaflor, a World Neighbors volunteer in the Philippines, reviews the "Fish Farming for Food and Profit" filmstrip with Bob Curtis (right), a World Neighbors communications staff member. Such discussions help local field workers to better use audio-visual materials in motivating rural people to try new ideas. Below, a local field worker in Guatemala uses a flannelgraph to explain the importance of good nutrition during an infant's first year. Because she is "one Indian talking to others," the Cakchiquel nurse is listened to—and believed. Such indigenous leaders are the key to multiplying the impact of any community self-help program.

American Friends Service Committee

Russia, 1920—in the wake of World War I, a Quaker relief worker rides on a sled bearing clothing. Below, in Essen, Germany, Quaker volunteers cooked and distributed food to the townsfolk during the hunger crisis following World War I, using trolleys clearly marked "Amerikahilfe Quaker."

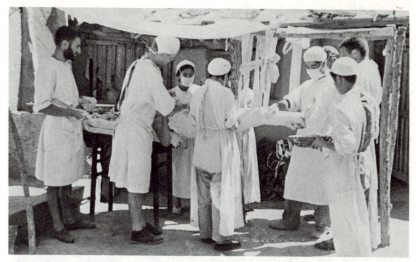

In the wake of World War II, at International Peace Hospital #1 in Shansi Province, north China, Friends Service Unit volunteers help to put on a plaster hip-spica. Below, blankets provided by the committee are handed out to Arab refugees in Palestine in 1948.

The American Friends Service Committee (AFSC), over a period of more than half a century, has sponsored a broad range of projects around the globe. Above, a Zambian woman shovels mortar into a form for making housing bricks in a 1978 self-help program. Below, a Mexican sewing co-op started with the help of an AFSC loan in 1980.

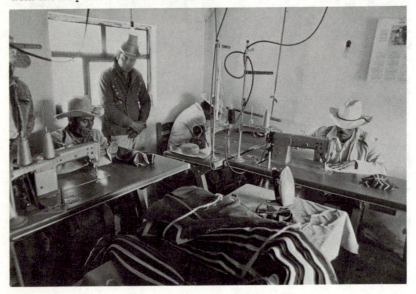

Here a woman makes prostheses in an AFSC-assisted rehabilitation center in Qui Nhan, Vietnam. Below, local men learn about farm machinery maintenance from an agricultural repair instructor in Laos—another AFSC-assisted program.

Africare

Members of the United Methodist Committee on Relief's Kansas West Conference (UMCOR) inspect corn grown in the Niger village of Tara. The crop resulted from a six-year multi-million-dollar project funded by UMCOR, the Lilly Endowment, World Vision International, Ramapo College, U.S. AID, and the government of Niger. Concluded in 1981, the project was highly praised by independent evaluators, and more importantly, by the people of Tara, who have reaped the benefits of enormous changes in all facets of their lives.

Africare's Yvonne Jackson, shown at top, managed a feeding program that saved countless lives in the drought-stricken Sahel region in the early 1970s. Since then, Africare has emphasized helping Africans feed themselves, sponsoring projects to improve irrigation systems, to provide agricultural training, to upgrade health care, and to raise the general level of literacy. Below, Africare's Kevin Lowther and his African counterpart inspect one of more than 100 Africare-built wells in Zambia's Chipata District that provide the water essential to agriculture and to daily life.

Save the Children

In 1978, Save the Children began a primary school in the village of Selbo in Upper Volta. The next step in the program will be the purchase of additional reading and writing materials, as well as sports equipment. Below, community members work on the first paved road through the village of Barqa, in Lebanon. Before the road was constructed, there was only a rough path connecting Barqa with a series of other villages, and it was often impassable in bad weather. The road now makes it easier for village children to reach the new school built to serve the area.

Redder

In the village of Deurali, in Nepal, Save the Children has helped the local farmers learn different methods of plowing, sowing, and harvesting their crops. Below, in 1980, one of many Save the Children projects included much-needed medical care for the masses of Indonesian "boat people" who sought shelter in refugee camps like this one at Gulang.

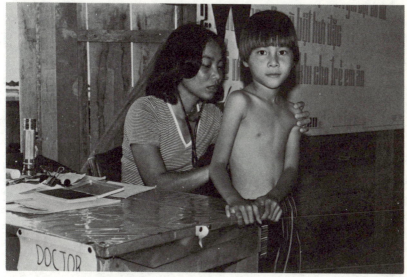

M. Novell

World Vision

World Vision chartered its own ship to patrol the coastal waters off the Indo-Chinese Peninsula, picking up the "boat people" fleeing from Vietnam and Cambodia. Its representatives provided food, medical care, and transportation for thousands who escaped from hunger, political harassment, and pirate attacks on their route to freedom.

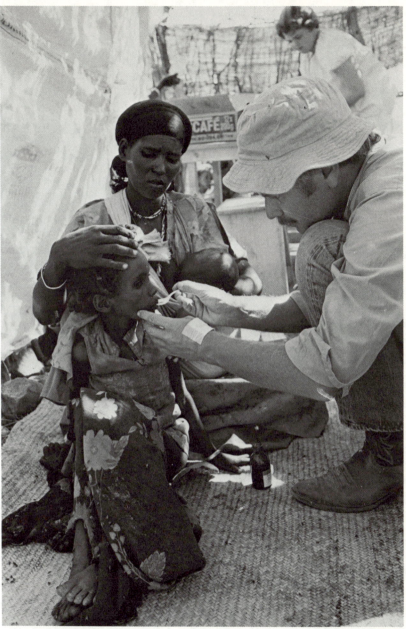

Among the private U.S. agencies that responded promptly to the needs of the starving refugees in Somalia, World Vision was a principal distributor of emergency foods. With more than a million and a half ethnic Somalis leaving the war-torn Ogaden Province of Ethiopia for Somalia, the Horn of Africa was one of the world's chief sites of human suffering. Here, a World Vision worker feeds a severely malnourished Somali child.

PART THREE

The Private Voluntary Organizations

6

PVOs:
What Are They?

Of all the private instruments of foreign aid—including churches, foundations, and business corporations—potentially the most significant are in that ill-defined category of internationally inclined agencies called private voluntary organizations, "the PVOs," a term supposedly invented by the U.S. Agency for International Development. Originally it was applied to those nongovernmental agencies that received grants or contracts from AID to help carry out certain U.S. objectives in development assistance. Now it has taken a very broad meaning, covering all manner of private and public service entities, domestic and international, financed by or wholly independent of government. A competing term, sometimes used loosely as interchangeable with PVO, is NGO (Nongovernmental Organization), an invention of the United Nations. Strictly speaking, there is a difference: the NGOs have a recognized status as consultative to the UN and are primarily engaged in study and advice on international issues. The PVOs are oriented more toward action and service.

The PVOs are the oldest of the private nonprofit groups interested in overseas relief and development, and some of the newest. They are numerous and diverse and they handle great amounts of money—far more than most people may imagine. They also have become more deeply enmeshed in governmental policies and funds than is generally known. Conceivably, their role in foreign aid may grow to be vastly more important than it has ever been before.

PVOs are the most crucial link between the broad American public and the peoples of the developing world. At their best, they provide very convincing demonstrations both of private initiatives for public service and of disinterested, popular goodwill. Their linkage to the vast and complex American voluntary sector suggests an enormous potential for involving additional millions of American citizens in international projects beyond those millions who have already given of their time and money. Moreover, the government's growing recognition of the political and economic advantages of providing foreign assistance through voluntary agencies, rather than through government bureaus, gives them increasing status and power. The PVOs can do things that government can't do—or can't do very well—and often those are the things that need doing most. As believable expressions of people-to-people concern, they have achieved a legitimacy in the eyes of private contributors, aid recipients, and governments that is indeed rare in a cynical and distrustful world.

PVO representatives distribute dried milk to starving children in refugee camps on the Somalia-Ethiopia border; they help to drill wells in the desert scrub land of Upper Volta; they teach Guatemala Indians how to grow and market avocados; they train poor urban workers in Zaire to build their own modern homes; they educate mothers in the Fiji Islands to improve the diet of their families; they help local Brazilians set up village health care programs in the Central Amazon jungles. Their activities circle the globe and reach into some of the most remote communities on earth. They touch the lives of millions of the most needy. They labor with some of the most hopeless of human situations, and with some of the most hopeful.

The number of U.S. organizations engaged in such people-helping services abroad is hard to pin down. It is sometimes said that there are about 1,950 national nonprofit organizations that devote a "significant" amount of their energies and funds to transnational issues. Of these, it is calculated that about 400 focus primarily on the problems of the developing Third World, but not all are involved in development work as such. Only about one-fourth of them appear to have well-established fundraising and management capabilities and operate relief and development projects exclusively. On the average, these 100 organizations receive about one half of their annual budget support from the U.S. government through AID, although a few of them refuse to accept any tax funding at all.

One of the most difficult decisions about the content of this book had to do with choosing which PVOs to write of from among the many varied and fascinating PVOs we studied. Every one of them, it seemed, had a story worth telling. In the end, we have selected a few for rather extended profiles, have given abbreviated identification notes about others, and have had to leave undescribed many more that we wish we could have included.

Profiles of Some Major PVOs

We have selected seven organizations to describe in some detail in order to illustrate the great diversity and organizational strength among the PVOs. Moreover, taken together, they account for a very large share of the total amount of overseas relief and development assistance provided by private American agencies. They demonstrate a broad range of public involvement, as shown by their contributors and volunteer workers. They also exhibit considerable contrasts in styles of operation.

We have chosen the American Friends Service Committee because it is one of the oldest and (as a Nobel Peace Prize winner) one of the most respected and imitated. We chose CARE because it has household-word recognition and is one of the largest. We chose Africare (which has no affiliation with CARE), for it typifies a new brand of technically oriented PVO, closely allied with AID, which emerged in the 1970s. We chose the Institute of International Education because, as the dominant higher education exchange organization, it has much to do with the flood of Third World students into the United States—a highly important aspect of American involvement with Third World development. We chose the American National Red Cross because, even though it operates primarily in the U.S., it is well connected to a strong international network and is an enormous resource for relief during crises anywhere on the globe. We selected Catholic Relief Services, the largest of the PVOs related to a religious denomination and with a truly global reach. We chose World Vision because it has strong links to the Evangelical Christian groups and because it has shown great flair for fundraising through the electronic media.

American Friends Service Committee

There has always been something unusual, at times pioneering, and on occasion down-right radical about the Quakers.

Founded by an English dissenter, George Fox, the Society of Friends proclaimed a doctrine of the Inner Light as a guide to faith and social action, protested against hierarchies of power in both church and state, denounced frivolity and ostentatious living, and encouraged its members to refuse to bear arms in any military cause. In the early days, many of them were beaten and imprisoned for their beliefs, their plain-spoken words, and their behavior. Over the years they came to be tolerated, and many of their protests eventually had some effect in helping to promote social change—e.g., in prison reform, improvement in the treatment of the insane, and the abolition of slavery. Although most of them have refused to fight in time of war, many volunteered to do service for the wounded, sick, and needy in various combat zones, during and after various wars. In 1947 two of the PVOs spawned by Quakers—the American Friends Service Committee (AFSC) of Philadelphia and the Friends Service Council of London—were given the Nobel Peace Prize, the only private relief and development organizations ever to win that famous award.

The Quakers are an extremely decentralized body of Christian believers, with great autonomy for their "monthly meetings" (individual congregations), and many of their social "concerns" are expressed through local and regional *ad hoc* projects. Nonetheless, the principal vehicle of American Quaker social service work since the end of World War I has been the American Friends Service Committee. From the beginning it has been deeply involved in international programs. No global problem has been too large, no government too powerful, no people in need too remote to keep the Quakers from trying to respond to their perception of a human need. To the extent that they could muster people and financial resources, they would tackle almost any conceivable social problem, particularly if the efforts were compatible with their underlying commitment to peace and brotherhood and human understanding.

At the end of World War I they undertook massive child-feeding programs in both Germany and the chaotic Soviet Union. They drove ambulances and relief supply trucks in China in World War II. They sent a delegation to Berlin early in the Hitler era to plead the cause of the persecuted Jews—most people knew little about that unfolding tragedy, and the German authorities didn't want anybody to know. They aided Jewish refugees to escape to the New World through France and Spain and assisted them in resettling. At the time of the first Arab-Israeli war, and afterward, they gave aid to the Palestinian refugees in Gaza and Jordan. They ran youth workcamps to help build village schools in remote Mexican villages. They sent teams of physical rehabilitation specialists to help repair the mutilated bodies of South Vietnamese children and older people injured in the war in Southeast Asia, and they crossed the lines to deliver medical supplies to North Vietnam. They worked on both sides of the battle line in Nigeria during its civil war. They were on the scene with some of the earliest relief supplies allowed into Cambodia (Kampuchea) after the forces of Pol Pot were driven out of Phnom Penh. They continue to work on many community economic development and health projects in a variety of countries around the world.

Like the Ford Foundation and Lilly Endowment, they have been accused of "scatteration." A Quaker in the grip of a "concern" is a hard man or woman to stop. The AFSC is committed to helping people express their concern to help other people, anywhere, and that takes them into a lot of places around the world.

Founded in 1917, the AFSC has been the inspirer and precursor for a number of sectarian, ecumenical, and secular private agencies that have entered the relief and development field in the past half-century. Its budget currently is about $15 million a year—substantial, but far below the size of CARE or Catholic Relief or Hadassah. Virtually all of the money expended by AFSC comes from private sources, much of it from non-Quakers. However, on occasion it has accepted government moneys for urgent projects, as it did for its recent relief work in Kampuchea, and earlier when it was asked by the United Nations to take full responsibility for the Palestinian refugee camps in Gaza in 1949, and still earlier when President Harding's administration asked it to help with food distribution during the famine years in the Soviet Union just following World War I.

Although a vast amount of its activities over the past sixty years have been related to direct relief assistance in times of emergency, it is also concerned about a variety of long-term development programs: birth control and other health services, improvements in agriculture, expansion of educational opportunities, and other familiar approaches to socioeconomic advancement of poor people. Its staff believes that both relief and development work must be done in tandem in many parts of the world for a long time to come. Meanwhile, AFSC also carries on unrelenting campaigns to strengthen the peace process, to mediate disputes, and to prevent the recurrence of further wars. Peace among all the people of the earth is, unmistakably, its overarching purpose.

In collaboration with the Friends World Committee for Consultation, AFSC maintains a substantial "presence" in the immediate neighborhood of the United Nations in New York, keeping in touch with a broad range of diplomats and international civil servants there. It maintains a similar base in Washington, D.C., for contacts with the Congress and the State Department and other offices of the U.S. government. Over many years it has carried on an extensive program of seminars and conferences for several thousand diplomats in a number of places in Europe, Asia, and Africa; to these meetings it has deliberately invited representatives of countries known to be antagonistic to each other, but willing to meet on an informal basis in relaxed settings, to talk about neutral issues with an opportunity to edge into private discussions of critical problems of conflict.

Quaker teams of scholars and writers have produced a number of studies of critical international issues: arms control, the Arab-Israeli conflict, the North-South Dialogue, the conflicts in Southeast Asia, U.S.-China relations, and many others. The purpose is to provide an informed basis for discussions and publications that, it is hoped, will help educate the Quaker community (only about 200,000 in the entire United States) and the general public about world affairs.

Some of the more activist Quakers affiliated with the AFSC have, at times, conducted marches, picket lines, vigils, and fasts to dramatize some particular peace concern they have been caught up in. At times they have annoyed officials, high and low. But again and again, government representatives have turned to the AFSC to carry out relief or development or mediation missions. Theirs is an uneasy relationship with government, but that has been true of Quakers from the beginning. They did not do what they did out of a desire to be popular, or to win a Nobel Peace Prize, but to provide tangible "testimony" (another oft-used Quaker word) for their un-flagging concern for peace. Relief and development work is just one approach to that goal.

CARE

The offices are in an old brewery building on New York City's First Avenue, far enough downtown to be in one of Manhattan's lowest rent districts (a bargain at $3 per square foot), yet close enough to the UN for its staffers to sprint to the few crucial meetings of the General Assembly each year that are important enough for them to attend. Its elevator is an ancient relic that groans with each slow, reluctant inch. The walls finally received a fresh coat of paint, but it is the olive green color of Army surplus.

This is the unassuming and penny-pinching world headquarters of CARE, once known to most Americans as the distributor of CARE packages in Europe immediately after World War II. Today the organization, housed in this obscure warehouse, is the world's largest private, nonsectarian dispenser of foreign aid, with a budget approaching $250 million and a staff of nearly 500. It has ongoing programs in thirty-six countries and is as likely to be involved in the construction of sewage systems as in the dispensing of dried milk. Nonetheless, feeding the hungry is still a major focus of CARE's work: in 1980 CARE's supplementary feeding programs benefitted 28 million people.

After thirty-five years of functioning as a purely American institution, CARE has, like some other PVOs, become a kind of international federation. There is now a CARE-Canada, a CARE-Finland, a CARE-Germany, and a CARE-Australia. CARE-USA is now separating itself from a "parent" organization that is actually its child: CARE-International. Broadening the base of contributors and participants, of course, has been the objective of these organizational expansion moves.

Yet CARE is still an American story. CARE was formed in November 1945, just six months after V-E day, by twenty-two American religious, relief, labor, civic, and service groups as a cooperative emergency relief organization to get food packages to the people of war-devastated Europe. The original CARE package was the Army "ten-in-one" ration, which was designed to feed ten soldiers for one day or one soldier for ten days. CARE began by giving away the huge surpluses of these rations that were left after the war. For $10 (later $15), a donor could arrange for a gift package to be sent to a designated individual or organization, with guaranteed delivery within 120 days. In the beginning, CARE served only Europeans. Nonpolitical from the start, CARE delivered its first package in Bavaria to a German widow. By 1948, General MacArthur requested that CARE include Japan, Korea, and Okinawa in its operations. Then other countries in need were added, not necessarily as a result of war.

Even though it was intended to fill only a temporary need, CARE did not phase out of existence when the postwar emergency ended. As stocks of rations dwindled, CARE diversified. It started to create food parcels of its own, and to include items other than food: clothing, linens, knitting wool, school supplies, and medicines— even midwife kits. Over the years, 100 million packages of all sorts were sent, and the term "CARE package" entered the everyday vocabulary.

Some of CARE's board members, representing established PVOs such as Church World Service and American Jewish Joint Distribution Committee, were not enthusiastic about CARE's refusal to cease operations, and, according to some, did not welcome the competition. Some of them resigned in protest. With Europe largely recovered by 1950, contributions began to drop to the point that the worldwide network for delivering assistance could not be supported. CARE responded to these developments for reasons that were both humanitarian and self-preserving. In the early 1950s it shifted its operations from relief to development and self-help, thus becoming eligible for new kinds of public and private funds. The Food for

Peace program began in 1954 when, as Carl Bakal says, "a surplus of American generosity coincided with a surplus of American grain." CARE was the choice to become the program's largest distributor, sending abroad more than $100 million of commodities yearly. Catholic Relief Services and CARE together are responsible for the distribution of more than 90 percent of these commodities handled by private agencies. Some of the recipients are given allotments through a "Food for Work" program, in which low income people are paid in commodities for their labor on construction projects.

CARE's Vice President for Operations has explained that the key to its survival and success has been its relationships with governments; first, of course, with AID, but also with the thirty-six host countries where CARE operates. CARE does not solicit customers. What often happens is that the people in a nation that borders one in which CARE is already at work will look at their neighbors, realize the value of CARE assistance, and request it. CARE then explains that several things must happen before it will agree to enter the country: the government must allow entry for CARE commodities duty free, must arrange and pay for inland transportation of those goods, and must protect CARE against legal suits and entanglements while operating in that country.

The country must also agree not to intervene by redirecting contributed goods away from those recipients designated by CARE. CARE must also be allowed to conduct a survey within the country to analyze whether there are true needs that CARE can meet and whether the citizens are sincerely ready to join with CARE in self-help programs. Finally, CARE and the foreign government sign a basic agreement, which clearly defines the relationship between them. Only then will CARE establish a mission in the country, usually with a mission chief and a small staff. Their first responsibilities are to conduct the agreed-upon comprehensive survey of specific needs, to develop detailed proposals for projects, and to design with the government a long-range plan. For each project, the CARE staff urges the foreign government to provide as much money and labor as possible. CARE itself provides money, expertise, and supplies and often solicits third-party funding. If the agreement with a host government is violated, CARE's mission will simply pull out. For this reason, CARE claims, it has not had the problem of government confiscation of supplies even in countries that are widely considered to be corrupt.

Relations with host governments appear to be excellent, with an increasing share of each year's CARE budget actually derived from national government funds, some of which may have come from loans by the World Bank or one of the regional development banks. Over the years CARE has been cultivating its relationships with these international banks' mission officers who now urge, at times, that governments write CARE into their budgets. In some cases, governments ask CARE to do things previously contracted to international or local profitmaking firms. "We can reduce the cost of building a school or building a road by 20–32 percent below what a government would have to pay a commercial subcontractor," a CARE official declares. One reason, in some cases, may be that some commercial firms occasionally build kickbacks to government officials into their bids; CARE will not.

The fact that CARE is a secular institution is frequently an advantage in establishing good relations with governments that are suspicious of church-related agencies. Religious PVOs generally offer their services to anyone, not just the faithful, but many governments perceive the opposite to be true, and would rather not enter a partnership with a religious organization, which they fear might offend religious constituencies of other faiths.

Although it has achieved excellent relations with governments, and substantial funding from them, CARE continues to rely heavily on private contributions, which amounted in 1980 to $26,884,000 in cash and another $13,906,000 in in-kind contributions. Most donations come from middle- or lower-income donors—two million of them in 1980, and most of those giving in response to repeated direct mail requests.

Despite the continuing strong support CARE receives from its broad constituency, the staff and board are quite concerned about efficient management and organizational image. There is continuous awareness of the hard reality that in recent years inflation generally has risen more rapidly than contributions. There also has been a lingering sense of unease about the possibilities of adverse public reaction to a headquarters administrative scandal.

In 1979, CARE's President, Louis Samia, was discovered by CARE's internal auditors to have signed a series of unauthorized checks. New York's district attorney was called in, made an investigation, and charges were filed, citing graft of $110,000 in CARE funds. Mr. Samia was convicted and forced to sell his property to repay CARE in full. The shocked staff trembled over the possible effects of the revelation. Would donations drop? "The next year we got about what we expected—about 5 percent more in contributions than the year before," is the official word at CARE. "Of course we don't know what would have come in if the scandal hadn't happened. Most people seemed to have understood that it was a problem of an individual and not an institution. Nonetheless, our accounting system now has been made as tight as any in existence in any PVO office."

Africare

Black Americans have found many ways during recent years to explore their roots and reaffirm their identification with Africa. Relief and development assistance for the hungry and needy in Africa increasingly has become an expression of that concern, and a PVO called Africare has emerged as its principal channel.

C. Payne Lucas and Joseph Kennedy, the founders and leaders of Africare, were among a small number of American Blacks who enlisted in, and then quickly moved into the administration of, the Peace Corps in Africa in the mid 1960s. Exposed to the harsh realities of life in some of the poorest countries of West Africa, particularly in the arid regions of the Sahel, they resolved to continue and expand the work of humanitarian service they had begun in the Peace Corps. The result, in time, was Africare, a unique product of collaboration between African government leaders and Americans, particularly Blacks. Ten years after its founding, Africare had become one of the most sophisticated and respected private development agencies in Africa, operating in close partnership with African governments and U.S. AID. With an annual budget close to $5 million and a largely U.S.-based staff of sixty-seven, Africare has become an established part of the PVO community. It has also acquired a unique unofficial diplomatic function. While hardly the black counterpart of the United Israel Appeal, Africare represents a voice and conscience for Africa in the American black community at a time when good relations with Africa are highly important to the United States.

The story of Africare began in 1965 in Niger, where President Hamani Diori, a French-educated visionary, was so delighted by the presence of the Peace Corps in his country that he invited the volunteers to his presidential mansion on Sundays to teach him English. Diori also got to know and like Lucas, who at that time was the national Peace Corps director in Niger, and William Kirker, a white physician for the corps. After his tour of duty, Kirker stayed in Niger, on Diori's urging, to conduct a private nonprofit health care project in one of the country's rural regions. They called the new organization Africare, and although it lasted only eighteen months, it was the precursor of something much broader.

When the Niger health project ran out of money, Diori and Kirker dreamed of the rebirth of Africare on a scale that could respond to human needs through all of Africa and at the same time be a funnel for support from black America. In 1970, President Diori got in touch with Lucas, who by that time had been promoted to Regional Peace Corps Director for Africa, to ask him to direct the new organization out of donated offices in the Niger Embassy in Washington. Lucas accepted, quit his government job, and brought in Kennedy (a former national Peace Corps director in Sierra Leone) to be his associate. Kirker was asked to serve on Africare's board, and Diori himself assumed the chairmanship.

The first step for Lucas and Kennedy was to formulate the Africare "concept," aided by friends in the African embassies and among the private "development community" around Washington, including other returned Peace Corps volunteers. They decided that their organization would provide more than relief and technical assistance abroad; its real mission would be to introduce new processes of problem-solving in the poorest of African countries. They would promote new patterns of participation that would bring leaders of rural villages directly into the development process, rather than treat them as passive recipients. If the village leaders would get involved as active partners, they maintained, the projects would work. The other part of the Africare concept was to develop a strong base of support in the U.S. black community itself. An early priority, therefore, was to elicit the support of national black leaders.

By 1971 they were ready to launch their organization in a way that would compel the media and the black community to pay attention. The "inaugural" event was held in Atlanta, with the backing of a number of local and national black leaders. Thirty African ambassadors to the United States and the UN showed up to pay their respects, and the Atlanta mayor gave Africare a key to the city. Some festivities were held in the Ebenezer Baptist Church, emphasizing the spiritual connection with its famous ex-pastor, the Rev. Martin Luther King, Jr. Black politicians from around the country were there, and, sure enough, television cameras were rolling.

That event, together with the deepening of social problems in Africa, gave Lucas and Kennedy the momentum they needed to launch a public information and fundraising campaign. "There was hardly a Sunday that Luke and I weren't speaking from the pulpit of a black church. For two years, particularly as the news of the African drought was reaching us, we were on TV talk shows constantly discussing Africa," said Kennedy. "Of the 24 million people who lived in the Sahel region (covering the northern two-thirds of Africa), ten million of them were predicted to die of starvation unless relief reached them quickly." However, Africare could do little about the problems unless it raised funds, and its early efforts did not produce substantial results.

Its first significant foundation support came from Lilly Endowment, the large Indiana-based foundation that was just beginning to expand its funding of international projects and had initiated a quiet exploration of what it might do to aid drought victims in the Sahel. The first result of that inquiry was an unusual special grant of $50,000 on a matching challenge basis to the government of Niger, with Africare advising. This money paid for the services of an Oklahoma aviation firm to fly three small planes across the Atlantic and undertake a month-long experiment in cloud seeding along the Niger river. It worked — at least, the rains came. The government of Niger was delighted and launched an intergovernmental project with its drought-stricken neighbors to train an African "weather modification" team for possible further use.

This rather exotic project was quickly superseded by a much broader involvement of Lilly with Africare. Charles Williams, then a Lilly vice president, followed up on the initial contacts with Niger and Africare and put the question to Lucas and Kennedy: "If you had a million dollars to do something about the drought in Africa what would you do?" The answer: "not direct relief, but wells." Water for the parched, emaciated cattle and people, and irrigation channels to expand the scanty crops — that became the central objective of the Lilly partnership with Africare, with grants that finally totalled nearly two million dollars. The Lilly support not only paid for well construction and irrigation projects in Chad, Niger, Mali, and Upper Volta, it also brought Africare to the attention of AID's Office of Private and Voluntary Cooperation. AID awarded Africare one of its first Institutional Development Grants, which provided funds to upgrade its technical and managerial capacities — in addition to project support totaling several million dollars.

The AID funds, moreover, have provided Africare the opportunity to refine its own approach to development assistance. Lucas hired a team of economic development specialists who tested Africare's ideas about exactly how to stimulate the participation of the ultimate beneficiaries of assistance, incorporating new ideas into the design of projects that Africare would carry out later. Rather than dream up the projects from their desks in Washington, the

Africare pattern is to send a team into the field to conduct inter-views and workshops to discover from the local people what sorts of projects they think should be undertaken. The first stop in such an Africare field survey is normally the capital city, where discussions are held with top national government ministers to determine the high priority areas for the country's regions and the services that most need development. The team then conducts workshops for lower-level staff members from the appropriate national ministries to fill in the details. Next, the team goes out to consult the provin-cial or regional leaders in the areas to be serviced. The crucial last stops are in the villages earmarked for the projects to find out what the local community leaders feel should be done, and why. Finally, the Africare team brings together representatives from all three levels—national, regional, and local—to meet face to face and arrive at a consensus on exactly what is being proposed, how the funding would be handled, and how the whole group will work together in its implementation. A single project for a few villages might be designed to include the coordination of any number of tasks, such as building wells or irrigation systems, promoting gardening or ranch-ing and reforestation, developing credit or marketing structures, and building roads, schools or health facilities. This process typically re-quires four weeks for shuttling back and forth between villages and the capital to produce an agreed-upon plan.

It is then up to Africare to write all this information into a grant proposal and seek the funding—from AID or any of a number of private funding sources, or even from a national government itself. Africare has received funds from a total of twenty-eight sources in seven years for projects that often run concurrently. In early 1981 the majority of its funds came from AID. Under its normal arrange-ment with AID, Africare does not actually conduct the project itself, but relies on the manpower within a host country. Africare signs an accord with the national government leaders, clarifying how much money would be turned over to the government by Africare to cover each of the project's phases. After each transfer of funds, Africare's field staff members monitor the projects to assure that the contract specifications are being adhered to. Only when they are satisified that past agreements are met does Africare release further payment. Using this approach, Africare does not have to manage a huge and expensive overseas staff. Instead, Africare helps African leaders, at various levels, develop skills as administrators of development proj-ects.

Evaluations of Africare's projects show that, despite delays in the completion of some projects, they pass their funders' criteria for effectiveness. But the Africare staff members feel that their real success does not show up in tests based on the levels of service provided. They claim their real value lies in evoking participation from those in the hinterlands and also in cultivating good relationships with national government leaders, many of whom have had histories of conflict with other European and American development specialists. These good ties with African leaders have had diplomatic value as well. President Carter sometimes used Lucas and Kennedy as unofficial "ambassadors without portfolio." Even after Diori was overthrown in a 1974 coup, Africare continued to maintain excellent ties with the military leaders who overthrew him and with other high officials in various African countries. The Vice Chairman of Africare's board, Oumarou Yousoufou of Niger, is also executive secretary of the Organization of African Unity (the association of fifty nations that is that continent's counterpart to the Organization of American States) and is OAU's Ambassador to the United Nations.

What of Africare's connection to the black community in the United States? With black American leaders, it has been a smashing success. Africare's newsletter and organizational brochures are as star-studded as *Ebony* magazine. Entertainers Roberta Flack and Sammy Davis, Jr., were early members of the board of directors, serving on its entertainment committee. Ms. Flack, Al Green, and Sanford Brown all have made TV public service announcements soliciting contributions for Africare's famine relief operations in the Sahel. *Roots* author Alex Haley led an Africare delegation to show the real plight of the descendants of Kunte Kinte. Commentator Carl Rowan's testimonials to Africare are written across its brochures. Marion Barry, Mayor of Washington, D.C., declares one day each year as Africare Day, an event that involves an address followed by fundraising receptions in an embassy. The 1980 speaker was UN Ambassador Donald McHenry. McHenry's predecessor, Andrew Young, joined the Africare board in April of 1980.

Muhammad Ali and his manager, Don King, picked Africare and UNICEF as recipients of part of the proceeds of a championship fight a few years ago in Zaire, providing charitable contributions of more than $100,000. Such expressions of black American support, particularly the gift from Ali, have special impact in Africa. When an Africare representative visited a small village in the Agadez region of Niger and explained that the highly prized donkeys they had received from Africare were the result of contributions from the heavyweight champion of the world, the villagers broke into broad smiles and started jabbing the air with clenched fists to show they know who Muhammad Ali is; the village chief gave a signal and every man, woman, and child present slowly knelt to the ground, hands extended, palms upward, while the chief recited in Arabic the appropriate verses from the Koran, asking Allah to bless the American boxer for what he had done for thirty-five poor families in a remote village in northern Niger.

Only slowly is that kind of spectacular support from prominent American Blacks being translated into contributions from the great mass of the American black community. Kennedy and Lucas are deeply concerned to broaden Africare's base. They fear that their success in getting large-scale support from government and foundations may have led the small givers to feel that their contributions are not important. Moreover, they reflect upon the fact that Blacks have a tradition in philanthropy that revolves primarily around the church and that their social concerns are almost exclusively domestic. Their ties to particular countries or communities or tribes in Africa are lost in the mists of the shameful slave chapters of history. The building of a broad base among American Blacks for philanthropy overseas will take much time and effort. The Africare team is determined to keep working at that task. Just as they are convinced that their success with the programs they have inspired in Africa has come out of the broad participation of the grass-roots villagers in Africa, so do they believe that, in the long run, their financial viability will be linked to strong continuing support from the grass roots of black America.

Institute of International Education

Today one-third of the world's places for students in higher education are in the United States. Yet young Americans' demand for higher education fell in the 1970s and is predicted to fall still further in the 1980s.

Meanwhile, as inflation has hit higher education perhaps harder than any other sector of the economy, student financial aid has been curtailed. Planners of the American Council on Education predicted the closing of scores of colleges and universities beginning in the mid-1970s. As if by miraculous coincidence, foreign students now bang at the doors of virtually every U.S. university and college. Their numbers jump by 12 percent annually. At the beginning of 1981 there were 250,000 of them; by 1990 they could well number 1 million.

A perfect marriage of surplus capacity and rising demand? Not quite. The flood of foreign nationals into American higher education has some potentially explosive "side effects," as was painfully evident in the uproar over the Iranian students during the long months of the American Embassy hostage crisis. The experience of foreign students in American colleges and universities and the relationship of their education here to political and socioeconomic developments in their home countries present some intriguing issues. The Institute of International Education (IIE) is, inevitably, in the center of any discussion of those problems.

The largest and most powerful private student exchange organization in the world, IIE is more than 60 years old. It did much to promote the first trickles of foreign students coming to the United States. Over the years, it has carried out major services for the U.S. government, for governments abroad, and for the American higher education community in arranging orderly processes for facilitating educational exchanges. Now that the floodgates are open for foreign students to come to American institutions, IIE's work is no longer that of advocacy. At times, part of its role is to help police and even hold back the flow. Always, its task is to assist in harmonizing the interests of the incoming students with the interests, patterns, and requirements of the host insitutions. For example:

• Frustrated by the nation's seeming helplessness to resolve the hostage crisis, many Americans wanted to send Iranian students (who numbered over 50,000) home. President Carter responded to the pressure by a directive to the Immigration and Naturalization Service not to allow the students to renew student visas. IIE, strongly believing it was in U.S. interests not to set the precedent of punishing foreign students for the actions of their home governments, lobbied successfully to allow the Iranians to finish their current degree programs.

• The financial desperation of some colleges has created demand for a new service: "head hunting" by third party organizations, for a fee, for each foreign student delivered to the colleges' doors. IIE has opposed this practice and has taken steps to coordinate the setting of standards for recruitment and admissions of college students from abroad. IIE undercut competition among colleges by setting up joint informational and recruitment sessions overseas and by distributing their literature.

• The fact that more foreign students are entering U.S. higher education does not mean that U.S. education is becoming accessible to the *neediest* students. Responding to the problem of favoritism for the full-pay affluent, IIE set up many scholarship programs that allow able but needy people from the Third World to study in the United States. Such a program allows tuition waivers for South African black students, for example. IIE designs or administers many scholarship programs for the United States and foreign governments. In each case it tries to help shape these programs so that they are accessible to low-income students.

• Many state governments have scrutinized state institution policies toward foreign students to see if they represent an economic drain on the states. Some legislators moved to regulate foreign students by imposing quotas. Others hiked fees for foreigners. Still others prohibited entry of students from countries with whom the United States does not have diplomatic relations. The IIE viewed all these developments with alarm, claiming that they represent an emergent xenophobia that runs counter to the organization's belief in open-ended people-to-people relations. It commissioned studies to determine the short term financial impact of the foreign students on educational institutions and their state treasuries. "We will show in the state legislators' own terms whether foreign students are a drain or a contribution," says IIE Vice President Dr. Joan Joshi. She explains that the Canadians and the British, who are also coping with reborn nationalism, are conducting similar studies and will share results.

• The superior appeal of American universities has caused an international brain drain from much of the rest of the world. Many students, particularly from the Third World, don't want to go home at all, or they drag out their studies over many years. The loss of these trained young people, or long delays in their return, may hamper the socioeconomic development of their countries. While remaining an advocate for open educational exchanges involving all countries, IIE has been working for decades to respond to this problem. There are several ways to do so. One, based upon careful investigation, is to recommend to Third World students local or regional universities in the Third World that are adequate to provide the training they seek. Further, IIE supported the creation of J-1 visas, which stipulate that graduated foreign students must return to their home countries for at least two years before requesting a new residence permit in the United States. In recent years, IIE has been helping provide fresh incentives for U.S.-trained foreign students to develop careers in their home countries by assisting foreign corporations and U.S. transnational corporations to recruit for employment students who come from countries where the companies operate. (These efforts have been particularly successful with Mexicans.) Furthermore, IIE has helped U.S. colleges design special technical programs for foreign nationals that can be replicated in other countries, thus encouraging foreign students to return and complete their training in their home countries.

• When the President's Commission on Foreign Language and Area Studies made its report in 1980, documenting a decline in the international education of Americans, IIE was one of several U.S.-based organizations that responded with ideas to use foreign students as a resource for community education. IIE has inaugurated a speakers bureau that matches foreign students with appropriate expertise with community groups in need of specific types of information. IIE is also watching closely the fast moving developments in "global education" and exploring ways to get more foreign students involved in grass-roots community efforts to broaden American understanding of the outer world.

Dealing with all these modern-day problems of global higher education, IIE's vision has understandably evolved far from its modest beginnings in 1919 as an administrator of student exchange programs between the United States and Europe. Located in a gleaming $12 million office building on New York's First Avenue, next to the U.S. Mission to the United Nations and across the street from the UN building itself, the IIE is an active force in the formation of a kind of worldwide higher educational system, one that responds with increasing attentiveness to the enormous technical needs of the developing countries. Dr. Joshi explains that educational costs have soared all over the world, to such an extent that "we now know that some countries just won't be able to develop their own university systems to meet their own needs. Some countries are too small. Others can't afford it. Some countries are strong in some areas but may always be weak in others."

As there gradually emerges something that approaches a single international system of colleges and universities, rather than isolated national systems, IIE expects to continue evolving new services as necessary while not discarding the old ones. The organization already counsels about 200,000 students through its regional offices in the United States. It also provides brief counseling sessions each year to another 85,000 prospective students through its worldwide regional offices. IIE also administers several scholarship programs that support more than 6,000 students from 134 countries. The biggest of these is the prestigious Fulbright Program, which benefits 2,000 students.

IIE's budget for 1979 was $56 million, a decline of $10 million from the previous year, largely due to the expiration of a major contract with the Venezuelan government. Moreover, the institute's private revenues from fundraising decreased by more than $1 million, and federal funding also fell.

Can the IIE budget keep pace with the organization's expanding vision? That is an unanswered question.

American Red Cross

One way to describe the American Red Cross is to call it the largest and the most enduring of all the U.S. PVOs. It was founded on May 21, 1881. Its annual budget, mostly raised from blood-bank fees paid by hospitals and through United Way contributions to local chapters, is in the half-billion dollar range. It had (as of January 1981) 3,082 local Red Cross chapters, a paid staff of 18,353, and more than 1,400,000 "service volunteers." Moreover, it draws about four million adults into its blood donor program, while four million school children participate in elementary and secondary school Red Cross programs.

Still faithful to the original concerns of its famous nurse-founder, Clara Barton, the Red Cross is committed to providing emergency care for the sick, the wounded, and the needy victims of man-made or natural disasters. However, it has expanded its services over the years into other broad areas of health maintenance, safety, and preventive medicine. Its Red Cross swimming and life-saving classes, its classroom demonstrations of procedures for dealing with a variety of physical emergencies, its programs of home care for the shut-in, its concern for the extension of the role of nurses and paramedics in providing various medical and health education services—all these activities, during many generations, have given the American Red Cross a rootage among the people of the United States scarcely found in any other private secular organization. It also, by the nature of its recurring participation in an assortment of crisis situations abroad, has provided a strong, continuing linkage between Americans and the peoples of many other lands.

The Red Cross movement, of course, is not strictly American—it had already been established in Europe before it was organized in the United States. The American Red Cross, moreover, is not completely private, for it was created under a federal government charter and has its international status defined by a convention of national governments. In time of war, it is virtually conscripted by its own government and works closely with military authorities. Yet the private dimensions of its character are unmistakable and powerful. Its huge budget is almost entirely derived from private sources. Despite its large professional staff, the vast bulk of its work is carried on by hundreds of thousands of unpaid volunteers.

Today the Red Cross movement is the most world-embracing of all PVOs, and the overarching League of Red Cross Societies (LRCS) has 122 national members. Even the Soviet Union and the People's Republic of China have Red Cross societies. Obviously, the extent of government involvement varies from country to country. However, for any national society to receive and retain its international charter it must demonstrate its ability to attract volunteer participation and to act in a nonpartisan, humanitarian manner in times of disaster. Some Muslim countries have comparable Red Crescent Societies, and there is a similar organization in Israel that carries on its work under the Red Star of David and goes by the name of Dagen David Adam.

One of the functions of the LRCS during the past twenty-five years has been to provide counsel and technical assistance for the emerging Red Cross societies in the developing countries. The aim is to see that they function under trained local leadership, that they enlist a broad group of volunteer participants, and that they have responsible management and meet all the qualifications for membership in the International League. Each country views the Red Cross as its own indigenous organization, not a foreign import. This local identity gives the Red Cross movement a legitimacy and a basis for claims on grass-roots support that is hardly matched by any other international institution.

At the same time, the international linkages within the movement give great advantages to each national society. They all function under the watchful eye of the International Committee of the Red Cross (ICRC), which sets standards for all Red Cross activities and monitors performance. The ICRC, a neutral body governed and administered by the Swiss, operates certain programs directly, but only during or in the immediate aftermath of international conflicts. It is this body that claims (and usually gets) the right to interview prisoners of war, makes public reports about their treatment, and brings pressure to bear upon governments that do not live up to international standards concerning POWs and refugees.

One of the major factors that sets the Red Cross apart from other PVOs is its continued emphasis on preparing and providing direct relief in times of disaster. Although it may work with other private and governmental agencies that have shifted to a primary concern for community development, the Red Cross makes clear its basic and sustained commitment to relief when it is needed. Red Cross administrators believe that its success and longevity are due to its limited but vital and professional role as an always-ready, always-available, quick-to-mobilize relief agency.

On a day-to-day basis, Red Cross activities are largely domestic, with each national society and its chapters involved in local programs and problems. When a war breaks out or a natural calamity occurs, however, the Red Cross network becomes quickly "internationalized." National societies raise special contributions and collect special supplies to ship to the affected area. Now, often only on the basis of news reports, people start sending in gifts to help the people caught in whatever tragedy has befallen them. For example, within a month after the serious Italian earthquake in 1980 the American Red Cross had received special contributions of more than a million dollars to forward to the Italian Red Cross. That kind of spontaneous outpouring of private giving for Red Cross emergency relief projects abroad happens again and again.

As with other PVO networks, the Red Cross since 1960 has given increasing attention to the new nations of the Third World. Extraordinary efforts have been required and new approaches of American Red Cross assistance have been explored. By and large, these countries do not have large numbers of affluent ethnic counterparts in the United States who can be counted on to organize the initial support, as is true concerning needs that might develop in Italy, Poland, Israel, and some other countries. Moreover, the relief problems in certain parts of the Third World seem to be long-term, as in Bangladesh, Somalia, and Haiti. These realities have made it necessary for the Red Cross to get into development work on a substantial scale. However, as Red Cross officials explain it, "To us 'development' means developing the capabilities of the local Red Cross societies in the Third World. The League of Red Cross Societies has a huge technical assistance effort aimed at beefing up their ability to raise funds from private sources in their own countries, handling their relations [and] their own national disaster-preparedness systems."

In some cases the Red Cross societies in developing countries have undertaken broad health-care services, sometimes in partnership with national health ministries and sometimes as competitors or alternatives. The Brazil Red Cross now operates rural health clinics and family planning centers and has become, in short, a full-fledged development-oriented PVO. Other national Red Cross societies are moving in the same direction.

Meanwhile, on the international level, the League of Red Cross Societies appears to be settling in for a long-term relief endeavor in the Horn of Africa. The horrible conditions that threaten the survival of more than one million refugees along the Ethiopia-Somalia border challenge the humanitarian concerns of the world community, and have overwhelmed the local governmental and private agencies. In contrast with the massive outpouring of aid from scores of PVOs that rushed to assist the boat people and other refugees from Southeast Asia, only a relative handful of private relief agencies responded to the needs in Africa. The Red Cross is one of those agencies.

As the largest and most active member of the worldwide network, the American Red Cross is, inevitably, a key participant in the global activities of the Red Cross movement and a vital link between millions of American supporters/volunteers and the needs of the Third World.

Catholic Relief Services

One of the giants in the field, Catholic Relief Services (CRS) has a staff of about one thousand and commonly operates with an annual budget of more than a quarter of a billion dollars. In 1978 it had a budget of $291.5 million and provided assistance to people in eighty-six countries. It works through counterpart Catholic agencies, usually in Catholic countries, but it serves large numbers of non-Catholics as well, including many in Islamic countries. In 1978 the agency reported that its work "touched over 14 million lives" and helped to alleviate suffering caused by thirty-five major emergencies in thirty-one countries.

Founded in 1943 as War Relief Services, to coordinate relief efforts by a variety of Catholic agencies, CRS has been headed from the beginning by a Bishop and receives nearly ten million dollars a year ($8.3 million in 1978) from 18,000 Catholic parishes through a special annual appeal, and several times that much from other collections and gifts.

More than half of the CRS budget has for several years come from U.S. government sources, the largest portion of which consists of surplus foodstuffs. Host governments, international organizations, and the U.S. government provide additional millions in cash grants and contracts.

More than two-thirds of CRS expenditures support self-help

development projects. In 1978 they totaled $215 million, while another $43 million went for disaster relief.

Heavy emphasis is placed upon service to families: child health, nutrition, and the care of pregnant women and mothers with small children. Wherever it is appropriate, CRS tries to link its assistance from the outside with work projects undertaken by the local beneficiaries, often on a "food-for-work" basis. These self-help arrangements have resulted in new or rebuilt roads, bridges, sanitation facilities, and irrigation ditches in many rural communities in Asia, Africa, and Latin America. In Morocco, CRS was called upon to help set up a nutrition education program through a training institute in Marrakech. By the time CRS completed this assignment and turned the program over to the local government it had established a nutrition training service that reached about 120,000 mothers.

In Senegal CRS was instrumental in establishing a highly successful agricultural cooperative, the Wassadou Agricultural Development Program Consolidation. More than 430 families in two villages were helped to work out a cooperative landholding scheme, to bring in modern farm machinery, to install irrigation pumps, to build satisfactory grain silos, and to provide year-round work and sufficient food for their needs.

Other types of rural cooperatives were fostered in Latin America. To solve a serious credit problem for market vendors in Tegucigalpa, Honduras, CRS helped set up a kind of credit union that provided a revolving loan fund on which market women could draw and thus escape the controls of extortionist moneylenders.

In Bolivia, one of the poorest countries in South America, CRS worked with a farmer cooperative to rebuild the market for a native grain substitute, the seeds of a common weed, *quinoa*, which is high in protein but bitter in taste, and once an important part of the diet of the Incas. Modern Bolivians had come to avoid it. Encouraged by research findings that the husk was the source of the bitter taste, CRS contracted with a vocational institute to develop an "appropriate-technology" machine to remove the husks. This brought new life to the cooperative of 12,000 farmers in the high plains of the Andes. With cooperation from the government, a nutrition education and marketing campaign was undertaken to popularize consumption of "the food of Incas."

In poor villages in Kerala, India, CRS workers found that an important part of their health service activities involved combating ancient folklore about various foods locally available: the belief that green leafy vegetables have no food value and shouldn't be eaten, that fish causes worms in babies, that liver causes blindness, and that a pregnant woman will miscarry if she eats papaya.

Although CRS gives major attention to long-term development programs, it is still heavily involved in emergency relief—for drought victims in Africa and for refugees in Asia and in Africa. It also expends as much as $15 million a year, and sometimes more, on care for the traditional objects of charity: lepers, orphans, the aged, and the mentally and physically handicapped.

CRS has an impressive record in management efficiency, calculating that its general administrative expenses are less than 2 percent of total program costs and that its fundraising costs are less than 1 percent of the funds contributed from private sources.

World Vision

In the two most highly dramatized refugee crisis situations in the world in recent years—Southeast Asia and the Horn of Africa—the principal private source of emergency assistance was World Vision, based in Monrovia, California. It is an organization that very much marches to its own drum.

Its leadership and inspiration come out of the Billy Graham evangelistic movement and the Campus Crusade for Christ, yet it carefully avoids activities that would get itself branded as a religious proselytizing agency. Its staff and its backers are representative of conservative Middle America, yet it refuses to allow itself to be used in any way for U.S. political purposes. It is one of the few private American organizations permitted to do its work of mercy freely in three Marxist countries: Ethiopia, Vietnam, and Cambodia.

Founded in 1950, World Vision operates on an annual budget of about $125 million and carries on activities in eighty-five countries. Its organizer was an itinerant missionary, Robert Pierce, unaffiliated with any denominational mission board, who became concerned about the plight of orphans in Korea and Hong Kong. The care of children is still one of the agency's strongest commitments, and it provides regular assistance, through individual sponsor arrangements, for approximately 300,000 children. Sponsors donate $18 per month for each child, and some support as many as 10 children.

As with a number of other PVOs, World Vision is determined to try to handle its assistance in such a way as to avoid creating long-term dependency. It directs its support funds as much as possible toward helping recipients get vocational training, including training in agriculture, in order to become self-sufficient. Relief for children, as rapidly as can be managed, is phased into broad programs of community development. Even so, about one-half of its work involves emergency relief.

In the late 1970s World Vision was one of the first private agencies to recognize the significance and expanding scale of the flights of the "boat people" from Vietnam and Cambodia. Its response was daring and for a time unique. It bought a 20-ton freighter and set it to sweeping the seas around Indochina looking for the often desperate and threatened refugees. Those whose crafts were unseaworthy they took on board, some they towed, others they simply guided to temporary refuge on an island chain along the coast of neutral Malaysia. At times, in dramatic confrontations, they snatched these miserable people from the hands of looting, raping pirates. Eventually, a few governments, including the United States, directed naval vessels to assist in this rescue mission. And though World Vision no longer gets much media coverage for its sea rescue work, its rusty old freighter, as this is written, is still sailing those troubled waters.

Use of the media by World Vision has probably been more extensive than by any other PVO. It has filmed a number of one-hour documentaries about its work and bought substantial amounts of air time to broadcast them to vast numbers of American television viewers. Sometimes it puts on a five-hour "telethon," in which it presents a series of documentaries about its work in various parts of the world. Always, World Vision unabashedly makes a vigorous appeal for money.

Such fundraising activities are expensive, but they work. Close to $100 million, or about 75 percent of its annual revenues, come from individual donors. In its 1981 budget, only 6 percent of World Vision's resources were provided by AID, and that included a $4 million shipment of seed rice for Cambodia. Corporations and foundations provide 2 percent of the budget and a network of churches another 17 percent, including substantial gifts in kind.

Total costs for fundraising and administration take up slightly more than 21 percent of the funds raised. From the broadcast of a one-hour film on its work among the refugees in Somalia, World Vision raised approximately $14 for each dollar spent on production of its televised program.

At its headquarters in California, World Vision operates with a staff of about 500. Overseas it has 1,000 employees, of whom only about 25 are U.S. citizens. Wherever it sends its supplies and money, World Vision works through existing churches to handle the distribution of assistance. Although most of the funds are collected in the United States, World Vision branches have now been established in Canada, Europe, Australia, New Zealand, and South Africa.

A Sampling of Other PVOs

With so many private voluntary agencies involved in relief and development programs abroad, it is difficult and perhaps unfair to try to select a few for listing here. This sampling can only hint at the diversity of their programs and sponsorship, and the range and importance of the human services they provide.

Christian Children's Fund

Founded at the end of World War II by a group of church people in Richmond, Virginia, it distributes more than $30 million a year to aid children in need, mostly through a person-to-person correspondence relationship between donor and child. Some are in orphanages, institutions for the blind or the deaf, or vocational centers. Most are helped in their own homes. Largest expenditures are in India, Brazil, the Philippines, Mexico, and Indonesia. Full-page advertising in national magazines is used to solicit funds, with actress Sally Struthers, head of the national sponsors committee, often speaking for the program.

MAP International

A Boston-based interdenominational agency, Medical Assistance Program International gives major attention to helping Christian missions throughout the Third World improve the quality of their medical services and community development programs. A major concern is to provide short-term medical and paramedical personnel to assist and train local staff members in mission hospitals. Projects in nutrition education, family planning, the development of safe water supplies, and the increasing of food production are seen as logical extensions of its original commitment to medical service.

Church World Service

An Arm of the Division of Overseas Ministries of the National Council of Churches, Church World Service is at the center of a network connecting thirty-one Protestant and Orthodox churches in the United States and numerous church groups around the world for purposes of overseas relief and development. Sample projects:

rehabilitation, in cooperation with two local Christian groups, of thirty-five Indian villages wrecked by a cyclone; craft training, in cooperation with the YMCA in Dakar, Senegal, for farm youth who have migrated to the city; and food-for-work projects in rural Korean villages to build mountain roads, bridges, and irrigation ditches as part of programs supervised by the Korean Church Service Association. In addition to more than $12 million in donated food supplies, CWS in a recent typical year expended more than $25 million in its various overseas relief and development activities. Beyond these direct services, it acts in an educational and catalytic role in encouraging the various churches with which it is affiliated to expand and improve their assorted efforts "to improve the quality of life around the globe."

The Protestant Episcopal Church

The Presiding Bishop's Fund for World Relief, affiliated with the Domestic and Foreign Missionary Society of the church, is the official channel by which American Episcopalians are encouraged to respond to human need for relief and rehabilitation in times of catastrophe. The overall missionary endeavor is heavily involved with programs in housing, education, agriculture, and small industry development. Mission centers are widely scattered in Africa, Asia, and Latin America.

World Neighbors

The Oklahoma City church origins of this organization have been described, and reference has been made to its firm policy against accepting any government support. Mention should also be made of its insistence on local participation in project planning, direction, and financing. In the words of founder John Peters, it has been, from the beginning, "a program which majored on long-term development rather than short-term relief," and "has been manned by those whose pride would not be eroded by our assistance—and whose identity would not be erased by our participation." It also has been a program that, despite its deep roots in Christian churches and its administration by an ordained minister, has consistently undertaken to "have fellowship with peoples of other faiths . . . to include literally everybody in my circle of concern."

That far-reaching ecumenicity caused severe problems for World Neighbors in the beginning, because some Christian groups in this country and in the developing world accused the group of a lack of religious orthodoxy and refused to cooperate with it or provide financial support. That kind of opposition has dwindled as World Neighbors representatives have demonstrated their compassion and spiritual sensitivity—and as their projects have produced practical benefits at the village level in one poor region of the world after another: South India, the mountains of Guatemala, the deserts of Ethiopia, the Masai grasslands of Tanzania.

Central to the World Neighbors approach is the training of local village development leaders, and the training of local trainers of such workers. Along the way they have worked out some "guiding principles": (1) Find out first what changes the village people *most* want; (2) select a *few* problems on which to concentrate; (3) try out solutions and stay with a few of the *best*; (4) select the local leaders who will make the best trainers; (5) design the program so that its success also rewards the trainer; and (6) keep the training and communication going.

Operating in twenty countries with a budget of only about $2 million, World Neighbors has provided direct services, catalyzed other giving, and stimulated local initiatives far beyond what its own budget would suggest.

International Executive Service Corps, Volunteers in
Technical Assistance (VITA), Technoserve, and
Partners in Productivity

These four agencies undertake to help with the creation and improvement of business and agricultural enterprises in a variety of developing countries. Technical advice and managerial consulting services are provided to help develop the kinds of skills that are essential if local economies are to advance. The Executive Service Corps makes substantial use of recently retired business managers and technical experts. VITA enlists mid-career professionals, as well as the retired, for what are often only short-term assignments to help with technical problems. At times, its assistance is provided in long-distance communication on specific problems. Technoserve has had success in a few countries in helping create producer cooperatives in Central America. Partners in Productivity has helped to train brand-new entrepreneurs in East Africa and elsewhere in the basic rudiments of accounting and marketing.

Assistance to Israel: United Israel Appeal
and Hadassah

Private support for the state of Israel and its many institutions is a most special case in the story of overseas assistance. Most reports on U.S. foreign aid tend to ignore it, and our mention of it here is entirely inadequate. Of all the American ethnic/religious groups, the Jewish community is the one most deeply engaged and most generously supportive in foreign aid. With a budget of approximately $300 million, almost entirely from private donations, United Israel Appeal is by far the greatest consistent fundraiser among all the PVOs. It is centrally involved in helping to finance the immigration and absorption of new settlers in Israel. Working through the Jewish Agency for Israel in Jerusalem, it extends assistance in housing, health care, youth care, and training in agriculture, industrial trades, and social welfare.

Hadassah is the Women's Zionist Organization of America; it supports programs of preventive and curative medical services in Israel. Hadassah Hospital in Jerusalem is one of the finest hospitals in the Middle East. The organization is involved in the financing of other health centers and medical schools, and it participates in a variety of social welfare and land reclamation projects. In a recent year its annual budget was $32 million, almost totally raised by private contributions.

Population Planning Agencies:
Planned Parenthood Federation of America,
the Population Council, the Population Crisis Committee,
and the Population Resource Center

Many of the experts on the development problems of the Third World have repeatedly warned in recent years that all the energies and resources that have been poured into trying to help the less developed countries to advance socially and economically will, in the end, come to nothing more than the delaying of disaster unless drastic steps are taken to curb the global population explosion. A large percentage of the PVOs include some involvement in family planning in their development programs. In addition, there are active and committed groups that concentrate on population issues and services related to the Third World. Some, such as the Population Council, have given particular attention to research on demographic trends and patterns and contraceptive technology. Others, such as Planned Parenthood, concern themselves with extensive educational campaigns on family planning and the distribution of contraceptives. Most of them, in one way or another, are engaged in advocacy endeavors to arouse more public attention to the issue and to influence the development of more explicit and far-reaching public policies, here and abroad, on population.

Consortia of PVOs

One of the recurring criticisms of private agencies for relief and
development is that their efforts are overlapping, that there is not
enough joint planning, and that there is too little working together
on program services in the field. PVOs generally agree that they
need more effective ways of working together. But they can point
out that they have been moving in that direction.

As proof, three PVO consortia are cited: the American Council of
Voluntary Agencies for Foreign Service, Inc. (ACVAFS); Private
Agencies Collaborating Together (PACT); and Coordination in
Development (CODEL).

Founded in 1943, ACVAFS is the largest coalition of private
assistance agencies, with forty-five members. The other two coalitions, PACT and CODEL, are both voting members.

The stated purposes of this council are to provide a forum of
cooperation, joint planning, and the exchange of ideas and information in order to avoid duplication of effort; to improve effectiveness
of the relief, rehabilitation, and development programs of American
voluntary agencies; and to coordinate communication with government funding agencies. In addition, it serves as a source of information for the general public about member agency activities. It has affiliate councils in fifteen countries, including the Korean Association of Voluntary Agencies and the Danish Relief Council.

One of ACVAFS's most valuable services, particularly for grantmakers, is its Technical Assistance Information Clearing House
(TAICH). Organized in 1955 and supported under contract to AID, it
provides "information on the socio-economic development programs abroad of U.S. nonprofit organizations, including voluntary
agencies, church missions and foundations."

TAICH publishes a highly useful directory for the field, *U.S. Non-
Profit Organizations in Development Assistance Abroad*, listing 203
religious groups, 171 voluntary (secular) organizations set up specifically for philanthropic purposes and supported by voluntary contributions, plus 72 other nonprofit bodies, such as professional
associations and labor union and business affiliates, and 10 foundations.

ACVAFS is not a grantmaker itself, nor does it directly carry out
overseas development projects. However, it has played a major role
in negotiating terms and conditions under which some of its
members perform contract services for government agencies. It has
worked closely with two of its members, CARE and Catholic Relief

Services, in establishing the arrangements for distributing Public Law 480 surplus foods and in securing government reimbursement for freight charges. These two PVOs handle a very large majority of the resources made available for the American "Food for Peace" program. They and another PVO giant, United Israel Appeal, account for a large percentage of the total amount of U.S. private foreign aid.

The most unusual role of the council is its processing and record keeping for Indochinese refugees being resettled in the United States. With the cooperation of ten resettlement agencies that belong to ACVAFS and funding from the Department of State, the council operates a computerized system that maintains detailed information on each of the many thousands of refugees from Cambodia, Vietnam, and Laos who have come to the United States or are in the staging camps in Southeast Asia preparing to come to this country.

CODEL describes itself as a "Christian resource facility." It was incorporated in 1969, and functions as a consortium of more than forty church-related organizations, including American Leprosy Missions, Divine Word Missionaries, Lutheran World Relief, the Unitarian-Universalist Service Committee, and the International Division of the YMCA.

In addition to its information and consultative services, CODEL actually raises money for projects and makes grants to its members. It has negotiated funding agreements with AID that require it to raise substantial amounts of matching money from foundations, corporations, and its own members, and has received AID support for expansion of its administrative services.

One of the private agencies that is making a vigorous effort to enlist business contributors, CODEL has published a special brochure, "Corporate Social Responsibility in the Third World," through which it attempts to build a strong case for the view that it is in "the enlightened self-interest of corporations" to assist the advancement of peoples in the less developed countries of the world.

PACT, the youngest of these umbrella organizations, was founded in 1971. It attempts to provide secular volunteer organizations with services similar to those provided to church-related groups by CODEL. Its core membership consists of such agencies as ACCION International, International Voluntary Services (IVS), Volunteers in Technical Assistance (VITA), and Save the Children Federation—all PVOs based in the United States. In addition, PACT is reaching out to bring into its fold private development organizations in other countries. Of its three Latin American members, one,

SOLIDARIOS, is itself a consortium of sixteen national development foundations in thirteen countries scattered across the Caribbean, Central America, and South America.

PACT, like CODEL, raises funds from a variety of sources, including the U.S. government, and dispenses them in grants to its member organizations for project activities. It also supports programs to improve the technical and administrative competencies of its members and to promote communication among them.

7

PVOs and the
U.S. Government

As private endeavors in foreign relief and development programs have proliferated since World War II, the U.S. government's interest in the PVOs has also grown—and vice versa. Governmental assistance agencies, since the early days of the Peace Corps and several governmental bodies involved in various forms of foreign aid, have repeatedly used universities, research institutes, and many different kinds of PVOs—under both grant agreements and contracts—to carry out a broad range of developmental activities.

Thanks to that government funding, several PVOs have expanded their programs and their budgets far beyond any scale that was once imagined or was ever possible through private giving alone. In some cases, the PVOs have adapted themselves to the program interests, priorities, and operating procedures defined by the government. In other instances, there has been lively give-and-take negotiating between the PVO and AID, with adjustments by both sides reflected in the agreements finally signed. In a few cases, a PVO has decided, for various reasons, that it will steer clear of entanglements with government, pass up the possibility of government funding, and proceed with its own program objectives supported entirely by the private funds it can raise.

Scope of Governmental Support to PVOs

The extent to which the U.S. government has embraced private voluntary agencies in recent years is remarkable. In 1964 PVOs received about $80 million from federal sources, mostly in surplus products. By fiscal year 1981 the figure had jumped to over $700 million, including not only the cost of surplus products but also grants for institutional support. This latter form of assistance gives the PVOs considerable operational freedom—a kind of stature within the professional world of development activities they would not otherwise have—and enhanced respect from government circles in general. Perhaps the most revealing statistics about government support for the PVOs have to do with the rising share of the foreign aid budget assigned to the PVOs. In 1972 the PVO share was 1.5 percent of AID's annual budget. By 1981 the amount had risen to 13 percent of the total AID Development Assistance budget and continues to rise by about 1 percent per year. (The Economic Support Fund for security assistance is directly controlled by the State Department.) The amount of AID funding of PVOs has increased even as the overall federal contribution to development assistance has declined. That favorable attitude toward PVOs has continued into the Reagan era.

A few PVOs receive grants from federal agencies outside AID: from the Departments of Commerce and Education, from the National Endowments for the Arts and Humanities, from the National Science Foundation, and from various governmental lending institutions. Some grants come from Action, the federal agency that sponsors the Peace Corps. However, the vast share of government funding continues to come from AID, which provides slightly more than one-third of the combined budgets (including the massive food shipments) of all PVOs working in the Third World. (Excluding the surplus food, the government provides about one-fifth of the total PVO development funds.)

Provisions in the foreign aid bill oriented to PVOs have, in recent legislative sessions, been treated kindly by members of Congress and their staffers even as they slashed other sections of the annual AID budget. In 1980 the Congress recorded its desire that the president give "fresh attention to revised structural arrangements not only to serve the needs of PVOs and cooperatives, but also to enhance further their potential as effective development instruments" (from AID report to Congress, 1980). Subsequently, the report of the President's Commission on Hunger (1980) recommended doubling the earmarked PVO contributions over the next five years, a suggestion that was backed by AID itself.

AID's Programs for the PVOs

The language written into law for the federal government to make fuller operational use of PVOs came in 1973. Although AID funds had been flowing to PVOs for development projects for some years,

Senator Hubert Humphrey's considerable enthusiasm for PVOs and his irritation with other forms of federally supported foreign aid led him to become a vigorous champion of expanded government funding for the private voluntary programs of development. Since that time several initiatives have emerged from AID that represent sophisticated ways in which the PVOs have increasingly become the "development instruments" that Congressmen hoped to see. AID's funding of PVO programs has taken many forms:

1. *Ocean Freight Reimbursement.* This covers the costs of shipping equipment and commodities overseas in support of PVO relief and development programs.

2. *Excess U.S. Government Property.* Surplus U.S. government property and equipment is made available to PVOs for use in their programs—in some years several million dollars' worth.

3. *Food for Peace.* Under PL 480, Title II, PVOs are a principal means by which Food for Peace commodities are distributed for development purposes. While AID is responsible for supervision, the commodities and freight costs are actually financed from the Department of Agriculture's budget. This program seeks to reach needy groups in the poorest countries. The PVOs that participated in the Food for Peace programs distributed supplies worth about $400 million in 1980.

4. *Operational Program Grants (OPGs).* This program of grants, initiated in 1974, enables PVOs to carry out specific projects in the developing world, a two- or three-year program, typically. Those projects are usually initiated and developed by the PVOs (rather than by AID), and yet are fully compatible with AID's legislative mandate. Normally, 25 percent of the cost of the project must come from non-AID sources.

5. *Development Program Grants (DPGs).* These grants, also initiated in 1974, provided support to PVOs to upgrade their ability to function as professional development agencies. Although now terminated, this program was important in helping the organizations improve their capability for program expansion. During the period 1974–1980, thirty-nine grants were made for a total of $26 million.

6. *Institutional Support Grants.* There are a number of organizations that provide significant development services overseas and are supported in part by volunteer contributions, but which apparently cannot raise enough money from the private sector to enable AID to discontinue its broad support. In this category are several of the

cooperative development organizations (Cooperative League of the United States of America, Credit Union National Association, Volunteer Development International, National Rural Electric Cooperative Association), plus Volunteers in Technical Assistance, International Voluntary Services, Meals for Millions, Overseas Education Fund, Opportunities Industrialization Centers International, and International Executive Service Corps.

7. *Matching Grants.* These represent AID's most recent approach toward PVOs and allow considerable operational freedom to the grantees. In several countries the program may be as broad as the overall work of the PVO or as specific as a single community-based health service. The matching grant normally allows a PVO to expand its activities and to initiate new projects. Awarded only to those relatively few PVOs with well-established programs and with demonstrated private fundraising capabilities, this grant carries with it less AID oversight than is the case with other grants. Under this matching grant program AID will pay up to 50 percent of the costs.

8. *Management Services Grants.* These grants are made to a few organizations, which in turn provide management or program support services to other PVOs: accounting assistance, fundraising counsel, evaluation, etc. Technical Assistance Information Clearing House (TAICH), the New TransCentury Foundation, Planning Assistance, Inc., and CODEL have been the principal recipients of those grants to help PVOs improve their administrative performance.

9. *Consortium Grants.* AID makes a few grants to consortia of PVOs: Consortium for Community Self-Help, National Council for International Help, SOLIDARIOS, Private Agencies Collaborating Together (PACT) and Cooperation for Development (CODEL). AID's support helps each of these groups of cooperating PVOs to exchange information on operating experiences and to collaborate on specific programs. These grants are sometimes "wholesaling" arrangements under which small amounts of grant monies can be distributed to grass-roots projects ordinarily difficult or impossible for AID to reach through its cumbersome bilateral structure.

10. *Special Technical Grants.* There are some AID grants to a few PVOs to carry out particular technical programs in fields such as family planning, health, and energy. These grants are more tightly supervised by AID than many other programs. They may relate to emergency disaster relief and, therefore, be of short duration. Others may extend over several years.

Why PVOs Are Favored by AID

Why has AID chosen to funnel an increasing share of its funds through PVOs? Will the trend continue? Should it continue? Those questions were addressed in a 1979 study for the Office of Management and Budget by Elliot Schwartz. Responding to "rising levels of funding and changing program priorities under AID's regular program of support for the PVOs," the study took on the ambitious task of evaluating the effectiveness of the PVOs.

The study's conclusions give some revealing answers and suggest that PVOs may well occupy an increasingly important role in future AID budgets. Schwartz concluded that the PVOs fit in well with the prevailing foreign aid policy concern to reach the "poorest of the poor" in the most desperate regions of the world. The study found that AID, to implement its "Basic Human Needs" approach effectively, requires the building of indigenous "participatory institutions" to handle many small-scale projects in remote and impoverished areas where they are least likely to exist. Simply delivering large sums of money to central governments for broad national schemes is not a very satisfactory approach. PVOs, he concluded, were more effective in building or bolstering local community institutions and in working on a people-to-people level. According to Schwartz, the PVOs' relatively greater effectiveness, compared with government projects, is based on the following factors:

1. PVOs are particularly active in fostering self-help initiatives among the poor.

2. PVOs show themselves capable of mobilizing substantial financial and human resources, not only among U.S. citizens but also among the citizens of the host country.

3. Because they are freer from bureaucratic restrictions than are regular governmental bilateral programs, some PVOs are able to stimulate innovative pilot projects that may be replicated later by others.

4. PVOs strengthen people-to-people contact, whereas governmental programs sometimes replace personal relationships with impersonal institutions, thus undermining the cordial ties between peoples.

5. One of the most significant contributions by PVOs has been their encouraging the development and strengthening of "indigenous participatory institutions."

6. Demand for PVO services by host countries and by international donor organizations is increasing, supporting the claim that their services are highly valued.

7. PVOs can take on a much lower profile than the U.S. government in development assistance efforts in the Third World. In regions that are sensitive to or hostile to U.S. intervention, PVOs are more capable of winning acceptance of the local governments and the people. In some cases the PVOs work under contract with the host governments and thus "blend into the local landscape."

Effectiveness in meeting basic human needs and psychological and political advantages are not the only factors on the side of the PVOs, the report makes clear. Highly important is their record of cost effectiveness. Apparently, one of the most convincing reasons why AID has embraced the private purveyors of development assistance is that, at a time when AID has been mandated to reduce the size of its own staff, PVOs often can do the same kind of work less expensively. Schwartz claims that funds given to PVOs go further to fulfill AID's purposes than funds spent by AID on its own staffs or through its bilateral government-to-government programs.

There have been too few hard studies documenting cost effectiveness of PVO versus government administered programs. However, the accumulated data now available and the main conclusions of Schwartz and others can be summarized as follows:

Lower Staff Salaries. People who love their work and are driven by a high sense of mission often work for less money than others less strongly motivated. PVO administrative and field staff members are willing to work for less money than their counterparts within AID and even those attached to host governments who might otherwise receive AID grants. According to one AID analysis of this question, the first year annual cost of one AID field staff member is $150,000, with all support costs added in. The same cost of a PVO field worker, with all support costs included, is just under one half of that amount.

Lower Overhead. When AID gives grants to a PVO, more of its funds are used on direct services for beneficiaries in the field than is the case with government aid operations. The reason: the PVOs' administrative costs are lower both at headquarters and in regional outposts than in any other "development instrument." A study of ten large PVOs (representing 75 percent of such AID funding in 1976) showed that the percentage of expenses earmarked for administrative costs and promotion was an astonishingly low 3 percent of total costs as compared with the 20–30 percent spent on overhead by most businesses and the estimated 20–30 percent spent on overhead by government-to-government AID programs. The figure is probably higher today, and has been artificially low due to

AID's prohibition on PVO use of funds for promotion and public relations activity. Other studies by AID have substantiated the wide gap between PVO and governmental overhead figures. One survey of the overhead costs of ten major U.S. PVOs operating abroad showed a high of 6.8 percent for overhead, and an average of 3 percent.

There are other reasons as well:

Saving the Costs of AID Supervisory Personnel. Another reason why PVOs offer economic advantages is that PVO projects are less expensive for AID to oversee than projects conducted by foreign governments. Schwartz claims that when AID passes money to foreign government agencies, AID's own personnel requirements increase because AID staff members must be added to cover the tasks of designing and monitoring the projects. PVO programs, however, are less expensive for AID to supervise because they operate more independently, with greater freedom to initiate and design their own programs and, in some cases, to monitor their own subgrantees.

More U.S. Resources Leveraged. Another advantage is that by channeling funds to the PVOs, AID can "leverage" additional funding for the same projects in the form of contributions from private U.S. citizens, foundations, and corporations that support the PVOs. Because several AID-funded projects are matched by "in-kind" and monetary contributions, AID frequently "doubles its money." Direct government assistance projects are, of course, unlikely to draw such matching private contributions.

Stimulation of Local Support. One of the most telling arguments for the private voluntary approach to assistance programs is found in the success of the PVOs in building up local participation and enthusiasm for particular development programs. In the long run, the true test of development efforts will be found in the degree to which they become rooted in the local culture and are sustained by local energies and local resources. As shown by an AID-funded study of development projects in Kenya and Niger, the projects administered by private groups are more likely to attract local volunteers and in-kind contributions and to be ultimately sustained on a voluntary basis by local citizens beyond the official life of the project.*

Improved Bargaining Position. When AID funds a PVO it is in a

---

*Development Alternatives, Inc., *Final Report: The Development Impact of Private Voluntary Organizations in Kenya and Niger*. Washington, D.C.: U.S. AID, 1979, p. 73.

good position to bargain over program cost. Such is not the case when AID funds a host government to conduct a project. Why? Because AID can solicit proposals on a competitive bidding basis from many PVOs capable of operating in a given country or region, and select the plan of lowest cost or highest quality. However, if AID wishes a national government to conduct a program in a given country, it must frequently consider a single proposal, and at times must settle for high cost, low-quality national government administration.

Varying Attitudes Among PVOs on Government Support

In the early 1970s, as the U.S. government became increasingly convinced of the political and economic advantages of enlisting PVOs to handle an expanding share of foreign aid operations, the PVO community reacted to this good news with ambivalence. "Are the Feds using us or are we using them?" one PVO staffer asked another.

The answer, perhaps once unclear, now is surely "yes—both are." The Feds *are* using the PVOs, encouraging them to change their purposes and styles of operation and become less private. On the other hand, the PVOs *are* using the Feds, by indirectly modifying the purposes and operational styles of government assistance. Some PVOs, particularly those with religious missionary ties, are uneasy partners of AID. Some PVOs see what they believe to be excessive national security preoccupations of the State Department. The truth is that tensions are simply inherent in the partnership. Both sides now know that *before* they start a new project they must try to negotiate a clear and mutually acceptable agreement and resolve in advance as many of their differences as they can.

How the PVOs handle this partnership is crucial, not just for their own organizations but also, indirectly, for the world's poor. As advocates for development in poor regions of the Third World, the PVOs are in some ways a special interest group. However, their causes, such as the elimination of hunger in Africa, require policies and action programs that generally are long-term, and it is hard to get Congress to make long-term commitments for anything. Moreover, because they serve people who are not American voters, there is very little "constituency pressure" for foreign aid on any basis. To be sure, there *are* Americans who favor overseas relief and development assistance. Many churches and synagogues and their affiliated bodies give support, as do secular humanitarian groups and academic think tanks. But the PVOs, clearly, have special respon-

sibilities and a tough challenge in building coalitions and constituencies around the foreign aid issue.

How do they feel about their government partners? What changes
in U.S. foreign aid policies do they advocate? What strategies do
they use to influence policies? How successful have they been as
lobbyists? What are their prospects in an increasingly get-tough
climate for U.S. foreign policy?

First of all, the PVOs are ambivalent about accepting government
money. The advantages are obvious. Government grants and contracts make it possible for the PVOs to expand and improve the services—what does it matter where the money comes from as long as
the job gets done? Why not put government money to "good use"
rather than reject it and let it be "wasted" on large, impersonal
government-to-government projects? These are the rhetorical questions often asked by PVO representatives. Furthermore, some argue,
the quality of their own work may be enhanced, for contracts with
AID often require the PVOs to make improvements in management
and technical skills. The result is that they become more busi-
nesslike, more objectively critical about what they are doing, more
deliberately involved in long-term development, and less influenced
by a slap-dash emergency relief mentality.

These advantages are easily apparent, but the disadvantages of accepting AID money have appeared more slowly. Most of their fears
have to do with loss of independence—growing reliance on tax
dollars, increasing acceptance of government controls, and weaken-
ing ties to the private constituency that created them and gave them
initial support. (Africare, highly successful in winning AID support,
struggles with just those problems in seeking more private funds.)
Finally, they fear a loss of credibility and acceptance by the Third
World people it is their purpose to serve.

To some extent, success in private fundraising depends on the
perception that if the private givers don't contribute no one else
will. If those who volunteer their labor or funds feel their contributions are insignificant alongside "big money" from government
agencies, they drift away. World Neighbors is one PVO that had
itself "de-registered" by AID's Advisory Committee on Voluntary
Foreign Aid, and it accepts no government support. World
Neighbors' James Morgan feels that the capacity to elicit private
support is an acid test. "If we can't raise voluntary contributions, we
haven't learned to articulate our program well enough. The burden
is on us to find a way to educate the public so that people will say:
'this is important and I want to give to it.' " Acceptance of sizeable

amounts of government money reduces the need to demonstrate to the public the worth of the programs. Rapport with independent donors, which is crucial for the vitality of organizations that call themselves "private" and "voluntary," is inevitably weakened.

Another fear is that dependency on government support damages the PVOs' working relationships in the Third World. The American National Red Cross, for example, refuses to become dependent on government aid on the grounds that to do so would potentially undercut its role of monitoring government performance during wars or during disaster relief operations. Oxfam-America refused to accept U.S. government support during recent Cambodian relief operations, and its representatives believe that this show of independence gave it prompt entrance into that tortured and suspicious country when other private relief agencies were being kept out. They speak proudly of being a "truly private organization with sufficient independence from government policy to act upon humanitarian needs and not upon policy considerations."

Some PVOs are also concerned that by subtle or overt ways they may shift their priorities against their principles or better judgment because AID funds are available. On their own, they might go into Upper Volta, where the need is great and the United States has no vital political or economic interests; but, because of AID, they could decide to go into the Philippines instead. Or they may be encouraged by the offer of government funding to attempt to operate on a large scale when their common sense tells them they should stick to the work they have slowly developed in a few villages.

Influencing the System from Within

Despite all the reservations, there is broad (though not unanimous) agreement that the assets of partnership with government outweigh the liabilities. However, among the cooperating PVOs there is strong determination to be active shapers of the relationship and not merely silent and passive junior partners. Says Charles MacCormack, President of the Experiment in International Living, "The argument regarding using or not using federal funds is a sterile one — the significant influence of governments is a fact of life in international assistance. The key thing for voluntary agencies is to be thoughtful and selective in their relationships with governments, both in this country and overseas. . . ."

Once they have become a part of the overall foreign aid system, many PVOs use their close proximity to government to try to influence it from within. To these representatives of private organizations, the federal government is not solid and unbending, but porous, pliable, and susceptible to rational change. How they influence government policies varies, naturally, with circumstances. Sometimes PVO staff members act as *advisors*, as when they participate on the advisory committee on voluntary foreign aid or make their views known in less formal ways. Sometimes they are *policy researchers* (e.g., through their presentation of papers to the President's Hunger Commission). Sometimes they serve as *task force workers*, teaming with government officers to design or modify the implementation of a given policy. At other times they take the stance of *loyal opponents*, communicating grievances, demands, and objections by mail or phone and at any number of conferences and seminars attended by PVO staffs and their governmental funders. Sometimes they may circumvent and challenge AID by conferring with congressional staff members, by offering testimony to some congressional committee, and by helping to draft new legislation. They may, on occasion, even take their case to the White House. At times, and perhaps increasingly, they function as *lobbyists*, organizing broadly based coalitions around *ad hoc* issues, enlisting other lobbying groups from among the religious organizations, scientists, unions, and, in some cases, American commercial interests.

How do the PVOs want to change federal policies? In various ways, they seek to:

1. *Close the Gap Between U.S. Foreign Policies and Their Own.* PVOs would like American foreign policy to be more congruent with the beliefs and philosophies of the PVOs themselves, and particularly to give greater attention to the immediate needs of the rural poor.
2. *Increase Independence from Federal Policies.* However great or small the congruence on policies may be, the PVOs would like to be restricted as little as possible by federal regulations that burden their day-to-day operations or by federal policies that divert them into activities they do not wish to pursue.
3. *Increase Funds for Co-financing.* PVOs would like the federal government to further increase financial support to development assistance and to use the PVOs more extensively as channels for that assistance.

Let us examine these three objectives in some detail:

1. *Close the Gap Between U.S. Foreign Policies and Their Own.* Since 1973, the official purpose of U.S. development assistance administered by AID has, in considerable measure, shifted from support of large-scale, capital-intensive infrastructural projects to smaller-scale local efforts to improve the life of rural poor. These projects have tended to concentrate on "basic needs" (e.g., food, water, clothing, shelter) by helping the poor acquire the necessary skills to become self-sufficient. Thus it *seemed* that the U.S. government's purposes were finally coming into focus with the traditional concerns of PVOs. They were the experienced specialists in this form of development assistance and had much to teach the government people just beginning direct involvement with the poorest of the poor.

But the apparent congruity of interests is deceptive. AID is only one of several agencies involved in implementing the foreign assistance policies of the U.S. government. Those policies are also interconnected with the Defense Department and with the international policies of the Department of the Treasury, which oversees U.S. contributions to the World Bank and the International Monetary Fund. AID, in consultation with high-level officials in other departments, designates certain countries as candidates for development assistance and will develop a "country development strategy" for it. The strategy must fit into broad guidelines defined by the host country as well. All that high-level negotiating means that there is much that motivates U.S. foreign policy toward the developing world besides the altruistic purpose of advancing the interests of the very poor. This troubles some PVOs.

For one thing, economic aid has become an increasingly important alternative to military intervention as a way of influencing Third World events. Global competition between the United States and the Soviet Union is often expressed in a struggle for the allegiance of Third World countries, especially those that offer essential raw materials or a strategic geographic base. While the notion of intervening in the domestic affairs of Third World nations is anathema to them, running counter to doctrines of "self-determination" espoused by the 125 or so officially "nonaligned" countries, the reality is that the United States can avoid competitive efforts to acquire such influence only when it bows out of the contest—to the Soviet Union's advantage.

Under the administration of President Carter and his predecessors, the United States, at times, demonstrated an apparent ambivalence over how and to what degree it wished to influence Third World governments. Carter's Human Rights doctrine, combined with support for democratic reforms in Latin America and Africa, frequently ran counter to other U.S. foreign policy interests and domestic influences that favored support for authoritarian anti-Soviet governments, with not too many questions asked. Whether the United States took a cold war posture, a humanitarian posture, a social reformist posture, or one of strict noninterventionism was a matter to be handled country by country, sometimes with puzzling fluctuations toward a given country from year to year. The arrival of President Reagan was viewed by many as a turning point for U.S. foreign policy in the direction of greater consistency. Some foreign policy analysts expected clearer directives from the leaders of the new administration that would clarify for each area how development assistance will be meshed with other forms of financial and military security aid in a coherent expression of U.S. national interest and will. Others were not so sure.

History suggests that foreign aid has many advantages as an instrument of national policy. The offer of foreign assistance, or the threat of its withdrawal, can affect a wide range of Third World decisions: whether a country will make peace with its neighbors, whether a country will adopt narrowly protectionist or free-trade policies, where and how it will set prices on raw material exports, what its stand will be on human rights, nuclear proliferation, and other important issues. Or so it seems.

Of course, it is evident that the United States will provide assistance in ways to promote what is perceived to be its national interests and will not promote activities directly counter to its own policies. The trouble comes when there is confusion over what U.S. national interests are—and when the policies are not clear or consistently applied. Because there is always the temptation to link foreign aid to other international objectives—and those have changed from time to time—foreign assistance programs have appeared to be shaped by not-always-consistent policy objectives. Some countries are at one time in favor, and later they are not. In the total scheme of U.S. assistance abroad, resources are not concentrated on the neediest countries, as some assume. Israel and Egypt, for example, received over one-half of AID's total assistance budget in 1980. Understandably, they were being rewarded for their efforts to bring about a Middle East peace—and for their willingness to cooperate with overall U.S. desires in the region. Some countries have supposedly been denied U.S. aid on account of human rights violations while others get aid despite human rights offenses.

The religious call for world brotherhood, which motivates much private voluntary giving (whether the PVOs are linked to religious groups or not), often conflicts with AID's foreign policy guidelines. PVOs, for the most part, would like U.S. foreign policy to allocate aid strictly according to the needs of the people and without regard to politics. Some more radical PVOs, following the view of Latin American liberation theology, go further and call for foreign assistance to be used to support policies that run counter to the perceived U.S. economic and political interests in the Third World. Indeed, at times a few church groups (the World Council of Churches, for example) have channeled some of their private funds into support of revolutionary groups it was the official U.S. policy to oppose.

PVO attempts to influence broad AID policy have at times focused on efforts to separate AID from the military and short-term commercial interests of the United States. The Senate Foreign Relations Committee on occasion has sought to consolidate all assistance programs (including those handled through the World Bank and regional development banks, and all of AID's assistance programs and the Department of Agriculture's Food for Peace) under one separate nonpolitical umbrella organization. Such an umbrella organization would be funded by Congress but insulated somewhat from political pressures. The National Science Foundation and the Inter-American Foundation are cited as models adapted for the funding of international development programs.

This proposal has never had the necessary support for passage, and it is unlikely to be revived. AID itself has opposed the measure, largely on the grounds that it might result in lower congressional appropriations for development. In 1979 a compromise measure was worked out that put the bulk of U.S. development assistance activities under the supervision of a semi-independent body, the International Development Cooperation Agency (IDCA). The director of IDCA was made responsible for the coordination of U.S. economic assistance programs and became the president's principal advisor on all development-related matters. However, he was not given cabinet-level status and had to report to the secretary of state on all foreign policy questions. Moreover, it is the secretary of state, not the IDCA director, who controls the separate Economic Support Fund, which provides special economic assistance to countries that are strategically important to the United States, "in order to promote economic or political stability." This huge side pocket in the foreign aid budget is clearly a way to make sure that development assistance can be used at times for political and security purposes of interest to the United States.

Instead of separating development assistance from U.S. military and commercial interests, the tendency has long been to link them more closely, and there are no prospects that this will change. The congressional mood is clearly to attach new strings to all U.S. contributions, and not just to those from AID. U.S. funds for the World Bank and for projects of the United Nations may not be used to assist countries unfriendly to the United States. Such was the case in Ethiopia. AID gave a grant of more than one million dollars to World Education, Inc., for a four-year project aimed at developing a national curriculum in informal education for Ethiopia. After two years of collaboration with the Ethiopian Ministry of Education, however, the funding was revoked, in accordance with the Hickenlooper Amendment, and the project terminated because certain U.S. properties had been confiscated without compensation. World Education challenged the AID decision, arguing that PVOs' humanitarian projects should be exempt from the restrictions that ought to apply to government-to-government aid. But the PVO lost and gave up hope of reviving the project, even though its staff members argued that the project might well have benefited U.S. political objectives in the long run. However, in late 1980 the Congress, reaffirming its confidence in the PVOs' approach to foreign aid, voted to exempt their "people-to-people" projects from those automatic cut-off requirements.

2. *Increase Independence from Federal Policies.* The PVOs would like to reduce the controls exerted by AID on their own grantees. Recognizing that they are unable to influence the basic direction of AID policy, PVOs have focused on ways to increase their ability to design their own AID-funded projects and to expand their freedom from AID interventions in their own operations.

Agreeing to the PVOs' need for independence, AID offers them some opportunity to choose the degree of influence they are willing to accept. Presently, a PVO may work with AID through any of three types of agreements: (1) grant, (2) contract, or (3) cooperative agreement.

PVOs working with AID *grants* have considerable freedom both in design and operation of grants, and are able to address needs that they themselves have identified as long as they fit into AID's overall priorities for the country. After the grant has been approved, AID does not have the right to interfere with program implementation unless it has reason to believe the PVO is not living up to the terms of the grant.

Organizations that are working under *contract* to AID have far less authority in designing and implementing their projects. Here, essentially, the PVO agrees to do work that AID wants to have done, and AID's mission offices have substantial involvement throughout the life of the project. PVOs that receive AID funding prefer grant agreements to contracts.

Cooperative Agreements between AID and PVOs are part grant, part contract, and are negotiated case by case.

Although PVOs can choose from among these AID relationships, there are still disputes. PVOs want less interference by the AID staffers in the country missions where they operate. They contend that the high turnover rate among AID field personnel makes such relationships impossible to develop properly. Since AID personnel are being cut back for economy reasons, PVOs may have their way on this issue after all, and will then relate more directly to upper levels in Washington.

One major issue to the PVOs is authority to monitor their own subgrantees, freeing their indigenous counterparts in the Third World from having to deal directly with the complicated regulations of the U.S. government. AID has now agreed to fund consortia of PVOs, which can then pass the money through to their own member agencies without AID interference.

PVOs have also won concessions from AID in program design. A new matching grant program allows funded PVOs the discretion of targeting their projects to any number of countries and regions. The programs can be highly specific, focusing on some special technical aspect of economic development for a broad population, or they may deal with multifaceted development activities for a single community.

In other matters, PVOs have not yet succeeded in winning changes they want. They would like AID to do more to disseminate information about successful village-level projects in order to influence the large-scale developmental programs of AID and the World Bank. They would like increased funding to launch educational ventures in the United States to promote public awareness of Third World problems, as has been done through government funds in Canada and Sweden. (A step in this direction came in late 1980, when Congress passed the Biden-Pell Amendment calling upon AID to foster public discussion of issues raised by the President's Commission on World Hunger.) PVOs would like Congress to enact multi-year (at least two-year) appropriations for assistance programs. They also want protection against such a simple but important hazard as delayed receipt of AID checks. Moreover, they argue for removal of a stipulation that prevents any AID funds from being used to support essential fundraising that would enable the PVOs to secure far more private contributions and thus decrease their dependence on AID.

3. *Increase Funds for Co-financing.* The Organization for Economic Cooperation and Development has urged the industrial nations to increase the level of development assistance to .07 percent of GNP. PVOs would like to see even more funds allocated for development. Most of them hope that more AID money will be channeled through their own programs, although some PVOs feel they are already operating on as large a scale as they can manage effectively and do not seek larger funding for themselves.

The Hunger Commission's report, which reflects PVO concerns, recommended that allocations to PVOs double between 1980 and 1985. After assessing the burden that increased funding would place on PVOs, the commission maintained that PVO "absorptive capacity" was sufficient to handle the increased load.

A study of the AID–religious PVO relationship by the Center of Concern has suggested that for some of them there could be a problem of overfunding. The report cautioned that with still higher levels of funding, the religious PVOs might begin to design projects to absorb money available rather than concentrate on those projects that affect basic human needs. There is always the worry, also, over the possible harmful effects when big money is poured into Third World projects that are soon abandoned.

Other PVOs would like to see new funding programs earmarked for domestic nonprofit organizations that have special skills to work overseas, as is true with certain Hispanic organizations that could be enlisted for work in Latin America. Others stress the need for new mechanisms to channel funds directly to new groups of indigenous PVOs in the various foreign countries.

The AID officials' response to these pressures is that they can do very little to influence the appropriations they actually receive from Congress. They can, however, continue their practice of getting PVOs to take over new tasks once performed by AID field personnel.

Vehicles for PVO Influence

The PVOs and other advocates for development assistance reform have access to several instruments for exerting influence on federal policymaking. In recent years they have avoided overt lobbying, favoring subtler forms of influence as advisors and information gatherers. However, as opposition to foreign assistance has increased, the PVOs have moved in the direction of mobilizing citizen groups as advocates for their causes. Within the PVO community there was much thrashing about for a long time in the development of a common "case statement" and in the defining of a practical strategy for building broader and stronger public support. Nevertheless, there seems to be a more sustained thrust toward collaboration among them than ever before, as seen by several distinct forms of collaboration that have now emerged:

1. *AID's Vehicle for PVO Input: The Advisory Council.* Since 1946 the Advisory Committee of Voluntary Agencies for Foreign Service has acted as an intermediary within the PVO community. This committee was set up by President Truman as an association of representatives from the federal Departments of State and Agriculture. Its purpose was to mobilize the voluntary agencies in crash efforts for overseas assistance in the immediate post-World War II period. Later, the committee's main function was to deal with PVO claims on government funds for ocean freight reimbursements related to the shipment of relief supplies. As the membership of the committee changed to include primarily representatives of the grantee organizations receiving government funds, the committee's role shifted to that of ombudsman, handling problems PVOs experienced in administering AID money.

Once the PVO community realized the importance of the committee as a voice within the federal government, it pressured AID to expand the committee's policy role and to open its activities to PVOs outside the chosen circle of registered and funded voluntary organizations. Although the committee could never lobby for PVOs' special interests,* AID did reorganize and expand the committee. Today the members are all private citizens. Committee meetings are held four times a year on the eastern seaboard and in western and midwestern cities, and about 200 people attend them. Recommendations are made relating to the process of grants administration and other aspects of AID/PVO relations, to which AID prepares a response.

2. *PVO Collaboration with Each Other.* The advisory committee

---

*Advisory committees of the federal government are regulated by the Federal Advisory Committee Management Act of 1974, which clarified that they are to exercise their limited powers purely at the discretion of the administering officer of the agency they advise.

created a demand for a measure of collaboration greater than its own activities could satisfy. As the PVO representatives met, time after time, they realized the clear limits to what such a committee could do. It could discuss and recommend. Clearly, it did not serve as an expression of PVO long-term interests and aspirations. Its status within AID was uncertain. Its meetings tended to emphasize problems in working relationships with AID rather than broad policy issues and the long-range course of development.

So, before and after the official committee sessions, the PVOs began to discuss the need to get themselves together on an independent and open-ended basis, rather than within the structure set by government. They needed a new pattern within which they might work together more fruitfully, through which they could carry their story to the nation, and out of which they might develop a more effective, sustained strategy for influencing public policy.

3. *A New All-embracing Association: Private Agencies in International Development (PAID).* The PVOs finally decided that their concerns were so urgent that they would have to create a kind of trade association for the internationally oriented segment of the U.S. nonprofit sector. Now more than one hundred agencies have indicated their interest and contributed modest sums to get the project going, with a steering group under the initial leadership of Thomas Keehn, formerly president of World Education, Inc., and Elise Smith, executive director of Overseas Education Fund. The group includes some domestic U.S. groups that only recently entered into international programming.

PAID's first concern was to develop a joint "case statement" and put out a brochure to advertise its purposes and elicit broader financial support for PVOs in development.

Its other principal aims were to impress upon Congress and the executive branch the importance of development issues and to foster new initiatives in development education, a growing concern for PVO activity. Efforts were also launched to bring together a number of action groups for workshops for various categories of PVO professionals: financial managers, personnel managers, and fundraising administrators.

It is no easy task to create a new national association of diverse and highly independent organizations whose several interests are really scattered all over the globe and whose scales and styles of operation differ so widely. But as this is being written, the effort is being made, and the prospects are promising.

4. *One Ecumenical Lobbying Group: Bread for the World.* While

the PVOs try to get their "trade association" and lobbying endeavors going, it is worth noting that one unusual organization has already learned much about how to influence the public and the government on behalf of needy people overseas. Of the domestic groups that have worked on this concern, the most effective in reaching the mass of U.S. citizens are those that are religiously affiliated. And among the religiously inclined, the pre-eminent citizens' lobbyist group is Bread for the World.

This organization began as a high-minded idea in 1976 when Executive Director Arthur Simon wrote a National Book Award-winning analysis of world hunger under the title *Bread for the World*. By 1980 the organization had 34,000 members, organized by congressional district with district coordinators responsible for overseeing all local chapters. The organization chooses its issues carefully, and when it goes after a legislative change it usually wins. It initiated a Grain Reserve Program in the 1977 Farm Bill, a big step toward world food security. It sought and secured amendments to laws governing U.S. participation in the International Monetary Fund, thus helping to assure that U.S. contributions would reach the poorest of the poor.

In 1980, its big emphasis was to follow through on the recommendations of the President's Hunger Commission by drafting a Hunger and Global Security Bill. Rather than advocate reforms that run completely counter to the winds in Washington (such as the commission's recommendation that funds for development assistance be doubled), it selected the modest goal of making small improvements in the "best" programs and major changes in the "worst" of them.

Just how it conducts a lobbying effort is instructive for other non-profit human service groups. After finding sponsors for a bill, a notice goes out in a newsletter distributed to the entire membership asking them to write letters seeking other sponsors. To prepare the constituency, forums and study groups are organized in local churches. Hundreds of local groups, for instance, studied the Hunger Commission report with the aid of a Study Guide provided by Bread for the World.

When a given bill actually goes onto the floor of either the House or the Senate, the constituency will be primed for more letter writing by the organization's Citizen Action Network, either through an instant newsletter or a predesigned "phone tree" operation. According to that system, the national headquarters makes a few calls alerting regional coordinators to the need to write letters.

Each person who receives a call calls several other names on a prepared list. Within hours thousands of people are called and within a few days thousands of letters flood congressional offices. As a technique of last resort, used on special occasions, the network gets priests and pastors to ask their congregations to write letters during the church service itself and deposit them, along with their donations, in the collection plate.

Bread for the World's network is growing. Its success reflects one more facet of the increasing politicization of U.S. religious groups on all ideological fronts in the 1980s.

Occasionally a U.S. PVO and a foreign government cooperate to help the people of a developing country. Such is the case in the partnership between the Norwegian government, through its international development agency, NORAD, and the American Friends Service Committee in Laos. Working together, they have provided resources to expand and improve the Dong Dok Agricultural Mechanics Training School. There, scores of young men from all over Laos are being trained in the operation and repair of irrigation pumps, rice mills, sprayers, bulldozers, and tractors.

8

PVOs and Intergovernmental Agencies

"One-on-one relations," remarks Harlan Cleveland, discussing the state of international affairs today, "are a thing of the past: Nearly every issue now involves several countries. Decisions are made in multilateral negotiations at many-sided tables." The veteran observer/diplomat/scholar insists that this "multilateralization of international relations" is the most fundamental modern phenomenon in global politics. It is a phenomenon that, more and more, affects private foreign aid.

Some PVOs and the UN-blessed NGOs (sometimes but not always the same) now find themselves increasingly involved with intergovernmental bodies or the United Nations Development Programme (UNDP). The European Economic Community, the Pan-American Development Bank, and other regional banks and commissions have established a variety of working ties with a number of private American relief and development agencies that surely did not have any expectation originally of becoming partners with an intergovernmental institution.

Since the UN was formed in 1945 there have emerged sixteen "specialized agencies" to work on particular global problems. They are organically linked to the UN, but most of them have headquarters at addresses other than the United Nations in New York. Often referred to as members of the UN "family," these agencies are particularly significant for the PVOs. They include the United Nations High Commission on Refugees (UNHCR), the World Health Organization (WHO), and the International Labor Office (ILO), all centered in Geneva. There is also the Food and Agriculture

Organization (FAO), which is based in Rome. The United Nations Educational, Scientific and Cultural Organization (UNESCO) operates from headquarters in Paris; the UN Environmental Program has headquarters in Nairobi. A dozen others are scattered around the globe. The relationships of private relief and development organizations to these agencies involve consultation, advocacy of certain policies, parallel action, and even the raising of private contributions to help certain UN programs. On the other hand, sometimes UN funds are actually channeled to the developmental and educational work of the private organizations. It is likely that such public/private partnerships will increasingly affect the work of both the UN specialized agencies and the PVOs.

Nevertheless, the cloud of uncertainty that hangs over the United Nations keeps alive assorted doubts about the specialized agencies and about their capabilities for long-term effective collaboration with any group. The work of the specialized agencies is probably viewed more favorably by the general public, in the United States and elsewhere, than are the core activities of the UN itself. However, the fact that the bulk of their funding comes from the "voluntary" rather than the "assessed" portion of the UN's income budget means that their financing is never quite secure. As general dissatisfaction with the UN has grown, particularly in the United States and in some of the other Western affluent countries that pay a high percentage of total UN costs, and as stagflation has struck their economies, the temptation is strong to cut back on "voluntary" contributions to any branch of the UN. Moreover, large emerging needs for voluntary contributions, as in the case of recurring refugee crises, tend to undercut the claims of the regular programs of the specialized agencies for voluntary support—and may threaten UN collaboration with (and support for) PVOs.

The truth is that the UN as a whole and its subsidiary agencies need all the help they can get in building broad public understanding and special constituency support. They also need responsible advice and criticism on their work and outside help defining goals and strategies for the future.

That such roles could be played by people drawn from the private sector was anticipated in the earliest days of the UN. At the charter meeting of the United Nations in San Francisco, April 1945, forty-two U.S. private organizations were present and actually signed the final document as "consultants." Thanks to their lobbying, Article 72 was incorporated in the UN charter, recording that:

The Economic and Social Council (ECOSOC) made suitable arrangements for consultation with nongovernmental organizations which are concerned with matters within its competence. Such arrangements may be made with international organizations and, where appropriate, with national organizations after consultation with a member of the United Nations concerned.

Thus, there came into being a network of NGOs (Nongovernmental Organizations) that cluster around the UN and its affiliates and undertake to influence both their policies and the public attitudes toward them. NGOs, in the UN lexicon, have a rather special meaning related to their "consultative status" with the Economic and Social Council (ECOSOC), or some other UN specialized agency. To acquire "consultative" status they are supposed to commit themselves to "undertake to support the work of the United Nations and to promote knowledge of its principles and activities." The various national UN associations, sponsors of United Nations Day (October 24) and of model United Nations General Assembly and Security Council sessions for high school students, and purveyors of assorted printed materials, are in the forefront of public information services in behalf of the UN.

The majority of the NGOs, however, are concerned more with working on particular issues and problems that affect the world community than with disseminating information in support of the UN. Indeed, the United Nations Association of the United States itself has been gradually shifting its emphasis toward awakening public interest in various global issues rather than simply giving uncritical endorsement to the UN.

Perhaps the best known and most effective of all NGOs in building a constituency for the United Nations, or a particular part of it, is the U.S. Committee for UNICEF, United Nations International Children's Emergency Fund. This private organization, working with 50,000 volunteer groups in 15,000 American communities, raises more than $20 million each year through its Halloween "Trick or Treat" solicitations door-to-door and other "special events." Millions of Americans thus become directly involved, on a voluntary basis, in providing help for destitute children and their mothers in some of the most impoverished regions of the world.

The UNICEF example is by no means unique. Private nonprofit groups with similar national committee structures have raised funds and popular backing for UNESCO's literacy campaign, the Yaws Control Program of the World Health Organization, and

FAO's Freedom from Hunger campaign, which enlisted the co-operating efforts of eighty different private national NGO commit-tees.

Beyond such direct and tangible private support for UN efforts to help peoples of the developing world, NGO representatives have been drawn into a number of conferences, "international year" ac-tivities, and study projects that relate to relief and development needs around the globe.

In 1963 about one thousand NGO representatives met to discuss global problems of food and hunger in a World Food Conference sponsored by FAO. The sharing of information and concerns at that meeting helped build awareness of hunger as a world poverty prob-lem and strengthened efforts to bring about President Carter's Hunger Commission and its call in 1980 for more sustained atten-tion to global food needs.

In 1968 several hundred NGO representatives gathered in Paris for a meeting on human rights as a follow-up to the UN's International Conference on Human Rights held in Teheran earlier that year. The Paris meeting was sponsored by two consortia of NGOs, one in "consultative status" with ECOSOC and the other related to UNESCO. Here was further proof of the potential for collaboration between private associations and official UN agencies. Subse-quently, there developed a pattern of parallel international con-ferences, one public and one private. One consisted of official government delegations operating within the framework of the UN; the other was made of private and volunteer citizen groups (NGOs) concerned about the same issue under discussion at the official con-ference. Such dual and simultaneous meetings were held in Stockholm in 1972 on the occasion of the UN Conference on the En-vironment; in Bucharest in 1974 at the time of the UN Conference on Population; in Mexico City in 1975, and in Copenhagen in 1980, when the problems of women were under consideration; in Van-couver in 1976 for "Human Habitat," the UN Conference on Human Settlements. The "private" side of the Habitat conference attracted 6,000 NGO representatives, far more than the number who par-ticipated in the formal UN sessions; it gained much media attention with its films, exhibits, lectures, and press briefings.

Immediately prior to the opening of the UN Special Session on the New International Economic Order in 1980 several hundred NGO representatives met in New York to explore the same issues the UN was about to take up dealing with the so-called North-South dialogue. Neither the official UN session nor the gathering of nongovernmental representatives came to any significant conclusions—a fitting reflection of the tensions and disagreements that exist between the developed and less developed countries.

Whether the UN and the NGOs will carry further the idea of overlapping big conferences is not clear. The chances are that there will be more such large scale gatherings to deal with a variety of international issues, most of them relating in some way to the problems of development. With the majority of the votes in the UN General Assembly now in the hands of Third World countries, and with words the principal force they hold, it is not likely that talks and meetings and reports will diminish. Yet just as it is now recognized that UN resolutions do not solve many of the more difficult problems of the world, neither do great conferences—even if they attract a broad popular participation through the NGOs.

Meanwhile, a considerable number of NGOs go quietly along doing their normal, regular work of observing and consulting, as originally anticipated in the UN charter. They have access to the official national delegations, to commissions and staffs associated with the specialized agencies, and to the international civil servants of the UN secretariat. They attend endless meetings. They lobby in the corridors, the lounges, and the offices. They conduct their own independent studies that update the UN information base. They provide a generally credible link between United Nations officialdom and grass-roots constituencies and their needs, problems, and concerns. In short, the NGOs help the UN work better than it would otherwise.

Increasingly, official commissions attached to ECOSOC, WHO, FAO or other specialized agencies draw into their deliberations representatives of the NGOs. The NGOs make presentations at hearings or other public meetings. A major part of their work, of course, is to communicate with their private constituencies and with appropriate agencies of their home governments about what they have learned from their observations of the UN.

Beyond seeking advice from the NGOs, UN agencies sometimes call upon them to help implement certain UN plans and programs. They have been very much involved in planning and carrying out such projects as the International Year of the Child, the Decade of Development, and comparable special UN events in other fields. Amnesty International, which has NGO "consultative status" with ECOSOC, was awarded the Nobel Peace Prize, in part because of its influence on the application in various countries of human rights policies affirmed earlier by the United Nations.

Although it was originally assumed that the NGOs would provide moral and financial support for UN agencies and their programs—and that has happened, conspicuously, in the case of UNICEF—the NGOs themselves are now, in special circumstances, receiving UN funds to help carry out UN programs. The United Nations Fund for Population Activities (UNFPA) allocated more than $17 million from its nearly $150 million budget in 1979 for grants to NGOs to assist family planning clinics and related educational programs in impoverished rural areas in a number of developing countries. The low profile of the private organizations made such a course preferable to direct operations by the UN, or even by the local governments. UNESCO spends about three million dollars each year in contracts with more than 500 NGOs for research and training projects. UNDP and FAO encourage local governments to use PVOs in carrying out programs funded in part by these official UN agencies.

The United Nations Commission on Refugees and the United Nations Disaster Relief Agency are two intergovernmental bodies that have turned to PVOs to take on emerging assignments to relieve acute human suffering in times of catastrophe. In time, the NGOs (or PVOs) also find themselves engaged in intensive private fundraising and negotiations with their home governments for support that goes far beyond any initial funding from UN sources. All of this is simply more evidence of how intertwined private and public initiatives are in the realm of relief and development. However, uncertainty about funding for UN activities makes any prediction about the future course of UN/NGO partnership unreliable.

Of all the approaches to development assistance born during World War II reconstruction, none of them has become as large, as truly global, and as successful as the consortium of lending institutions known as the World Bank.

In 1968, Robert McNamara left his grim job overseeing U.S. military operations in Viet Nam, as Secretary of Defense, for the more positive relationship to the Third World as President of the World Bank. In the following thirteen years it grew from $3 billion in loans to developing countries to $13 billion. It now has over $35 billion in assets, regional offices in thirty-four countries, and about 5,000 employees. At the same time, it truly has become a world institution, and it has done so without becoming shattered along the confrontational line between North and South. It now has 122 member countries, including (since 1979) China. Even such Soviet-inclined nations as Ethiopia, Viet Nam, and Afghanistan are members. Only Soviet bloc hardliners are left out. Not all the new member countries are there just to borrow. Recently, seven "midlevel" developing countries, including Mexico and Venezuela, have joined the ranks of "net lenders." Significant contributions are now flowing from the Mideast countries, which seem to have designated the bank as their favored vehicle for Arab participation in international development assistance. Some observers of the Mideast economy feel that the 1980 Arab contribution of $3 billion to the bank will eventually seem like a trickle compared to the possible gush of future Arab contributions.

The bank won its highly favorable standing as a global institution with the backing of both business and government people. It doesn't give grants, but makes loans to those member countries that usually don't have good enough credit ratings to get reasonable terms from commercial banks. All loans are given at lower than market rates, but some rates are higher than others because the bank gets most of its money from the sales of bonds. The interest charged to the borrower varies according to what the bank itself must pay to get the money.

The World Bank has a special "soft loan window," called the International Development Administration (IDA), which now lends $3.5 billion annually to the poorest of the poor countries. Countries receiving IDA loans have up to fifty years to repay, and they pay no interest. Considering current inflation rates, the saving in interest will probably be worth more than the value of the loans by the time they are repaid.

Usually the loans are made in conjunction with other sources of funds that are to be used for some development project. Most of these non–World Bank funds come from financial institutions within the borrowing country itself. Other increasingly significant sources are banks in the developed countries, including the United States, West Germany, Great Britain, and Japan. Still other funds come from bilateral aid agencies such as U.S. AID and its counterparts in the sixteen other industrialized countries, and from such multilateral international agencies as UNDP. Because the World Bank has a lot to say about how the overall development programs are designed, it is in a strong position to influence how the funds from other sources are earmarked. Because it is able to coordinate the entire financing program, the bank, in effect, leverages its own contribution. For example, the bank estimated that the $13 billion it lent in 1980 would trigger many more billions from other sources. The bank's authority as the preeminent intergovernment financial institution may well increase. The passing of the bank's presidency from McNamara to A. W. Claussen (who already had vast international experience as chairman of the world's largest private banking enterprise, BankAmerica Corporation) appeared to signal continuing strong leadership for expanding financial assistance to poor nations.

The growth and efficiency of the bank during the past few years, however, has overshadowed another trend that signifies a basic shift in its philosophy. In the bank's early years its approach to eradicating poverty was tilted toward large-scale technology. Now its central mission is to help fulfill the "basic needs" of the world's 800 million people who live in chronic poverty. The construction of dams and highways once seemed to be a major thrust of any long-term development program, but the goal of national economic self-sufficiency always seemed to elude the planners and builders. In recent years, however, the bank has come to rely less on big technological projects and to search for modest ways to improve the lives of the village poor. Following in the steps of certain U.S. bilateral programs, the bank has changed its focus to the human dimensions of development to such an extent that sections of its 1980 Annual Report sound like readings from E. F. Schumacher's *Small is Beautiful*. The report boasts of launching forty-nine new projects aimed at developing small-scale enterprises among the poorest of the poor in the hinterlands. New bank projects focus on "nonincome aspects" of development, such as education and primary health care, and emphasize "human resources development" as the key to all other forms of development. Thus, the World Bank moves close to the thinking of many PVOs that have long stressed the importance of small-scale, village-level development projects.

This coming together of the powerful bank and the struggling PVOs was highlighted in 1980 when meetings between PVO executives and bank officials took place in Washington, D.C., and Paris. Bank External Affairs Minister Munir Benjink said to the group, "In our new framework, it is logical for the bank to turn to people's organizations, like the PVOs, that have practiced development at the grass roots and evolved models suitable for replication and expansion on a large scale."

The first meeting, held in the bank's huge, new Washington offices in June 1980, discussed "issues and opportunities for cooperation in selected areas of socioeconomic development." Top executives from thirty-six of the largest national and international PVOs based in Europe, the United States, Canada, and Japan, as well as executives from several World Bank departments, took part. The bank started out by identifying over fifty cases in which it had already worked with PVOs on an *ad hoc* basis, through consulting or contracting and subcontracting arrangements.

Most of the consulting has been informal and unpaid, usually initiated by the bank asking a PVO for information on a particular region or topical problem in which the PVO has practical expertise. The PVO provides the information or hunts for it — as in the case of Technoserve, Inc., which was asked to compile data for the bank on ranch operating costs in semiarid areas of Kenya. "Through these kinds of interchanges the PVOs have already made an enormous impact on bank policies," says the bank's liaison to the PVOs, Vittorio Masoni. "An increasingly significant percentage of all our projects involve this sort of consultation."

There are several contracting arrangements between PVOs and the bank, and they occur largely at the "macro" (national) levels. For example, the bank may formally request a PVO to assist the bank in designing or evaluating a national bank project, such as World Education, Inc., has done in Thailand. There, the PVO developed a national "educational model" for remote village schools, using funds loaned to the Bangkok government by the bank.

By far the most prevalent model of bank-PVO interaction is by a subcontracting arrangement in which a PVO carries out some portion of a given project, at some time in the life of the project. Following the establishment of a country's need for a loan, teams of World Bank economists and researchers explore many aspects of the country's needs and resources to identify where loans would be helpful and appropriate. Individual PVOs working locally may then be approached, particularly if they are the best qualified agency already working in that field. Eventually the PVO may be written into the loan application as a subcontractor, or the PVO may be asked to submit a bid to carry out the project.

For PVOs to find a place in this system of loan making, key bank staff members and key host government officials need to be acquainted with the PVOs, and there must be compatibility of interest and purpose. Whether the bank/government/PVO connection comes about also depends on timing. "We just happened to be at the right place at the right time," says Ed Bullard, President of Technoserve, Inc., explaining how his organization was written in as a contractor fulfilling the design of projects in Central America. Such was also the situation in Central Africa when the government's Department of Transportation submitted a plan for a new highway system. The plan included dozens of low standard "feeder" roads that connect remote villages to highways. CARE has been constructing such highways in that country for many years as a precondition for setting up its programs in the hinterlands, so it was written in as a contractor. Such bank/PVO partnerships tend to be concentrated in areas where the PVOs have a lead on the bank: informal education and training, nutrition and primary health care, rural water supply and energy, rural cooperatives, transfer of appropriate technology, and handicrafts.

A factor limiting PVO connection to the bank is the lack of effective linkage of small-scale projects to the larger overall plans for national development. Although the bank insists that projects at the village level are the heart of its program, it recognizes that too many diverse village programs may be counterproductive. Sooner or later, a host government must "combine village expansion programs into a national plan, avoiding duplication and sharing resources whenever possible." In this way "micro" projects become "macro" projects. But in the process the PVO may be left out.

At that crucial PVO/bank meeting in 1980 it was agreed that unless a PVO and a host government are willing to work with each other, PVOs can hardly play a role in bank operations, for the bank can only lend to governments for projects that carry governmental guarantees. Some governments are understandably reluctant to work with PVOs if they are perceived to be competing with their own civil servants and national contractors. Furthermore, many emerging nations are seeking to unify their countries after centuries of tribal conflicts and feel a need to centralize administration and keep tight control over funds. Some governments, moreover, may suspect PVOs that have religious or quasireligious connections.

PVOs have generally preferred to work with local government officials rather than with the vast bureaucracies of a central government, for they tend to fear they would lose the trust already won among villagers, who are often suspicious that their own national governments siphon off assistance funds for illegal purposes. One PVO executive depicted the national civil servants as "harried bureaucrats, traveling occasionally from the capital city to the villages, not likely to know how the proceeds of the loans could reach the grass roots, nor too much interested in ensuring that the benefits accrue to the poor."

Reflecting this sentiment, some representatives suggested that the World Bank set up an alternative to the triangular bank/PVO/government relationship and establish a "small loan window" (perhaps within the International Finance Corporation), as had already been done by the Inter-American Development Bank, or set up a loan guarantee program for the benefit of the PVOs.

The bank flatly rejected the suggestion, insisting that there is no way around the relationship with their governmental "clients" except when PVOs are called in at top level as consultants or contract agents. But the bank did agree to take a modest, if bureaucratic, step toward further ties. It agreed to set up a working group of representatives of fifteen organizations, selected with the assistance of PVO consortia, that would find ways to increase the information flow between the bank and PVOs. Further PVO–World Bank meetings were planned. Whether new opportunities will emerge for the PVOs remains to be seen. Perhaps the policies set by A. W. Claussen, a known PVO advocate, will make the critical difference.

9

The Special Case of PVOs and Refugees

Refugees do not have a home but they belong to everyone.
— Said Muhemmed, UN High Commissioner on Refugees

By the late 1970s it had become fashionable in some PVO circles to speak of overseas relief—the distribution of direct assistance—as a thing of the past. The Third World wanted trade, not aid. The relief agencies were told that their compassionate endeavors actually resulted in a demeaning dependency of the recipients on their benefactors. Many PVOs came to feel that perhaps their historic mission, indeed, was over, that it was time to move away from relief activities and to concentrate on technical services for long-term economic development. A few concluded that they should focus on changing American attitudes toward the Third World and thus build greater support for funding development programs.

"The 'giver/receiver' relationship of the aid-giving era is fading," said Irene Pinkau in one of her reports on voluntarism. "We have come to realize that the gaps between rich and poor nations . . . cannot be eliminated and friends cannot be won by giving charity from 'us' to 'them.' " Meanwhile, all kinds of attempts have been made to shift voluntary North-to-South contributions for relief to such new or enlarged development strategies as:

1. encouraging *locally* run development programs in the Third World;
2. instituting a transnational "development tax" to be paid by citizens of the technically advanced countries for support of UN-administered aid;
3. creating centralized grain reserves on which the whole world could draw as needs arise; and

4. setting up technology transfer schemes under which advanced skills acquired anywhere could be disseminated everywhere.

Any and all of these actions, it was hoped, could reduce the sense of dependence of the poor nations on the rich, minimize the sense of prideful benevolence of the rich toward the poor—and, of course, curtail the influence of the powerful nations over the weak.

The recommended alternatives to relief, however, failed to materialize. The developed countries didn't buy them. Meanwhile, the need for relief increased on a staggering scale. Despite all the talk about interdependence between the rich and the poor, and the economic self-interest justifications for foreign aid, it can be argued that ultimately the real motive that evokes the giving of relief is compassion. If this is true, then compassion is what is needed now, in greater measure than ever before. The "relief" problem is not solved and no end to the need for "relief" is in sight.

The underlying reason is that poverty is affecting more people than ever before, and national disasters and war and revolution continue to create homeless and hungry refugees. Of today's 4.2 billion people, over one billion suffer from hunger and twice that many are undernourished, according to a 1979 World Bank survey. But relief efforts are rarely mobilized unless poverty is compounded by either natural or man-made disasters. The impoverished surviving victims of those disasters make up the vast numbers of refugees, and they have been the main beneficiaries of relief programs in recent years.

Some studies suggest that the number of disasters will rise significantly in the years ahead. The UN Convention on the Status of Refugees, which tries to keep track of dislocated persons, counted 9.5 million of them in May 1980. By September 1980, the total had jumped to 12 million and later estimates suggested that the true number was closer to 17 million and rising by tens of thousands each day. No end to the expansion of this human tragedy was in sight.

Natural Disasters Are More Disastrous

The number of natural catastrophes has remained fairly stable in the last two decades. Each year the world suffers about the same assortment of volcanic eruptions, earthquakes, forest fires, storms, floods, tidal waves, and avalanches. To be sure, some world disasters have diminished—fewer plagues, for example. But that reduction is balanced by the inevitable and ominous appearance of "technological disasters" and the unending experiences of ethnic, ideological, and intergovernmental violence.

The problem is not increased incidents, but the intensifying effects of disasters on those least prepared for them. The forty-four poorest countries of the world can afford disasters less than ever before. Natural disasters affect the poor in unplanned, huge Third World cities more than any other group, and urbanization on a vast scale is taking place everywhere.

Furthermore, many of those poor areas are showing acute signs of what Stephen Green calls "ecological overstress" – a combination of overpopulation, overgrazing, deforestation, and soil and water depletion, all factors that exacerbate the effects of any serious change in weather, water, or social upheaval. Poor countries are, each year, more disaster prone. Between 1972 and 1976, 64 percent of the poorest countries of the world suffered major disasters requiring international assistance.

Climatologists predict weather changes in the coming decade that will actually shorten the growing season over most of the earth and cause droughts and floods in areas that had rarely known them before. A devastating experience with catastrophic "desertification" occurred in the Sahel in the early 1970s. During that period a relatively minor change in the rainfall level over three growing seasons resulted in 250,000 deaths in Ethiopia and many thousands of deaths in other countries across the continent. That drought has abated, but many scientists predict a new drought in the Horn of Africa and maintain that catastrophic climatic problems for much of Africa and Asia will occur by the end of the 1980s.

An Epidemic of Political Disasters

Just as the combination of poverty and earthquake compounds the effects of a drought, so does the combination of poverty and warfare. According to one State Department calculation, 90 percent of all wars in the past ten years have primarily involved Third World peoples. Unlike dislocated victims of Third World clashes in previous eras, such as in the conflicts between Muslims and Hindus after the partition of India in 1947, most of today's refugees probably will never be able to return to their homes and are unlikely to be permanently resettled for years, if ever. All indications suggest that their numbers will rise steadily throughout the rest of this century.

Moreover, there is every likelihood that the countries that voluntarily or involuntarily receive such refugees will consider them less and less welcome. Already there are signs that political refugees are creating huge economic and social problems for their hosts, both in industrialized countries and in the Third World. In some areas refugees have already become scapegoats in a new rise of nationalistic sentiment in the countries to which they have fled.

The issue of refugee immigration is so politically explosive that some governments in position to respond to the problem are now paralyzed. The U.S. liberal policy on the acceptance of political refugees led to an enormous influx of Cubans in 1980 and created an antirefugee backlash in Florida and elsewhere. Indochinese resettlement in the United States cost U.S. taxpayers $4 billion in 1980 alone. West Germany, which once held open arms to homeless Vietnamese, now wants no more of them. New restrictions on immigration have been established by Great Britain and other European countries, and the Reagan Administration has pledged to "do something" to stem the tide of immigrants.

The problem, of course, is far more complex and far more troublesome than antirefugee sentiment at home. A profoundly disturbing fact is that the recent waves of refugees are often the results of regional conflicts that are intensified by the ideological struggles between the superpowers that are being played out, shiftingly, through Third World countries. Involvement of the United States with the estimated 1.7 million Palestinian refugees in the Mideast, or the 1.5 million Afghani refugees in Pakistan, or the 200,000 Cambodian refugees in Thailand, or the more than one million Ogaden refugees from Ethiopia in Somalia may involve us also in the violent conflicts that produced the refugees, with risks of provoking retaliation in various forms. Refugee camps for these unfortunate people often double as safe staging areas for guerrillas trying to launch revolutionary or counterrevolutionary movements aimed at liberating their homelands. Frequently, to help refugees is to help "freedom fighters," or "terrorists," whichever you choose to call them.

Overt official government relief efforts can infuriate governments that rule the lands from which the refugees fled. The Phnom Penh government, backed by Vietnam, considers the Thai border refugee camps to be enemy territory, just as the Soviet-backed Afghani government resents the Pakistani camps, and the Ethiopian government opposes international aid to Somalian refugees who include soldiers at war with Ethiopia. The Castro government, similarly, has always charged that aid to Cuban refugees in America is really aimed at encouraging the U.S.-based Cubans to conspire to over-throw Castro.

The Response to Disaster

Before anyone ever talked about "international crisis management" or "disaster preparedness systems," the Red Cross was well-established as the first PVO to develop a compassionate, global approach to disaster assistance. For a long time it was the primary agency for dealing with prisoners of war and refugees. That monopoly no longer exists.

Scores of intergovernmental agencies, dozens of PVOs, more than one hundred national governments, and even media organizations now form an interconnected relief system for refugees, of which the Red Cross is only one part.

In the UN there are twelve separate agencies, most of which have separate bureaus for relief problems. They include UNICEF, which coordinates the fundraising activities of its many national chapters; the FAO, which offers advice on food and nutrition aspects of disasters; WHO, which gives counsel on the public health implications of disasters; and UNDP, which draws heavily on its local technical staffs to handle the transition from relief into the development phases of a project in which income-producing programs are launched. Recently several other technical UN agencies have joined in this work, including the International Telecommunications Union and the United Nations Center for Housing, Building and Planning. The involvement of these agencies in crisis activities is coordinated by two separate agencies—which may someday themselves require an overriding supercoordinating body. One of these coordinators is the United Nations Disaster Relief Organization (UNDRO), the other is the United Nations High Commission on Refugees (UNHCR). In recent years the budgets of both agencies have skyrocketed, especially that of the High Commission, which has jumped tenfold in five years to nearly $500 million—and that is only a small part of the costs of actual relief operations, and an even smaller part of what is needed.

Where does the assistance come from? As contributions to the UN by industrial countries have slowed, and as the costs of UN operations and the political roadblocks among UN members have increased, both UNDRO and UNHCR have relied less on their coalition of UN agencies and more on bilateral government grant assistance and on private donations, most of which have been funneled through the PVOs. Today, just as in the earlier days of Red Cross preeminence, the UN agencies regard PVOs as a key element in responding to victims of disasters, and there are more demands for their services than ever before. Can the PVOs handle this responsibility? Can they depend on an ever-flowing stream of compassion from their constituencies back home? Are they so preoccupied with their existing overseas projects that they don't have the flexibility and manpower to improvise to meet a new crisis? After all, they are not volunteer firemen, primed to respond whenever a sudden alarm is sounded. Since they must raise funds from separate constituencies, their operations are fragmented. Can they join forces effectively when the need arises?

The PVOs' recent involvement in two world crises, one in Southeast Asia and the other in Somalia in East Africa, suggest different answers to those questions.

The Cambodia Crisis Committee: A PVO Instant Coalition

Few Westerners knew what was going on in Cambodia (now Kampuchea) during the ominous four years 1975–1979. In 1975, Lon Nol, the leader of a weak pro-American government installed after the end of the Vietnam war, was overthrown by forces commanded by the Communist Pol Pot. Yet not until early in 1979, when Vietnam forces expelled Pol Pot from Phnom Penh, was the truth revealed: the greatest mass atrocity since the Nazi Holocaust. A combination of deliberate mass extermination, prolonged civil warfare, and starvation had reduced a population of nearly eight million to a mere five million, disproportionately female. Hundreds of thousands more were still dying as bloodshed continued in the hinterlands, with fighting between Soviet-backed Vietnamese forces and the remnants of Pol Pot's forces backed by the Chinese. Cambodian peasants, once exporters of rice, could produce only 20 percent of the food needed for their own survival. Cambodia itself was closed to outsiders, but a steady stream of refugees flowed into camps in Thailand, many of them having been raped and robbed by pirates by the time they reached the refugee camps.

Foreign affairs departments of Western governments and UN agencies deliberated at great length. But the only group that instantly responded was a team of international private voluntary organizations: OXFAM (the international organization based in England with a U.S. affiliate called Oxfam-America), the International Rescue Committee, the American Friends Service Committee, and a few others. These trailblazers negotiated their way directly into Cambodia in the summer of 1979 to deliver the first relief shipments.

Following these initial missions of mercy there began a broad-scale, unprecedented national relief effort. It succeeded on a scale hardly believable, and showed:

- that almost instantly a coalition of private U.S. relief services could be activated for effective action;
- that despite stagflation, fears of long-term leveling or decline in the U.S. standard of living, and widespread irritation with Third World demands, massive funds could still be raised for Third World causes;
- that PVOs could learn how to complement U.S. government and UN funding and services, rather than duplicate and compete;
- that PVOs could respond to crises by using their independent status and diverse approaches to overcome political obstacles that constrict official U.S. and UN efforts;
- that the PVO consortium's new efforts to involve recipients in income-producing ventures in even the earliest stages of a relief effort could help reduce the dependency syndrome among relief recipients;
- that the PVOs' strength does not lie only in ties to their traditional constituencies but also comes from their abilities to tap other resources from the whole broad private sector, including the media, large corporations, organized labor, the domestically oriented nonprofit organizations — and even from governments. The PVOs also secured large in-kind contributions that greatly expanded the PVOs' capabilities for accomplishing their mission.

In October 1979, a coalition of State Department officials formed a Kampuchea Working Group. Father Theodore Hesburgh (Father Ted), President of Notre Dame and Chairman of the Overseas Development Council, realizing that immediate action was needed, urged First Lady Rosalynn Carter to travel to Thailand to view the refugee camps. On five days' notice she went, with the president's backing. After her return, Mrs. Carter invited all relevant federal agencies and PVO leaders to the White House, and a relief agreement was reached quickly. The federal coalition pledged $69 million, drawn from the budgets of various federal agencies. International organizations, including UNICEF, were challenged to contribute $300 million. The U.S. private sector was asked to raise $100 million within nine months. (The only comparable effort was in support of relief efforts in Bangladesh during the early 1970's, when $30 million was finally raised with much effort.)

In January 1980 the National Cambodia Crisis Committee was established under the sponsorship of the Indo-Chinese Refugee Action Center, created a year earlier by a consortium of private foundations. The first task was to select co-chairmen: (1) Jean Young, already experienced in coalition building as the Chairman of the Commission for the 1979 International Year of the Child; (2) Lane Kirkland, who had just been installed as the head of the AFL-CIO; (3) Walter A. Haas, Jr., chief executive of Levi-Strauss, a large and socially progressive San Francisco-based corporation; and (4) Father Ted Hesburgh. With the help of representatives of about 130 broad private constituencies, they went to work to launch a major, sustained nationwide information program, and to carry through an intensive, massive fundraising campaign. Out of their imagination and energy came:

- A steady stream of press releases, Op-Ed commentaries, and news reports;
- A "hot line" service ensuring that the news media were informed of day-by-day developments in the Cambodian crisis, often even before those events became known through regular press services or government channels;
- A public service announcement featuring Rosalynn Carter was offered to all television stations and provided the Crisis Committee with a highly visible means of promoting the fundraising effort. The "spot" urged contributors to send money earmarked to any of nineteen churches or synagogues and relief agencies;
- The Advertising Council, a corporate-supported public service, distributed bulletins, advertising copy, and other promotional materials to more than 13,000 media outlets—radio, TV, newspapers, magazines—throughout the country. Ads appeared on hundreds of radio and TV stations and in magazines, trade publications, and newspapers throughout America.

The institutional fundraising was highly organized and sophisticated. The committee conducted specialized campaigns drawing in four categories of leaders and workers: civic groups, state governors, labor unions, and corporations. Leaders who agreed to participate were asked to inform their membership, employees, or constituents about Cambodia and the relief effort and to urge them to contribute promptly to the agency of their choice.

Some of the results: approximately twenty-four national *civic organizations* agreed to participate in efforts to inform their membership. The Lions Club International gave $120,000 to be funneled to Cambodia through Save the Children. B'nai B'rith Women sponsored numerous local fundraising events. The American Legion convinced its members that their aid to the Indochinese was an expression of patriotism. The Girl Scouts underscored the fact that a disproportionate number of refugees were, in fact, girls. Through speeches at many weekly luncheons, the Rotarians exhorted local businessmen to contribute. Through articles in magazines and journals, speeches at conventions and before executive councils, special mailings, brochures, etc., hundreds of thousands of members of many, many organizations began to feel that their agencies had a special relationship to starving Cambodians.

The leadership role of state *governors* was appealed to by Ambassador Victor Palmieri, official Coordinator for U.S. Refugee Policy, and by Mrs. Carter during the annual national Governor's Conference in Washington. Several governors and/or their spouses initiated full-scale statewide media and fundraising campaigns handled through the governors' offices. Other governors did not directly attempt to launch campaigns but they did issue proclamations calling on the citizenry to support the Cambodian people and urging them to "Give to the church, synagogue or relief agency of your choice." Still other governors assisted by hosting meetings of key business or labor leaders to coordinate state campaigns.

An extensive and unprecedented *labor* campaign was directed by Lane Kirkland. With the active support of key staff members within the AFL-CIO, and several presidents of large international unions, the campaign involved many of the affiliated unions in both public information and fundraising. It was the first time the unions gave to a nonunion cause on such a scale.

Forty-five international affiliates and thirty-three central councils and state organizations conducted their own special fundraising drives—including the International Ladies Garment Workers, the United Steelworkers, the Communications Workers, and the Plumbers and Pipefitters. In addition, the AFL-CIO produced a film in support of the campaign and distributed it widely for use in affiliated union campaigns, conventions, and meetings.

A Corporate Steering Group, composed of twenty leaders of the largest American corporations, was formed under the Cochairmanship of several chief executive officers: John D. deButts, AT&T (Ret.); Walter A. Haas, Jr., Levi Strauss & Co.; William May, American Can; and J. Irwin Miller, Cummins Engine. During the summer, CEOs within the Corporate Steering Group—from such corporations as Standard Oil of California, Xerox, General Foods, BankAmerica, Pillsbury and National Steel—wrote personal letters to each of the top 500 CEOs in their industries and followed up the letterwriting with telephone calls. The result was a CEO-instigated campaign that was eventually extended to hundreds of thousands of employees who were asked to match contributions that were made by companies.

Within six months after the campaign began, $64 million had been raised and funds continued to pour in. Fundraising costs were less than two million dollars. The $100 million goal was eventually reached.

Meanwhile, the Cambodia Crisis Committee developed a mechanism for collaborating with its counterpart PVO associations in other countries, with Indochinese resettlement organizations and with relevant UN agencies.

But not everything went smoothly. The most politically sensitive aspect of this effort was entering Kampuchea itself. Vietnam's attitude toward the relief efforts varied between ambivalence and hostility. It was not anxious to let the world know the extent of the continued starvation and displacement within Cambodia. But the greatest reason for Vietnam's antagonism was concern that the relief camps along the border in Thailand were aiding the Pol Pot forces who were continuing to fight against the Vietnamese and their anti–Pol Pot allies.

OXFAM was successful in maintaining a base for relief efforts inside Cambodia only after it agreed to cease its relief operations in Thailand. Other PVOs expressed shock at this "sellout" to Vietnam. OXFAM justified its actions on the practical grounds that few other groups were responding—or could respond—to the starvation within Cambodia. Other PVOs stepped in to replace OXFAM's phased-out efforts in Thailand. Eventually two coalitions of agencies, those in and those out of Cambodia, emerged to confront each other over a range of specific operational details that carried heavy political overtones.

There was no way the agencies could avoid being enmeshed in increasingly complicated disputes between bitter enemies. Relief agencies operating inside Cambodia complained that those working from Thai bases with refugees along the border were indirectly supporting the Pol Pot forces by feeding Khmer Rouge fighters among the refugees. The Thai-based agencies made counter charges: that those agencies working inside Cambodia had been duped by the Phnom Penh regime, that their movements inside Cambodia were so restricted by the government that independent monitoring of the distribution and use of the relief supplies was impossible, and that much of them were being siphoned off by government workers.

Despite the complications imposed by the political crosscurrents in Southeast Asia, the relief agencies themselves felt they had been able to do their job remarkably well. By December 1980, a satisfactory rainy season had finally brought in a good local rice crop. The need for imported basic staples quickly declined, making large food deliveries from the outside no longer so necessary.

From Cambodia to Somalia and Beyond

As the nineteen participating PVOs concluded their collaboration in Cambodia, the obvious question was asked: Had the committee developed a model for a concerted PVO approach to crisis intervention that might well be applied to future emergency refugee situations? To be sure, they had overcome their own political naivete, learned to negotiate with governments, discovered how to interrelate with other PVO consortia in Europe, and learned how to take advantage of their consultative status with the UN High Commission. And they understood how to make the transition between relief and self-help efforts. They had also survived deep divisions within their own ranks, which grew as the complications of assistance grew.

Would the PVOs that worked in Cambodia do it again? If so, would they do it differently? The agencies were soon being asked these questions with considerable urgency, for an escalating human catastrophe was already begging for their attention: the refugees in Somalia. Representatives from four organizations—CARE, OXFAM-America, American Friends Service Committee, and the U.S. Committee for UNICEF—were appointed to evaluate the experiences of the Cambodian Crisis Committee to determine whether it provided any useful model for the handling of other refugee situations, and what alterations should be made for the crisis of refugees in the Horn of Africa. Their response seemed surprising in light of the urgent needs in Africa.

Perhaps the answer lay less in the inconclusive evaluation of the Cambodia effort than it did in the enormity of the African task. The Somalian crisis made the Cambodian dilemma look like an easy one to solve. The victims of a border war between Soviet-backed Ethiopia and U.S.-backed Somalia over the disputed province of Ogaden, nearly one million Somalis were crowded into camps with about 60,000 persons in each—compared to a total of 300,000 in Thailand—and these camps were scattered over a distance of 1,600 miles. It was estimated that another 600,000 ethnic Somalis from across the Ethiopian border had been more or less integrated into Somalia's 3.5 million native population. In short, one in three persons in Somalia was calculated to be a refugee, surviving on an average of ten ounces of food per day, or less than 1,000 calories.

Somalia itself was and is a destitute country, with an average per capita income of $110. (In Cambodia, per capita income is calculated to be three times as high.) A naturally arid country, it had suffered a two-year drought. The refugee camps were accessible only by dirt roads. Provisions of relief required heavy-duty trucks and plenty of gasoline. Gasoline? Compounding all the other problems, Somalia lost its entire source of petroleum supplies when Iraq became embroiled in its own border war with Iran. The UN High Commission managed to secure enough gasoline to continue operations for a short period, but the long-term prospects were bleak.

Unlike the Cambodian situation, for which American guilt still lingered because of the 1971 bombing of that country, the United States had no real historical legacy in Somalia, which might explain why U.S. private agencies responded much more slowly. The Somali government itself sounded the first alarm; it declared a state of emergency in September 1979 and made a desperate appeal for assistance. UN Secretary General Kurt Waldheim was among the first to respond by putting together a task force of ten intergovernmental agencies (the UN Economical and Security Council, UNICEF, UNDP, World Food Programme, UNHCR, the ILO, the FAO, UNESCO, WHO, and the World Bank). The group formulated a program and appealed to governments to fund it, and asked for help from the PVOs related to the governmental and intergovernmental agencies.

The problems were seen immediately to be overwhelming. There was not enough grain for the supplementary food program. Three airlifts of housing and household materials, tents, and plastic sheets simply created widespread demand for more of them. The task force soon determined that a comprehensive new water supply system was needed, requiring water purification facilities, wells, reservoirs, and tank trucks for potable water. UNHCR collected a scant $5 million for all of this, and recruited PVO experts to oversee it. Medical supplies were needed at once for health clinics and TB centers. Hundreds of health posts were set up, and thousands of sick refugees were assigned to each health professional. As soon as the health system was in place, the transportation program had to be expanded. Hundreds of ten-ton trucks were needed to transport supplies, and repair stations were needed to keep them rolling. But before the trucks could reach the camps, more and better access roads had to be built. At the same time, primary schools had to be set up for refugee children, requiring hundreds of new classrooms and teachers who had to be recruited and trained. Income-producing agricultural schemes had to begin so that the refugees would not become dependent on outside support.

The news of the vastness of all these problems must have made even the most venturesome and the most concerned PVO staffers and volunteers hesitate. In this case there would be no tidy one-year cycle of assistance, as had been their experience in Indochina, before the refugee population would produce a good crop and income on their own and the PVO representatives could go home.

In Africa the problems are long-term and multi-faceted, and they are being duplicated in more and more regions. Conditions in the neighboring countries—Sudan, Ethiopia and Djibouti—are not much better than in Somalia. In Zimbabwe, where thousands of former refugees have returned home following the election of Mugabe, there are 660,000 destitute and misplaced persons who are of "immediate concern" to the UN High Commission. Huge numbers of repatriated refugees and displaced persons huddle in camps in isolated places in Uganda and Zaire. Cameroon has 100,000 refugees from Chad. Any number of political conflicts in future years could force hundreds of thousands, even millions of other hungry, impoverished people to spill over into neighboring countries.

Despite the U.S. government's belief that it has vital security interests in Somalia (it has been negotiating for a military base there to help guard the sea lanes to the Mideast oil fields), only $12 million in economic assistance came from the United States in 1980, little of it involving the PVOs. In 1981, shipments of $24 million worth of grain were scheduled to boost U.S. involvement significantly, but far more was needed. Those U.S. PVOs already in

Somalia are there independently of the U.S. government and are delivering assistance largely provided by their own contributors. (These include the Seventh Day Adventists, Church World Service, Catholic Relief Services, the Mennonite Central Committee, American National Red Cross, Catholic Medical Mission Board, United Methodist Committee on Relief and MAP International, and Save the Children Fund.) So far, their efforts have not been coordinated or boosted by an effective collaborative effort in this country. However, the Hunger Project, the voluntary agency that grew out of Werner Erhard's *est* program, seems to have made an important first step. It has placed ads in the ten highest-circulating and most prestigious newspapers in the United States to inform the public about the plight of refugees in Africa and particularly Somalia. It has urged readers to donate to the PVO of their choice and listed the PVOs' names and addresses.

Where will it all end? Another five million refugees are scattered over various parts of Africa. The Afghani refugees who fled into Pakistan at the end of 1980 were estimated at close to 1.5 million (10 percent of their country's population), with no indication of when they could return home, if ever.

The massive refugee problems of the world make it clear that the statements, so often proclaimed, that the era of relief has ended — that our only real problem now is development — were, to say the least, premature.

10

Future Issues: Indigenous PVOs in the Third World and Global Education at Home

Since the days of the early missionaries the work of the PVOs has been divided into two distinct operations: one within this country, the other overseas. The two parts have been linked in an endless cycle: first gathering money and volunteered labor in the United States, then carrying out the program abroad.

In the past ten years important aspects of this cycle have changed. On the domestic side, the PVOs have moved away from emergency relief ("starving children") appeals in their fundraising to educational programs, for their supporters, about overseas problems. A broadened understanding among their U.S. contributors has been thought essential to enable the PVOs to change the nature of their role in foreign countries — to shift from direct delivery of relief assistance toward helping to build local self-help institutions.

In the 1980s these two trends will undoubtedly continue and accelerate. But the striking prediction is that overseas many PVOs will go beyond building local "citizen participation," and actually turn over the files, the desks, and the funding agreements to Third World staff members of independent *indigenous* PVOs. As some U.S. PVOs phase themselves out overseas, it is believed, many more will enlarge their educational activity at home. Not limiting themselves to building awareness among their own traditional constituency contributors, the PVOs will launch new educational efforts that they hope will produce more informed long-range thinking about international affairs. As the key U.S. agents of "global education," these PVOs may help usher in a new U.S. role in world affairs that, despite America's pull toward greater nationalism, could be both more realistically informed and more compassionate. There is a widespread feeling among PVO staff members that they are at an historic turning point. For their long future they face two key issues: the rise of "indigenous PVOs" (IPVOs) in the Third World and the emergence of "global education" at home.

Indigenous PVOs

The very same reasons given for preferring development programs run by U.S. PVOs over those administered directly by the U.S. government—that the PVOs respond faster, are more successful, more cost-effective, more acceptable to the local people, and are more capable of producing benefits that last beyond the life of the project—are said to apply even more to PVOs that are native to the Third World. According to one AID-funded study, the IPVOs in the Third World countries:

1. can respond to emerging needs faster (because they are already there);
2. are more likely to win, or already have won, the support of the intended beneficiaries (because they themselves may be among the targeted beneficiaries);
3. are more likely to win the cooperation of a local government (for they are one of its constituencies and often express their government's zeal for national self-sufficiency);
4. are in a better position to fit into the planning of national and intergovernmental agencies (because they are expected to remain for the long term);
5. can operate less expensively (because they usually have fewer middlemen); and
6. are more likely to follow through on completed projects (because they must live with the results of their own efforts).

The chief drawback of the IPVOs is that few of them have the technical and administrative capacity, or sometimes even the inclination, to take over completely what American PVOs have started or to be partners with government-sponsored development efforts. The question is: How can outsiders "gear up" the IPVOs as full-fledged manager-agents of development programs without being guilty of too much outside interference?

The United States and other international PVOs from the developed world have justified their interventions overseas on the grounds that no appropriate local group could do the job. They also have known, however, that once operating overseas their work was likely, even if inadvertently, to result in psychological and economic dependence of the recipients upon the givers. Most American and international PVOs have tried to build antidotes to this "dependency phenomenon" into their programs by deliberately stimulating local community involvement. Rather than compete with local groups that they have helped to establish, most foreign PVOs try, with varying degrees of success, to complement and reinforce the local ones. Increasingly, the U.S. PVOs pull out altogether when the local organizations have acquired sufficient administrative and technical skills and can negotiate with government agencies and private organizations their own partnership arrangements. In time, these native PVOs can expect ongoing working relationships with their own national government's development agencies, with official bilateral assistance agencies (such as U.S. AID and its counterparts in twelve other developed countries), and with multilateral agencies such as UNDP.

How U.S. PVOs Encourage IPVOs

U.S. PVOs stimulate local independent initiatives among citizens of the Third World in a variety of ways. Basically, they use four approaches.

One way is to establish a local office in the Third World, hire local staff, form a local board of directors and then, over a number of years, divert decisionmaking and financial responsibilities away from the U.S. PVO, leaving the local counterparts with funding sources and linkages to international organizations. This has been the approach of many Christian missionary groups that have increasingly devolved responsibility for mission projects upon the local church organization.

Another approach is for a U.S. PVO to bolster an existing IPVO, which usually has local support but may have little experience in operating development programs, by offering assistance in developing managerial skills. As soon as the IPVO staff has achieved the desired experience and skill, the Americans phase out of the picture.

A third approach is for the U.S. PVO to enter into a partnership with a well-developed existing Third World PVO for the operation of a particular project. As rapidly as possible, the U.S. PVO passes along its advanced technical know-how and broader relationships with outside funding sources to the local PVO, which then continues existing programs or starts new ones on its own.

A fourth approach is for a group of PVOs based in the developed world to organize an international conference or committee in which Third World PVOs are invited to participate. Typically, the IPVO representatives return home with a new developmental perspective and the incentive to launch new projects, perhaps in association with counterparts in the industrialized world. This has happened in relation to such issues as aging, women, the environment, and children.

How Funding Sources Fund IPVOs

The PVOs are not alone in promoting the transfer of responsibility to local voluntary groups in the Third World. Most national governments in the Third World prefer to work with their own indigenous organizations, and virtually all government-sponsored development agencies in the Third World try to elicit voluntary participation of local citizens in their programs. According to Dr. Irene Pinkau, after surveying the rise of the IPVOs in Third World development, "the request for foreign personnel, including volunteers with technical skills, will decline in the years ahead." She emphasizes that it is the policy of dozens of Third World countries in the "mid-level" stages of development to elicit, as rapidly as possible, participation and responsibility by their own people through their own organizations.

According to one spokesman of UNDP, many Third World governments have been most anxious to incorporate U.S. PVOs into their short-range and mid-range development plans, but insist on relying on their own indigenous PVOs for the long term. The UNDP, the FAO, and other intergovernmental agencies also prefer IPVOs, when they can be found, over PVOs from the United States or from other advanced countries. Even private funding sources in the United States that once supported American PVOs exclusively are now on the IPVO bandwagon. The Rockefeller Brothers Fund and a few other U.S. foundations conduct investigations to make sure that no local group is capable of providing a given service before funding a proposal from a U.S. PVO; increasingly they choose the IPVO. The Asia Foundation pursues a policy of funding only Asian organizations in self-help projects. Transnational corporations with operations in the Third World generally support local community groups, even those that do not have a truly "developmental orientation," in preference to foreign PVOs. By funding IPVOs the U.S. transnational corporations can neutralize the charge that they represent alien values and that they are undercutting indigenous institutions. After U.S. corporations provide grants to such local groups, they sometimes supply them with consulting services and in-kind contributions through their local employees.

The virtues of the IPVOs have not been ignored by the U.S. government. Despite its close ties to U.S. PVOs, the U.S. International Development Cooperation Agency has been flirting with many such local organizations in the Third World. One semipublic U.S. agency, the Inter-American Foundation (IAF), is widely hailed as a model mechanism for funding indigenous groups; IAF makes no grants to U.S. PVOs. Instead, the organization searches for a local or regional nonprofit organization in Latin America capable of winning local community support and able to deliver technical assistance. After it has worked out successful relationships with a number of such local organizations in a given country, IAF then uses those agencies as intermediaries, passing funds to them so that they in turn can provide funds or technical assistance to other organizations directly. This approach, widely applied in Central America and the Caribbean, has in turn stimulated the building of networks of new local volunteer agencies. Of all U.S. initiatives in support of development, IAF wins the most praise in Latin America and is often mentioned as evidence that U.S. funding sources can bypass completely U.S. PVOs if there is sufficient local initiative.

This model, developed by the Inter-American Foundation for the Western Hemisphere, was to be adapted in Africa through the African Development Foundation (ADF), as of early 1981, with an initial budget of about $5 million. Because some members of the Reagan administration have expressed strong early opposition to any expansion of foreign aid, its future is uncertain.

For a long time, AID dealt with IPVOs in only a random and *ad hoc* fashion. Most of the funding arrangements grew out of decentralized relationships between AID's individual country missions and the IPVOs. In 1979, "several millions" were made available, mostly in Latin America, by the AID missions through operational program grants to the IPVOs. AID has also used the consortia of PACT and CODEL in this way. PACT actually includes within its membership a mix of American PVOs, IPVOs, and associations of IPVOs. For example, one of PACT's members, SOLIDARIOS, is itself a consortium of "national development foundations" that operate as separate national PVOs in Mexico, Costa Rica, Dominican Republic, Nicaragua, and other countries in Central America and the Caribbean. AID money goes to PACT. PACT funds SOLIDARIOS, which, in turn, funds the individual national development foundations. They then distribute the money to small local organizations in Latin America. PACT has already worked out similar arrangements with associations of IPVOs in Africa, and may eventually do so in Asia.

In 1980, AID showed its commitment to the IPVOs by funding an American PVO, Planning Assistance, Inc., to provide management counseling strictly for IPVOs in Latin America. That arrangement parallels AID's grant to the New TransCentury Corporation, which provides management assistance to U.S. PVOs. Planning Assistance, Inc., has opened offices in Costa Rica, Honduras, and Guatemala, and seems to have created more demand for such services than it can meet by itself.

A New AID Policy Toward IPVOs

There is a feeling among AID staffers that its efforts in relation to IPVOs are piecemeal and minuscule compared with what is needed. One factor limiting AID's involvement is the lack of common agreement on exactly what the term *IPVO* refers to. Should it apply to religious organizations, trade unions, and neighborhood support groups? Without a consensus on what the IPVOs are, it is hard to know which ones are eligible for assistance. There is as yet no comprehensive inventory of IPVOs. Some nations have published directories of private nonprofit organizations working in their countries, but these seem weighted in favor of the local affiliates of such international organizations as the Red Cross. There is no comprehensive listing of the entire national networks of church and neighborhood-level associations that already do, or could, function as agents of development. (CODEL, it should be noted, has been compiling a partial inventory of the church-related IPVOs throughout the Third World.)

Despite the rapidly growing interest in and support for IPVOs, certain cautions are being expressed. Some informed observers, such as Irene Pinkau, warn that the global "development community" may be placing too much hope in the IPVO idea, too soon, since most Third World private voluntary associations are still small neighborhood support groups. She claims, moreover, that most such local groups do not have the economic freedom to act as true volunteers in relief and development efforts. She points out that the indigenous groups closest to being counterparts of U.S. PVOs are actually government agencies and are regulated to such an extent that they are unable to make independent decisions or enter into flexible collaborations of the sort that characterize the U.S. PVOs' projects. She also argues that for U.S. government and private efforts for development to be transformed into an almost exclusive financing relationship with Third World governments and local organizations, would be to erode seriously—or destroy—the very important, if often intangible, people-to-people relationships that grow out of the partnerships of U.S. PVOs with indigenous individuals and organizations.

Another caveat, sometimes expressed by outside observers well acquainted with IPVOs, is that they are often affiliated with some political party or faction and that any funding organization that supports one group will be accused by rival groups of political interference. Moreover, it is sometimes said that if an IPVO succeeds with its program it is very likely to be co-opted by the government, which always wants to take credit for or be perceived as related to successful public service ventures.

In any case, AID has commissioned research papers on the IPVO question to determine just how far it ought to go with these organizations. Should AID bring local governments into the review and evaluations of IPVOs? Should AID interrelate U.S. and indigenous PVOs' efforts in the future? How much control should AID exert over the design of IPVO projects? Should AID use U.S. PVOs as intermediaries in the support of IPVOs? Should IPVOs funded by AID be encouraged or required to "buy American" when they purchase goods and services for implementing their development projects? These are some of the questions about U.S. relations with IPVOs that need answering. AID officials say they are moving cautiously and are concentrating on what might be called the elite IPVOs.

A Question of Pluralism

As the U.S. moves into the Reagan era of foreign policy, ideological arguments regarding IPVOs are to be expected, along with disputes over technical matters. How important is it for the United States to help build pluralistic institutions in the Third World? How significant are IPVOs as expressions of pluralism? To what extent does U.S. support of IPVOs infringe on the sovereignty of Third World governments? To understand the background of these questions some broader political issues must be examined. The struggle today between the United States and the Soviet Union for influence in the Third World revolves in a substantial way around the issue of pluralism versus centralism.

Both the United States and the Soviet Union claim to favor development in the Third World, but each has in mind very different development processes, styles, and ultimate objectives. The Soviets give emphasis to building a strong centralized national government unencumbered by competing power centers within the country. To some nationalistic leaders of new Third World countries in Africa and parts of Asia, this centralized "statist" approach is appealing. They want to concentrate power in their own hands. Some of them see a strong state as a precondition for breaking down petty tribal factions, building the infrastructure of a sound national economy, and carrying through a government-administered national development program. Hence, some of them welcome funding by the Soviet Union and accept the Soviet model of central government dominance.

The development process for the Third World advocated by the United States is one that works through strong and diverse private institutions. Although some countries provide conspicuous exceptions, encouragement generally is given to making political decisions through bargaining among diverse groups. Efforts are made to evoke the creative energies of many individual entrepreneurs and private groups and associations.

Transnational corporations are, of course, a highly visible and controversial expression of pluralism implanted in the Third World. Another expression, not yet so controversial but perhaps just as important, is the expanding domestic voluntary nonprofit sector. As manifestations of the independent will of citizens, these voluntary groups (labor unions, neighborhood councils, church groups, even liberation movements) have a legitimacy (at least in the eyes of their own followers) that is lacking in national governments, whose power derives ultimately from an ability to coerce citizens through taxation and police and military controls.

By promoting IPVOs, the U.S. government may be doing more than simply gearing up local well-meaning organizations to be agents of development assistance. It is also affecting the internal affairs of foreign countries in a way that could have major consequences. For example, a small grant ($75,000) made by one U.S. PVO (the international arm of the AFL-CIO) to a kind of IPVO (Solidarity, the Polish federation of labor unions) created an international incident and may or may not have helped strengthen that independent union movement in its dealings with the Polish government. It was attacked, however, as a challenge to the authority of the government leaders and was cited by the Soviet Union as evidence of "capitalist interference" in the internal affairs of a socialist country. To the United States, the grant was simply a gesture of support from one independent PVO to another. The American view was that the open indigenous federation of unions in Poland had every right to receive open and above-board support from a fellow trade union movement in its efforts to establish its independent status. But such experiments in pluralism are, of course, anathema to the Soviet Union.

It happens that over the years AID has funded that same AFL-CIO division, which in turn has provided subgrants to regional IPVOs—the Asian Labor Center, the Latin American Labor Center, and the African Labor Center—all of which support national labor movements in the Third World. Because the United States was officially involved in such cases, the political fallout potentially could be even greater than in Poland. Of course, the charge of "foreign intervention" runs both ways. When the Soviet Union also supports IPVOs (by providing funds and technical assistance to Third World liberation movements, sometimes using Cuba as its intermediary), the United States insists that such foreign support cancels out the liberation movement's claim to be a legitimate indigenous endeavor.

In any case, the issue of U.S. government funding of indigenous PVOs could become a very touchy issue within the State Department and between the United States and Third World governments.

Global Education

As the funding agencies and the PVOs themselves push IPVOs into center stage as major actors in the development drama, another question arises: Are we seeing the beginning of the end for the U.S. PVOs? Some of them are already phasing out much of their work in Central and South America and the Caribbean where indigenous groups now proliferate, while Africa and Southeast Asia are becoming regions of expanding activity for some U.S. PVOs. But even in a few of the most destitute areas the process of transfering responsibility to local nongovernmental groups has begun. Some PVO staffers believe that by the end of the 1980s the role of American PVOs in these areas might be limited to short term interventions following natural and man-made disasters. Others speculate that after the 1980s, regional Third World systems of preparedness for and prevention of disasters might be so advanced, and intergovernmental funding so extensive, that there no longer would be a need for help from outside private agencies.

That vision of the coming demise of the PVOs might make sense if it were not for one vexing issue: public information. For years, PVOs have worked on "constituency education," more recently called "development education" or "global education" in the current jargon of the PVO community. What is meant is a comprehensive effort to help the American public gain a fuller grasp of global issues and problems that affect the lives of all of us. Going beyond traditional concern about European and East-West issues, now special stress is given to efforts to increase Americans' understanding of the Third World countries and the impact of their problems on the vital interests of the United States, on Big Power rivalries, and on the peace of the world.

At first blush, "global education" seems to run against the current tide, for the United States seems to be growing more nationalistic, not less so. Our preoccupations in the 1980s are domestic, and the popular approach to education is to return to basics, not to a proliferation of studies of complex issues in distant lands. Moreover, "global education" sounds like one more concept pushed by the education lobbies, and to some it conjures up images of new bureaucracies, new teachers' union demands, and new pressures for more funding. So why "global education" at a time like this? The truth is that despite the sound of the term, this is not an ideological issue. Greater awareness and understanding of world problems is a high-priority interest to a broad coalition of groups—some quite conservative, and all concerned with American vital interests. All of them are certain that the revitalization of the U.S. economy will depend on the capacity of Americans to come to terms with global economic realities, and that U.S. security requires greater public knowledge of the world as it is and the threats of what it might become.

The Internationalization of America

The internationalization of the U.S. economy, proceeding under our noses for many decades, has caught many people by surprise. Few seem aware that one of every six U.S. workers is engaged in manufacturing products for foreign consumption, and that one of every three acres of U.S. farmland grows food for export. The biggest and most successful U.S. corporations are the multinationals whose growth results from overseas operations and foreign investment. Those overseas relationships keep moving toward the Third World, which is now a bigger trading partner with the United States than all of Europe. As the productivity of the U.S. worker has declined and the rate of growth of the American GNP has diminished, productivity has been skyrocketing in the Third World, particularly in Asia (Singapore, Taiwan, South Korea, and Hong Kong). The Third World has been organizing itself rapidly into regional producer associations to promote the so-called South's bargaining position with the North. Successful Third World coalitions have formed along product lines

(OPEC) as well as regional lines (Association of Southeast Asian Nations). By their sheer numbers the Third World countries now control the United Nations agencies (and other forums operating under the one country–one vote principle) and are using them as a base for trying to reshape the global economic order in their interests.

The U.S. response to such events often has been to make no response at all, or to react defensively, or to make countermoves half-heartedly. As long as we were the preeminent advanced nation, the rest of the world would just have to meet us on our cultural, economic, and political terms. However, while we may have thought we could indulge ourselves with the luxury of remaining relatively ignorant of many foreign peoples and their interests, other countries were becoming shrewd internationalists. In effect, we forced them to expand their own thinking by forcing them to speak English and to learn our ways better than we knew theirs. At times they were able to ignore the differences among themselves and to team up with each other to deal with us as a unified bloc.

Too slowly we have come to realize how much our lack of a global view has cost us. Each year lamentations on the topic emanate from new quarters. For example, Senator S. I. Hayakawa commented on the Senate floor that "there are 20,000 Japanese businessmen in New York who speak English and about 1,000 American businessmen in Tokyo, most of whom speak no Japanese. No wonder that Japan has a favorable trade balance vis à vis the United States." Congressman Paul Simon added a more tongue in cheek comment that made the same point: "When General Motors, when Chevrolet, comes out with a car named Nova and it doesn't sell in Latin America because *no va* means "doesn't go" in Spanish, you know that it is a simple lack of knowledge. . . ."

The new concern for U.S. economic self-interest is not the only factor today that explains the growing concern for "global education." The make-up of our population continues to become more international and interracial, perhaps faster than our cultural attitudes. In 1980 alone the United States received an estimated one million legal and illegal immigrants, and there seems to be no end to future waves of political refugees. While the immigrants have been well received in the past, in Florida and elsewhere there are new signs of bitterness over the continuing influx. Foreign students in the United States are the fastest growing segment of U.S. higher education: 250,000 today, perhaps one million by the end of the decade. Foreign visitors supply increasingly large sums of foreign exchange, although few services have been set up to accommodate their special needs. Foreign businesspeople have found U.S. real estate and corporate stocks to be good investments as the U.S. dollar has declined, raising the spectre of foreign control of much of our land and many of our businesses.

Why the Schools Are Unprepared

The fact that Americans have not always greeted this new internationalization with understanding and enthusiasm can be explained partly by the nostalgic "we're number one" mentality. But a more fundamental cause may be found in recent changes in the educational system, which today produces fewer foreign language speakers or foreign specialists than it did ten years ago and far fewer than the schools in other advanced countries. The numbers of American students in higher education enrolled in foreign language or foreign studies courses have declined by 30 percent since 1973. High schools across the country have dropped the foreign language requirement, and so have many liberal arts colleges. Despite the influx of international students, universities have cut back their "area studies" curricula, largely due to a decline in grant support. For some years, international programs were supported by outside money—particularly by the Ford Foundation grants, which, in the international studies heyday period from 1951 to 1973, provided colleges and universities an average of $14 million a year for this purpose. That figure rose as high as $27 million during the 1960s. Now Ford has all but pulled out of the field, leaving the beleaguered U.S. Department of Education as the chief and somewhat reluctant patron. That federal department has been unable to give adequate support to even the best of the existing campus programs, and university administrators resist requests to dip into their scarce general funds.

Outside the schools, in the "informal education system," other explanations account for America's inability to respond well to the demands of new international conditions. In comparison with other countries, the U.S. media are attuned overwhelmingly to domestic rather than foreign news, unless there is a hostage crisis or its equivalent. The number of U.S. foreign correspondents has been steadily declining ever since World War II. In 1980 there were only 429 of them stationed throughout the world serving television, radio, and the printed media—altogether a number now exceeded by several European countries and Japan. According to one survey of the broadcasting content in one-hundred countries, less than 2 percent of U.S. television programming presents international topics, the lowest in the survey. Of the larger countries of the world only the USSR and China were more isolationist in their news coverage.

The extent of America's lack of preparedness for its new international role was documented in a 1980 report of the President's Commission on Foreign Languages and International Studies, which recommended changes in the formal education system. The report was closely timed with those of two other presidential commissions: the Report of the Presidential Commission on World Hunger and the Global 2000 Report to the President. The World Hunger study emphasized North-South interdependence and a number of "win-win" strategies in which policy changes in the interest of the South would also benefit the North. The report contained a separate chapter on "development education," which advocated federal support for raising consciousness about world hunger. The Global 2000 study stressed the need for the United States to take a long-term view in setting its policies because pursuit of existing policies in the U.S. and abroad would bring about a range of disasters, which the report enumerated in 800 pages of detail. Other less official studies also reached the attention of policymakers, with declarations that the key to revitalizing the U.S. domestic economy was to produce a citizenry more capable of adjusting to, and taking advantage of, the international economy.

The Federal Response Focuses on PVOs

The results of this new information were quickly felt in the federal bureaucracy. Secretary Hufstedler, President Carter's Secretary of Education, was a convert to global education after viewing the foreign languages report. She commented, "What is needed is a conscious effort to overhaul our educational experience, to take a fresh look at existing curricula offerings, at text books, at syllabi, at the quality of language teaching and, indeed, at the capabilities of teachers" ("A World in Transition," in *Educating for a World View*, Washington, D.C.: Council on Learning, 1980, p. 9). Despite huge funding cuts in most of the Department of Education's programs, Hufstedler proposed a 50 percent hike in appropriations for its international studies programs, a new administrative unit to "coordinate international education policy," and a plan for major international initiatives in upcoming years. Reagan's election cast doubt on how far these academic changes would go; the president-elect had announced his intention to do away with the Department of Education, eliminating as many as possible of its initiatives.

Outside the Department of Education, rumblings in three other federal agencies already reflect this new direction. All of them are gearing up PVOs as the most likely "agents" of global education in this country.

One of these is the International Communications Agency (ICA—the old U.S. Information Agency). ICA coordinates dozens of scholarly exchange programs for the State Department. It also promotes the idea of "cultural diplomacy," with each citizen, as the occasion arises, concerned and able to represent the country responsibly. Since 1979 ICA has given about $7 million to private nonprofit groups to help them build international perspectives into their domestic operations. One ICA grant studied 350 of the largest national nonprofit networks to find out how they inform their own members about global issues. Reviewing the outcome of the study, the ICA staffers were excited at the idea of using PVOs more fully as resources for international information at the local community level.

ACTION, the federal agency that sponsors the Peace Corps, also is exploring ways to further this community-based approach. ACTION sees the possibility that it might link up some of the 72,000 returned Peace Corps volunteers with some of the 27,000 VISTA volunteers currently assigned to nonprofit groups in the service of global education. It cosponsored with the Kettering Foundation a report written by Irene Pinkau called "Volunteer Services in the Global Learning Process." The report recommended some bold programs that would bring together the domestic and foreign-oriented voluntary organizations with the educational system, the Peace Corps, VISTA, and certain foreign exchange programs. AID contributed to these efforts by proposing a pilot program in global education to be awarded in 1981 to a single grantee on a fifty-fifty matching basis.

Clearly, the federal government is aware that the PVOs have already set up mechanisms for influencing millions of Americans about global issues, not just through their own local chapters but also through their ties to the domestic U.S. voluntary sector. No other aspect of society seems better suited to reaching out and influencing the entire American population on global issues than the nonprofit, nongovernmental voluntary sector. Perhaps its greatest asset is its pervasiveness. There are three million local voluntary organizations, counting both the religious and the secular. They have combined total memberships of 331 million, which means that the average U.S. adult is a member of at least two such groups. While the majority of these affiliations (210 million of them) are religious, a substantial number (131 million) are secular. Their activities are conducted by millions of active volunteers and about 500,000 paid staff. The monetary value of the annual activity of these organizations was calculated to be $50 billion in 1973, according to a study by the University of Michigan, and probably close to $80 billion in 1981.

The educational outreach activities conducted by these three million groups touch virtually every American adult, including many who actually belong to no organization. Closely related to fundraising, for years these activities have been called by the professionals "constituency education," viewed as particularly important for bringing a sense of immediacy to faraway problems. Such work makes up about half of what many PVOs do. The term understandably means different things to different PVOs: sometimes informing the public of a crisis in the world to evoke concern for the problem; sometimes involving people as donors, volunteers, and possibly as continuing members of the PVO and recruiters of other members. Sometimes explorations of Third World problems lead to discussions of how policies in the United States, as well as attitudes of U.S. citizens, could be changed to eliminate injustices and promote closer, more effective ties with Third World nations. Some observers believe that the PVOs—not the economic specialists or the academicians—may become the nation's most active informers about global interdependence.

The New Model of Community-based Global Education

Already certain elements of the new strategy for global education are being tried out. Some aspects of that strategy are already operating in piecemeal fashion: (1) community surveys, (2) citizen action lobbying and advocacy networks, (3) ethnic group involvement, (4) two-way exchanges, (5) PVO and government programs in international education. Following are some details:

1. *International Community Surveys.* An international community survey can be a powerful way of showing the nature and frequency of all contacts between a given community and foreign countries. The first such survey was conducted by Chadwick Alger in 1972 for the Kettering Foundation. Called "Columbus in the World, the World in Columbus," the project showed interrelationships between the citizens of Columbus, Ohio, and rest of the world. The findings confirmed the argument made years ago by Harlan Cleveland that the distinction between domestic and international affairs is largely a myth. In 1972 Columbus citizens bought 20,000 plane tickets to foreign cities, produced $134 million in

goods for export, welcomed 7,000 foreign visitors and 1,110 foreign students. But the most surprising evidence was the extent of globally oriented private voluntary activity. More than $3 million were sent overseas by Columbus churches during that year. Moreover, 21,000 man hours a month were spent on international activities by volunteers. Hundreds of nonprofit groups participated. These activities were fragmented, uncoordinated, and usually not related in any way to formal international studies in schools and universities. Within two years, fifteen other cities conducted similar surveys, and more communities are planning such local studies of their world relationships.

2. *Action Networks.* In every city that employed the community survey, a call to action was the spontaneous next step. In Columbus, a consolidated citizens effort called the International Council of Mid-Ohio was created to coordinate the commercial, educational, and people-to-people ties with the outside world. Subsequently, seventeen other cities adopted the survey method and similar international councils were soon established in eight of them. The first action was always to seek to create city-wide or area-wide international coordinating councils to build coalitions that do such things as:

- advocate that the local schools introduce more international and intercultural studies into the curriculum;
- collaborate on fundraising or education in support of world hunger projects;
- lobby for changes in federal foreign policies and foreign aid policies;
- help ease the refugee resettlement process;
- coordinate local responses to foreign disasters, such as the Italian earthquake of 1980.

The most comprehensive approach to such coordination, so far, has occurred in four U.S. metropolitan areas: Los Angeles, Seattle, Minneapolis, and Atlanta. The international divisions of the YMCA and other PVOs have been active in organizing this collaborative program.

3. *Use of Ethnic and Foreign Resources and Returned Volunteers Locally.* One of the findings of the community surveys was that huge numbers of local citizens have important first-hand information about foreign countries but are not being adequately involved in local international activities. These people include members of

certain ethnic communities, recent refugees, foreign students and workers, and returned volunteers. These people can be recruited as guest speakers, foreign language teachers, or presenters in inter-cultural programs.

4. *Two-way Exchanges*. In the coming years various exchange programs are likely to be coordinated with community-by-com-munity efforts at global education. Over 700 such programs exist at high school, college, university, and professional levels. Some of them relate the exchange programs with educational activities that take place during and after the orientations. About thirty of the pro-grams link specific communities to the communities overseas. Two of the best known of these are Sister Cities International and Part-ners of the Americas. Another that gained much attention in recent years is Friendship Force, which arranges home-visit swaps between a cross-section of citizens of an American community with the citizens of some foreign city.

Still another notable example of this type of program is the American Field Service, which operates in 2,100 communities. AFS involves students aged 16–18 from the United States and from all six continents in exchange, which are usually followed by com-munity service activities. At the higher education level a similar program called Experiment in International Living includes foreign study and service activities touching 1,100 U.S. communities. The largest of all the youth exchange programs is Youth for Understand-ing, which arranges for American high school students to live in private homes in foreign lands and attend local schools. It also organizes the same kind of home life and education experiences for foreign students in the United States.

Kettering Foundation showed how these kinds of exchange pro-grams could be integrated into ongoing local global education when it conducted a project called the "Findlay Story." Under a grant from Kettering, fifteen carefully selected civic leaders in Findlay, Ohio, agreed to spend twenty-four months doing local volunteer work of a broad civic education nature following a three-week study tour of Kenya and Tanzania. They wrote articles in the newspapers on North-South issues as they saw them from their experience, gave lectures, and took part in other events to bring the reality of East Africa into their city. Kettering furthered this approach by conven-ing a number of organizations, all PVOs that conduct sister-city–type programs, to find ways to collaborate with each other and broaden the educational aspects of their programs in their own cities and their overseas counterparts.

Sometimes these two-way exchanges link specific local organizations with the counterpart organization in the corresponding sister city abroad. For example, about one hundred YMCA local chapters in the United States have "sister-Y" relationships with other Ys in Latin America and Africa. Similarly, the United Way International, a recent outgrowth of United Way of America, is setting up sister relationships with United Way national and local organizations in Latin America and the Philippines.

5. *PVO and Government Programs in International Education.* The United States lags behind a number of other countries in officially sponsored programs of global education. The governments of Australia, Austria, Belgium, Canada, Denmark, Finland, France, Germany, Ireland, Italy, the Netherlands, Norway, Sweden, and the United Kingdom have made substantial efforts to promote broader public understanding of global issues among their peoples.

In those countries PVOs engage in a great variety of educational activities dealing with world affairs. Each of these countries also has an official public information program, operated by a government agency, to make the public more aware of the importance of development assistance; all of these countries consider PVOs important and effective institutions to inform the public about development issues. Canada was one of the first countries to fund global education programs to promote public understanding of the developing world. Of the $66 million spent in 1980 by the AID counterpart in Canada (Canadian International Development Authority), $3.2 million was allocated for educating the Canadian public on these issues. CIDA authorities see a direct correlation between its funding of the educational activities and the significant increase over the past three years in private contributions to Canadian PVOs.

The United States is increasingly faced with the necessity to decide whether its commitment to the continuance of foreign assistance does not require greater support for the efforts of many private organizations to broaden public knowledge of the international problems we face and the international responsibilities we carry. In a democratic society, an informed citizenry is essential for the carrying out of responsible, costly, and controversial policies. Nowhere is this truer than in the field of international and security affairs.

PART FOUR

Conclusions and Future Options

11

Rethinking Foreign Aid

There are many reasons for a critical reappraisal of foreign aid and its relation to development. Yet, somehow, a really searching, comprehensive, and objective examination of the issues is difficult. It is easy to get lost in debaters' arguments that have to do with international or domestic politics, with competing pressures in national budget making, with the protective defensiveness of established bureaucracies, with the ambitions of national leaders, or with the shifting perceptions of Western security needs. A thorough assessment of the nature and extent of the foreign assistance needed for any developing country is bound to be complicated and controversial. The actual effects of the assistance given, moreover, are hard to establish. The weighing of options among development strategies is puzzling and often inconclusive.

During the 1970s there arose a series of challenges to many of the long-prevailing ideas about foreign aid: spokesmen for the Third World made increasingly blunt attacks from various international platforms on the advanced, industrialized countries and their policies. Assistance to the developing countries was frequently denounced as too niggardly, with too many strings attached, with too little support for the industrialization ambitions of the emerging nations. Moreover, it was argued, whatever good might be done by foreign assistance was often cancelled by the gyrations in the world price level of the raw materials and commodities produced by the developing countries, and by trade and credit policies dictated by the industrialized powers, which had adverse effects upon the Third World. Calls for a North-South dialogue to negotiate a New International Economic Order (NIEO) became more and more insistent. Indeed, fitfully, such a dialogue began. However, it turned by stages into a confrontational stalemate rather than a serious process of negotiation. The appeals by the South for a New International Economic Order were repeatedly turned aside by the North, more by artful delays and evasion, it would appear, than by outright rejection. As the advanced countries have become increasingly concerned about their own domestic problems of unemployment and inflation, and as their governments have come more and more under pressure to reduce taxes and public expenditures, they have been inevitably less and less sympathetic to expanding their assistance to the developing world. And they have had their own criticisms of the ways in which many Third World countries have dealt with their development needs and the resources already made available to them.

Meanwhile, that disparate bloc of developing nations once called the Group of 77, and numbering now about 120, have indicated that they are more interested in "structural reforms" related to the NIEO than they are in foreign aid as such. Moreover, several nations of the South have made clear that their ideas about the kind of assistance they should have differ markedly from the current ideas of the Northern countries that provide the aid. They long have urged that industrialized nations contribute 1 percent of their annual GNP to development programs. That goal has been ignored by all except the Scandinavian countries, the Netherlands, and Japan.

On the point of "structural reforms," the South presses for: changes in international trade arrangements to raise and stabilize commodity prices; easier access to Northern markets for Southern exports; new and more generous policies by Northern creditors for the rescheduling of Southern debts (now totalling more than $400 billion); greater financial reserves to be made available to Southern countries, partially through monetary reforms; and a much prompter, more open-handed sharing of Northern technology with the South. Sensing the advantage the developing world has come to have through the one country–one vote pattern of the UN General Assembly and certain other international bodies, the Southern bloc pushes for greater influence and greater equity in the policies and operations of those agencies that grew out of the Bretton Woods agreements on the international financial system. The industrialized Northern countries, on the other hand, are not inclined to relinquish their dominance in the International Monetary Fund (IMF), the World Bank, the General Agreement on Trade and Tariffs (GATT), and other crucial institutions of the current international economic order. Clearly, they will not agree to shift to a one country–one vote pattern.

In successive and prolonged North-South sessions under UN auspices, the North has been willing to make certain gradual and modest accommodations to the desires of the South. But these gradualist proposals have been maddeningly frustrating to the countries of the South, which accuse the Northern countries, and particularly the United States, of "talking them to death." Some observers say that the North has been "playing for time" as it tries to co-opt the more advanced and the more affluent of the Southern bloc countries—Saudi Arabia, Mexico, and Venezuela, for example—by inviting them to join the Organization of Economic Cooperation for Development and other institutions dominated by the industrialized club of nations that jointly design that group's development policies.

In the early stages of the Third World development movement, there was a large measure of agreement on what the goals and processes should be. Nation building, institution building, health service delivery, agricultural modernization, leadership training, and infrastructure engineering—these were the high priorities. The World Bank, the national planning ministries, U.S. AID, assorted UN agencies, plus the Ford and Rockefeller Foundations all seemed in substantial agreement on the major tasks to be undertaken. There were certain basic beliefs about development, widely shared by both the providers and receivers of assistance as they planned their joint endeavors:

1. that creation of a modern national economy, based upon technically sophisticated infrastructures, would almost automatically bring a better life to almost all the people in any developing country;
2. that economic dvelopment would promote domestic political stability and peace among nations; and
3. that the developing countries and the developed countries that assisted them would benefit through an expanding symbiotic relationship.

These assumptions, largely confirmed by experience, underlay the highly successful Marshall Plan for the reconstruction of postwar Europe. In that endeavor, American investments of about $22 billion and the creative energies of the European recipients combined to produce a startling economic miracle within a decade. Benefits were widely shared among the masses of the people; political stability was encouraged; international harmony among the once-warring Western Europeans was restored with amazing rapidity. And the Americans profited mightily in the bargain.

One did not quite say that a Marshall Plan for the developing world would work the same way. Yet lurking in the minds of many champions of development was the hope that something roughly comparable to the Marshall Plan success story could be repeated through massive foreign assistance to the developing world. Moreover, many government leaders expected that, as earlier in Europe, the advancing new nations would build up antibodies against the virus of communism as their economic well-being improved. There were also many who, naively, thought that grateful recipients of foreign aid would and should join the Western powers in one of several military alliances.

A third of a century and $100 billion later, much of that early thinking about development has been scrapped. Most of the developing countries have made it clear that they do not want to be allied with either camp, or involved in either cold or hot wars. Although they might, at times, lean toward one side or the other, they prefer to be able to go their own way, sometimes playing one superpower off against the other, seeking assistance with the fewest possible strings.

In a sense, the developing countries are still wedded to the "nation building," "economy building," and "institution building" objectives talked about so much in the early postwar years. But they want to make their own definitions of those goals, set their own priorities, design their own programs, and, generally, build strong governmental bureaucracies in the process. Their concepts of development are very much linked to traditional aims of acquiring more factories, enlarging their GNPs, and expanding their export trade (including their own manufactured goods). They are less concerned about controlling population and improving subsistence farming—major goals of development as defined by grantmakers of the North. Northern bloc advisers, including AID (during the Carter/McNamara years), and many of the PVOs and the U.S. foundations have urged that primary attention be given to efforts to "overcome absolute poverty," that a key development strategy should be built around "basic needs" programs to provide minimum requirements of food, housing, and health care for the poorest of the poor, as well as population control. According to that view, the problem of world hunger could not be overcome until more of the food-deficit regions of the developing world substantially increased production by their own small farmers. It was absurd for predominantly agricultural developing countries to go on importing American grains, which they must pay for with scarce export earnings or borrowed dollars, when they could improve their own agriculture enough to feed themselves. Also, it has been argued that even those countries that have received free American food have thereby, at times, discouraged local food production and delayed self-sufficiency; therefore, all the more reason for a development strategy that emphasizes local food production.

The Southern bloc has tended to resist this strategy on the grounds that it does not give adequate attention to the need to build up their industrial infrastructures. To be sure, Southern leaders do champion food self-sufficiency. Yet, within the arena of North-South confrontations they are inclined to challenge what they consider an overemphasis by the North on agriculture for the South. Some of them see this as a plot by the richer, industrial nations to keep the poorer nations from experiencing industrialization and, hence, to remain primarily agricultural and permanently poor. They accuse the North of being unsympathetic to their desires for rapid industrialization and of being ultimately fearful of competition from the developing countries in the sale of manufactured goods on world markets. The impact of expanding imports of shoes, textiles, electronics, and certain other consumer products made in Hong Kong, Taiwan, Singapore, and Korea on markets once dominated by U.S. and European manufacturers gives some force to the argument. The rise of protectionist sentiment among broad segments of the American labor movement and some businessmen underscores the point.

Moreover, spokesmen for the Southern viewpoint charge that the North, including the United States with its long history of foreign aid, has not really demonstrated a serious commitment and a believable practical strategy for carrying out a program of "overcoming absolute poverty." If an effective strategy were to be undertaken, it would require a considerably greater investment than the North is willing to make in the development programs of the Third World, plus changes in trade and monetary and technology transfer policies.

A favorite rejoinder from the North is that many of the Southern nations simply cannot expect to overcome their development problems, and certainly cannot demand additional foreign aid, until they put their own houses in order. Corruption, political instability, and sheer wrong-headed economic policies—including romantic experiments with alleged forms of socialism—are cited as evidences that the leaders of some of the new nations are themselves to blame for the slow pace of development. Moreover, it is often argued that only determined, persistent programs to control population growth can, in the long run, make possible solid, sustained economic growth—and that many nations in the Third World simply have not faced up to that reality.

Such are some of the arguments and accusations that continue to be exchanged between the developed North and the developing South. Yet the stalemate is not hopeless. There are many leaders in the North who seek to bring about rapprochement with the South. Northern bankers and finance ministers are sympathetic to the rescheduling of debt payments. Even among critics of foreign aid there are those who would like to see it expanded. There are also new leaders in the South who are trying to make changes the North advocates, and some are converts to the "tougher" approaches to development advocated by the International Monetary Fund. On the other hand, some Third World leaders, including those in newly independent Zimbabwe, accuse the United States of "interfering with domestic economic and financial affairs" of developing countries through policies it is pursuing in the IMF.

Now that the global formulas for the New International Economic Order have been rejected, many of the leading advocates of the NIEO have shifted to practical, piecemeal negotiations that promise step-by-step progress for particular sets of countries and regions. The failure of the South to sell the North on NIEO as a total package has not meant that no changes are possible. A leading advocate for a new regional approach to international economic affairs is the European Economic Community. Together with the Association of Southeast Asian Nations (ASEAN), it has worked out a comprehensive economic aid plan on trade, monetary matters, and investment—a plan for economic aid meant to complement the other economic ties between the two blocs. The EEC is putting together other new and far-reaching interregional economic packages with still other groups of nations.

Japan, meanwhile, has undertaken to double its foreign aid to the countries of southeast Asia, and plans still further expansion of its direct assistance, while making a variety of changes in trade and investment policies that will benefit both that Asian economic superpower and its less affluent neighbors to the south. Like the EEC, Japan has come to view foreign aid as an important complement to its basic international economic policies.

One nation in the North or a bloc of nations may be able to help one of the developing countries, or a bloc of them, in ways that moderate the often harsh confrontations that arise between North and South in the debates in the UN General Assembly and in other multinational gatherings where economic issues are discussed. This bloc-to-bloc approach may, over time, temper the North-South conflict, though it is not likely to end it.

Meanwhile, the election of President Reagan introduced fresh uncertainties into calculations about the future of U.S. foreign aid. Early pronouncements from the Office of Management and Budget, the State Department, and the Congress indicated that there were strong initial pressures:

1. to reduce drastically the total dollar amount allocated by the U.S. government to foreign aid. OMB director David Stockman spoke of a 50 percent reduction, and Senator Jesse Helms, in a shrewd political maneuver, urged the Senate to vote to transfer $100 million from the foreign aid surplus grain program to the domestic child nutrition program in the United States (but the actual reductions were much lower than had been expected);

2. to curtail, if not eliminate, multilateral assistance in favor of direct bilateral grant agreements;

3. to tie U.S. assistance to Third World countries to economic and political principles and practices that reflect the American administration's conservative views — and to press the international funding agencies to adopt similar policies;

4. to continue to assign roughly half of all U.S. foreign aid to two countries — Israel and Egypt — obviously out of strategic and political considerations.

Secretary of State Alexander Haig, within the first months of the Reagan administration, announced that the United States would give precedence to "security assistance" programs (to deal with East-West issues) over "development assistance" (aimed at North-South problems). He also said that the United States would concentrate on making bilateral aid arrangements rather than providing assistance through multilateral relations. These comments shocked our European allies, provoked protests from many in the developing world, and predictably drew scornful criticisms from the Soviet Union and its satellites. However, from the beginning there were doubts within the administration about the wisdom of a drastic and immediate curtailment of U.S. participation in multilateral assistance — particularly the abandonment of a strong U.S. role in various aid programs developed through the World Bank and related international banking institutions.

Despite the initial attempt of Budget Director David Stockman to cut in half the U.S. contribution to the World Bank's "soft loan" window, the Reagan team, in the end, agreed to a substantial increase in the American contribution. Not only had the protest of allies been heard, but there had been fresh thoughts about the need "to maintain the leadership role of the United States" in the international financial system. Moreover, it had been argued successfully that the United States was "honor bound to deliver on international agreements" already made. However, some conservative supporters of the Reagan administration were outraged, including the *Wall Street Journal*, which editorialized that the authorizations for continued and expanded involvement in these kinds of multilateral aid arrangements would "open the floodgates for massive lending for exactly the sort of programs in other countries — nationalized railroads, cooperative lending, government subsidies in mass transit, government meddling in oil and gas production — that the administration is fighting at home."

The most dramatic departure of the Reagan administration from an ideological purist position of opposition to multilateral assistance came in negotiations among the Western donor nations over aid to newly independent Zimbabwe. The avowed Marxist prime minister, Robert Mugabe, an outspoken critic of Reagan administration moves of accommodation toward South Africa, won U.S. financial backing to an extent that at one point would have been declared impossible. Mugabe's request that the United States and other Western nations provide funding for a $2 billion Marshall Plan type of reconstruction program was not rejected out of hand, as might have been expected. Instead, the United States pledged a contribution of $250 million toward the World Bank planned program, even though it called for a considerable role for the public sector. This decision was clearly part of a multilateral aid agreement. Pragmatism apparently won out over ideological principle.

All of this, however, did not mean that the Reagan administration had given up its ambition to reshape U.S. foreign assistance programs and to redirect them to political goals compatible with the overall Reagan philosophy. In the very early days of the administration, plans were begun to give special attention and support to those countries that advocated a strong role for the private sector in their development plans. Rather than scatter U.S. aid to all countries requesting help, certain nations could be "showcased" as examples of successful appliers of free enterprise principles, including, perhaps, supply-side economics. The election of conservative Edward Seaga as prime minister of Jamaica over socialist Michael Manley gave President Reagan an unusual opportunity, and he invited Seaga to Washington as the first head of state he received. In short order, Jamaica was provided with $69 million of additional U.S. bilateral assistance, most of it directed to the strengthening of the island's private sector. In addition, the President requested retiring Chase Manhattan Chairman David Rockefeller to head a committee of bankers and businessmen to explore ways to expand private investment in Jamaica.

Hopeful signs of economic recovery in Jamaica under conservative leadership reinforced the Reagan administration's determination to exert a strong role throughout the Caribbean. As early as 1978 the Carter administration had identified the Caribbean as an area requiring major economic assistance and special security attention. Each U.S. president since John F. Kennedy has worried about Fidel Castro's possible radicalizing influence on Cuba's neighbors, and each has tried to counter it. Despite the Carter concern about the region, his administration was never able to get a coherent, comprehensive Caribbean aid program off the ground. However determined the Reagan team might be to cut back on assistance elsewhere, they were also determined to take strong action to assist the impoverished island countries to the south.

By mid-1980 a broad development assistance plan for the Caribbean was taking shape within the adminstration, with firm backing from President Reagan. Although the planning bogged down rather quickly in the common interagency quarrels, it was expected that loans and grants of more than one billion dollars and a variety of other measures would be taken to bring about significant improvements in life in the Caribbean basin. Not wanting to make this entirely a bilateral effort, the administration was trying hard to persuade Mexico and Venezuela, with their vast oil revenues, to assist with the regional development effort. Further multilateral aid through the World Bank and its affiliates was also being encouraged.

On a still broader front, the Reagan administration showed interest in beefing up the resources and activities of a little known aid organization, Overseas Private Investment Corporation (OPIC, too easily confused with OPEC). Its purpose has been to provide a kind of safety net for U.S. private firms investing abroad. For several years, some people have argued that OPIC could be used far more extensively than it has been for promoting private sector initiatives for development. There have been indications that the Reagan administration will indeed proceed in that direction.

Meanwhile, the role of PVOs in the implementation of new American approaches to overseas development was not clear in the early months of the Reagan administration, but the same impulses that led the Congress to promote PVOs in recent years appealed to the new team responsible for assistance programs. Private voluntary agencies seemed destined for continuing and perhaps expanding involvement in the foreign assistance enterprise—linked, if possible, to the activities of U.S. business firms. Just what kinds of partnerships could be worked out effectively between American profit and nonprofit organizations was not immediately evident. However, if the American aid programs are to emphasize agricultural self-sufficiency, the development of appropriate technology, and the strengthening of local capabilities for managing independent enterprise, then the training and other "human resources development" skills and experience of the PVOs would be much needed, as would the technical know-how of the business firms. Melding these two sets of competencies is an interesting challenge.

In any case, what does seem clear is that U.S. government support for large-scale public works types of projects in developing countries has been fading away. It is believed likely that increasing attention will be given to efforts to encourage grass-roots economic development in agriculture and small business and to enlarge and strengthen the local entrepreneurial class. Countries whose economic policies support that kind of development would obviously get a much more sympathetic hearing in Washington than those still wedded to large-scale public sector programs and infrastructure projects.

Meanwhile, not only in Jamaica, but in a number of other countries that have had disappointing flirtations with socialism, there are increasing signs of renewed interest in the free enterprise option and growing desire for U.S. business investment. Local Marxist-leaning intellectuals and Soviet bloc advisers have produced no economic miracles in the developing world; on the contrary, they are being blamed increasingly for the widespread economic chaos that has so generally attended their period of influence.

Responsible free enterprise advocates would, of course, be modest and restrained in claiming how much better they would have done, given all the complexities and difficulties related to local and international conditions that have affected the developing world. Still, they could hardly have done worse than the Marxist advisers on development.

Despite footholds in Angola, Ethiopia, and South Yemen, and faithful satellites and surrogates in Cuba and Vietnam, the Soviets and their ideology have not captured the developing nations. That they seek influence and ultimate dominance in the Third World may be taken for granted—if the price is not too high. The wonder is not that they tried to do what they did in Angola and Ethiopia, where they correctly calculated that the West would not do much to stop them. The real question is why they have not done much better than they have in extending their power throughout the developing world. They possess enormous built-in advantages, chief among them being the historical fact that they were never part of the European colonial system—at least not as it had been experienced in Africa and Latin America. By taking advantage of assorted discontents and rising demands for social change that the Soviets had little or no role in initiating, they have sought, and occasionally won, what have appeared to be easy victories. The arms and military advisers they have shipped abroad in large quantities have, at times, determined the immediate outcome of civil wars, as in Angola. Yet the overall Soviet record in trying to export their particular brand of revolution or in otherwise gaining decisive influence in the developing world has not been impressive.

After providing thousands of Soviet military and technical advisers and advancing billions of dollars to Egypt, the Soviets were unceremoniously thrown out by President Sadat in 1972. After long years of influence with leftist leaders in Ghana, Guinea, and other African nations, they gradually lost their favored position; their advice and assistance were finally treated as largely irrelevant. Neither their arms nor their technology had won for them wide acceptance as the architects of development. Cuba, which may be the showcase example of Soviet assistance, has obvious great internal difficulties and is sustained only by direct Soviet investments of several hundreds of millions of dollars each year.

All of this gives the United States no cause for smugness. The record of American involvement in the development activities of the Third World is also full of disappointments, both in countries where its assistance is still being given and in countries where Soviet influence is now ascendant.

In a time of intensified American concern over its rivalry with the Soviet Union, coinciding with a period of reassessment of governmental functions and expenditures, there is cause to reexamine the whole range of U.S. policies and programs related to development strategies. The temptation to cut back on economic aid and expand military assistance widely and on a large scale is understandable. Soviet subversion, it is said, must be met by strengthening the capabilities of friendly governments to resist terrorism and civil disorder—and that means arms and military advisers. Clearly, it is not that simple. Assistance that promotes economic growth and political stability is also urgently needed. But the nature of an appropriate, workable, and comprehensive strategy is not evident. Just pouring out more money is not the answer. Unfortunately, there has been, as this is written, far too little in-depth, sustained examination of just what any new official American plan for foreign aid ought to be and how it might be carried out. Meanwhile, there is continuing need for a clear-eyed evaluation of the ways in which the private sector can most significantly participate in development—and what national strategy can most appropriately encourage that participation.

12

The Continuing Need: Private Initiatives for Relief and Development

The future role of private institutions in relief and development programs abroad is complicated and shrouded in drifting fogs of uncertainty. Shifts in U.S. foreign policy, intensification of the Soviet-American military rivalry, continued inflation and mounting unemployment in the industrial nations, rising protectionist sentiment in response to unemployment and the declining fortunes of certain faltering industries that are being undersold by foreign imports—all these are significant factors that cast doubts over the future of foreign aid in general and of those overseas assistance activities financed, primarily or in large part, by private donations. Add the further reality of sheer human weariness and confusion over what does or does not help people in need, and there are abundant excuses to pull back, to walk away, to do less and less about the problems of the developing world and to fantasize that those problems will somehow vanish on their own.

Some rather discouraging facts can be summarized as follows:

- There is not enough money available from government and private sources together to deal adequately with the current claims for relief and development assistance that are put forward on behalf of poor countries.
- The needs of the impoverished peoples of the developing world are continuing and will increase more rapidly than the local and international resources available to meet them.

- Foreign interventions of technical advisers and money do not guarantee solutions to the problems of poor peoples and poor nations.
- Individuals and societies change primarily from within, and even the wisest experts are not always sure what it is that most effectively motivates people to change in ways that improve their lives.
- Donors and recipients are not always going to agree on the levels or strategies of assistance, and some seekers of assistance are difficult, demanding, and unappreciative.
- Military security considerations and political ambitions of the Big Powers will, inevitably, have great influence on the direction and scale of government financed foreign aid.
- The mood in the United States and in Western Europe, influenced by problems of inflation, high taxes, unemployment, and budget deficits, is not favorable to expanding foreign aid.
- Just as there has been a middle-class backlash against welfare state expenditures for the lower income people in America, so is there considerable popular opposition to spending public moneys for assistance to the poor overseas. That opposition may well increase.
- Foundation support for international programs, never large compared with funding for domestic programs, has declined substantially. Conceivably, it may increase, and there are some foundations that are so inclined, but the prospects are not favorable.
- Although U.S. corporate giving has expanded impressively in recent years, most transnational companies do not participate in philanthropic activities in the countries where they operate on a scale commensurate with their profits or the local needs around them.

These pessimistic observations may seem to indicate that there is little hope for foreign assistance programs, public or private. That is not our conclusion. Despite all the negative factors, we believe the possibilities exist for enlarging foreign assistance endeavors, for developing more successful programs related to those endeavors, and for increasing the significance of the private agencies in relief and development.

What is the basis for such hopeful speculation? Partly, that there is growing worldwide discussion—encouraged by private interventions—of the following realities:

1. *The human needs are there—and they won't go away.* Certain elementary facts are well known, but they bear repeating. More than one billion people, or about one-quarter of the world's population, live in Asian, Latin American, and African countries so poor that about 80 percent of their people exist in absolute poverty: chronically malnourished, diseased, without access to safe drinking water, doomed to high mortality rates for their children and low life expectancy for those who survive into adulthood, with literacy rates of less than 40 percent, and with average annual income of about $200. These are the "absolute poor"—perhaps a billion of them—today. By the year 2000 there will be many more. That reality shames the developed countries into helping change things, if they can, and it encourages Big Power rivalry in trying.

2. *The contrast between the affluent, industrialized countries and the poor, predominantly agricultural countries is enormous and ominous.* The developed countries, with 25 percent of the world's population, account for more than 75 percent of the world's GNP, have individual average annual incomes sixteen times higher than those of the average among the poorest billion, have five times the chance for their babies to live into adulthood, are able to spend four times as much as the remaining three-fourths of mankind on their education and health services. The industrially advanced 25 percent use more than half of all the oil, gas, coal, iron, copper, and countless other commodities that the world produces. They also grow and ship 80 percent of the food exported on the world market and provide virtually all of the food that goes to the food-deficit countries.

The contrast between the life of the peoples of the developed countries and life in the poorer nations is startling—and terrifying. In an earlier age, when poor people in faraway lands had virtually no notion of how people lived in other countries, the comparison would not be made or, if it were, would be shrugged off as the will of the gods. With instantaneous television communication worldwide, with rising levels of education and rising expectations of material progress, the humiliating comparison is made—and resented.

Among the billion neediest people around the world there is increasing frustration and anger, a predictable tendency to blame others, and a growing readiness to listen to extremist dogmatism, whether from radical Marxists or fanatical religious fundamentalists. Increasingly, the affluent minority can sense the possibility of eventual grave threats to their favored position from the impoverished majority, unless the material life of the majority is appreciably improved.

3. *The advanced countries recognize more and more that their own prosperity is linked to the economic well-being of the developing countries.* The United States now sells more of its export goods to the developing countries than to all the countries of Europe combined. Moreover, numerous raw materials essential to the operation of our economy make us dependent upon imports from other countries, mostly in the developing world.

Japan, until only a few years ago, was highly resistant to the idea of providing foreign aid. Today, largely out of calculated self-interest, it has become one of the leading donor countries, providing a considerably higher percentage of its GNP for development programs than the United States. The economic self-interest argument in justification of foreign assistance is still resisted, but it also is increasingly accepted in many of the developed countries as hard-headed realism.

4. *There is a growing sense of horror over the extent and import of the massive global expenditures for arms.* With the Soviet Union, the United States, and other countries spending together approximately $500 billion for military purposes each year—twenty times the amount spent annually for all development assistance programs throughout the world—there is a growing murmuring worldwide about the desirability of diverting some of those arms expenditures into development. That could hardly be done without serious moves by the Super Powers toward mutual disarmament, but they clearly have been going in the opposite direction. Moreover, a number of the less advanced countries have themselves been caught up in regional arms races, diverting scarce resources needed for their own economic development. The armaments burden is an enormous drag on the world economy, and it can be argued that it is the greatest single impediment to a more rapid advancement of the developing world. The arms control and disarmament problems are vastly complicated and no solutions are in prospect, but the linkage of disarmament with development is an idea about which we will hear a great deal more in the years ahead—the developing countries and dissenting critics in the developed countries will see to that.

5. *Public awareness of the plight of poor people in developing countries, particularly the refugees, has been steadily growing.* Despite widespread ignorance of and popular indifference toward international affairs, many Americans have become sensitized to the

sufferings of the poor in distant lands and are willing to do something about it. The overwhelming response of private givers to the needs of the boat people of Southeast Asia, stimulated certainly by an elaborate, organized campaign of information and advertising, demonstrated again the potential for private involvement in serious humanitarian endeavors. Refugees, more than any other group of the poor, stir the emotions and open the wallets of those who can help. The problem is how to insure a carry-over of interest from emergency relief to long-term development assistance by the people of the developed nations. One of the sad ironies of the present vast refugee problem is that 90 percent of the more than ten million individuals affected are people who fled from one poor country to another. At home or in exile, they are in need of long term development assistance.

Although Americans obviously differ over the question of what their government can do to oppose human rights violations abroad, they cannot be ignored. Again, it is a case in which the global communications revolution has changed our awareness of distant events that produce or accentuate the sufferings of millions of people, and has strengthened the human concern to become involved, even if we aren't quite sure how.

Despite all the humanitarian impulses that are stirred by an increasing awareness of homelessness, world hunger, and world poverty, voices are raised from time to time to question whether outsiders can really do much of anything to help other people make significant, lasting improvements in their lives. In times of natural or man-made disasters, immediate direct relief is often essential for the survival of thousands or millions of people. Individuals, private groups, and governments will respond, at times generously, with help that literally makes the difference between survival and death. For as long as emergency conditions last, such direct relief usually, and rightfully, continues. There is a danger, however, that some of the people helped may settle with being helped indefinitely. Such dependence on external assistance may slow the work of reconstruction and the rebuilding of the spirit and practice of personal and community self-help responsibility. There have been enough proofs of this human phenomenon in the history of both domestic and international relief operations that it need not become an issue of liberal/conservative dispute. But the larger question is this: Given the necessity to move, in time, beyond emergency relief to long-term development, how can lasting changes and real gains in the quality of life be achieved and sustained?

There are neo-Malthusians, "life boat ethicists," and plain cranky cynics who argue that people who have socioeconomic problems are best left to fend for themselves. Some well-trained biologists, economists, historians, and social anthropologists press this point of view. Some of them contend that China—backward, poor, overpopulated, isolated, and denied foreign aid—made vastly greater advances in the past forty years than India did in the same period with all the massive assistance it received from the United States, Great Britain, the Soviet Union, the United Nations, and the Ford Foundation (which once had 1,200 employees in India trying to help the Indians). The argument is that the Chinese, fending for themselves, made far more progress toward controlling their population, feeding their people, providing general health care, expanding education, and achieving other goals of development than did the Indians within the same period. The explanation, they insist, has nothing to do with Chinese communism or "Chinese character," but with the "sink or swim on your own" choices the Chinese had to make. People change when they have to. A nation improves its life when its leaders realistically face the problems before them and organize their people to deal with those problems. Outside help may simply confuse the issues and delay the changes people ultimately have to make out of their own convictions and with their own resources. So the argument goes.

There is no way such an argument can be definitively resolved. Immediate political considerations and humanitarian urges will inevitably interfere with carrying out any such hard-nosed advice on how to handle world poverty. Large-scale foreign assistance for development is going to continue.

All of this brings us back to the central question of this study: What is it that private groups, organizations, and individuals in the years ahead can most usefully do about the whole vast problem of relief and development? From our investigations, we conclude that there are essentially three major roles for private initiatives in relief and development: (1) *Education in the broadest sense*, (2) *Demonstration through limited-scale experiments of how people can help themselves*, and (3) *Emergency relief when it is required*.

Education

Whether the concern is for promoting sounder U.S. foreign policies, for stimulating private donations for overseas relief, for enlisting technical assistance workers, for promoting harmonious relations with foreign students and visitors, or for orienting American tourists and business people toward their experiences living and working abroad—the need is for more information to be made available to more of our own people on global issues. Whether it is a question of improving sanitation in primitive villages abroad, of training clerks and accountants to replace departed colonial service employees, expanding health care, developing new business, or improving farm production—the need in every developing country is for education.

Moreover, in the rarefied circles of the United Nations Secretariat and affiliated UN agencies, of the World Bank and the International Monetary Fund, of the State Department and AID—there, too, is a critical need for more accurate, comprehensive, and up-dated research data on a variety of issues related to relief and development.

In the gathering and disseminating of information about these issues, private initiatives are of critical importance. Official reports, government documents, and political pronouncements are often suspect and widely ignored. There will always be a significant place in a free society for gathering and distributing facts and opinions on public issues under nonofficial auspices. Nowhere in our search for sound public policies is there greater need for such initiatives than in the broad international field. Private grantmakers who are in any way open to funding activities related to international issues should give consideration to such educational and informational programs as the following:

1. *Research and the Dissemination of Research Findings.* Universities, free-standing research institutes and think-tanks, church bodies, and PVOs working abroad all have roles to play in gathering the data and informed testimony required for sound judgments about relief and development needs and about the diverse results from various kinds of foreign assistance programs. Ongoing studies of overseas development are of critical importance for the wise use of scarce resources, public and private.

Research, of course, is not enough. Academic libraries are jammed with masses of laboriously accumulated data, much of it valuable, which nobody has ever read, or is likely to read. Just gathering more data on international development is not enough. On matters of public policy, particularly on matters so controversial and so often misunderstood as foreign aid, it is essential that research findings be made available in such a format as to draw the attention and interest of opinion makers and policymakers, and in summary form, to reach the general public. Such information is critical in the building of private constituency groups that are indispensable in securing volunteer workers and private contributions for relief and development.

2. *Formal Educational Programs for Americans.* Schools, colleges, and universities are and will remain the primary instruments for educating the general population in virtually all fields of knowledge. Yet, by every relevant study in recent years, including one published in 1980 by the Presidential Commission on Foreign Languages and International Studies, American young people are finishing their formal education poorly informed about the history, geography, and cultures of foreign lands. The vast majority of them utterly lack any competence in any language other than their own, and most of them are woefully unprepared to make any informed judgment about America's overseas interests and obligations. They are particularly ignorant of the problems of the developing world. At the time of the most severe oil shortage, polls revealed that 40 percent of the general public did not believe there were real limitations to oil supply. More recently, over half of the people questioned said they were unaware that the United States has to rely on imports to provide part of its petroleum needs.

Public funding sources—local school boards, state legislatures, and the U.S. Congress—have tended to regard foreign language and international studies as of secondary importance, if not unnecessary frills. Private funding in this area is of genuine importance to the national interest. American foundations and corporations, particularly those operating overseas, ought to give renewed attention to either direct contributions to such educational programs or to the encouragement of strategies for stimulating increased public funding. With global interests and responsibilities that cannot be abandoned, the United States is severely handicapped by an educational system that is grossly inadequate in its preparation of young people to understand, communicate with, and work effectively alongside other peoples around the world. That is a problem on which progress can be made, and where private initiatives could be of major significance.

3. *Formal Educational Programs for Foreign Students.* There are nearly 250,000 students from Third World countries studying at U.S. colleges, universities, and professional schools. Fewer than 5

percent of them depend on U.S. scholarships and fellowships. They are funded almost entirely by their families and home governments. In recent years, this has meant great concentrations of students from the oil rich countries—Venezuela, Iran, Saudi Arabia, and the other Arab Gulf States—and from a few other countries in Asia, Africa, and Latin America that have high respect for American science and technology and want to expand rapidly the ranks of their professionals.

With the decline in the numbers of college-age youth in this country, American colleges and universities have embarked on aggressive student recruiting campaigns in foreign lands. Finding well-financed young foreigners has been a boon to many of them. Although there may have been failures and disappointments on both sides, the contribution that American colleges and universities have made to countries of the Third World through training their young people has been substantial. Yet there are nagging questions: Can the U.S. do a better job of educating foreign students than it has been doing? Can we give them the kind of training that will enable them to be most effective in contributing to the development of their homelands? Also, can the United States, in its own self-interest, do more to draw to our educational institutions a broader cross-sectional representation of students from the entire Third World, with not such heavy concentrations of youth from the oil-wealthy lands? The Soviet Union and the Soviets' most hard-line satellite, the German Democratic Republic, both provide relatively more opportunities for foreign study for people from the Third World than does the United States. So does France. In the years ahead the United States may come to believe it desirable to encourage more foreign students from more countries to come to this country, both for degree programs and shorter-term, more focused special projects. Private as well as public funding will be advantageous for carrying out such an expansion.

4. *American Educational Institutions Operating Abroad.* Dating back, in most cases, to missionary schools founded in the nineteenth century, there are a number of educational institutions in foreign countries that are under strong U.S. influence, expressed through American administrators, professors, board members, and financial contributors. Three of the most conspicuous of these are in the Middle East: Robert College in Istanbul; American University of Beirut, in Lebanon; and American University in Cairo, in Egypt. Despite the turbulence of the area and rampant anti-Americanism,

all three of these institutions have continued to make outstanding contributions to the host countries and have been highly positive symbols of American concern. There are several others.

Such American "educational representation" overseas has weathered the stormy accusations of "cultural imperialism" and has been enormously helpful in speeding social and economic development of the region. These universities have also constituted a humanitarian American presence of enormous political importance. Although they receive some U.S. government assistance, they deserve continued and expanding private support both because of the intrinsic worth of their programs and because of the importance of maintaining their identity and credibility as private, independent institutions.

5. *Cultural Exchange Programs.* There are many people-to-people exchange programs concerned with promoting reciprocal travel and personal visits involving Americans of various ages, social interests, and professional careers, and their counterparts abroad. In large measure, even for school and college students, these exchanges are self-supporting. They should not depend upon government favor and financing and they should be more widely available to the Third World. They could, of course, become more representative and have wider impact if they had greater financial resources. Relatively modest inputs of private funds would make possible both expansion and improvement of these valuable programs.

This is not to argue against the programs that are supported by the U.S. Agency for International Development or the International Communication Agency or the Fulbright Fellowships or the Hubert Humphrey Fellowships, all of which are supported by federal funds. Private financing should not be expected to substitute for government appropriations. But more private support clearly would be helpful in developing a full range of privately administered people-to-people exchanges that it would be desirable to maintain.

6. *Improvement of Journalistic Coverage of the Developing World.* One of the barriers to understanding and cooperation between the developed and developing countries is the inadequate information—and misinformation—that passes back and forth between the two worlds through newspapers, radio, television, films, and books. For years, throughout the Third World, there has been a smoldering resentment of what they consider to be distortion, sensation, triviality, and patronizing hostility in the way the media representatives of the industrially advanced countries report events and daily life in the developing countries. So angered have many of

the governments become over this issue that they have undertaken through the United Nations to secure a UNESCO "code of ethics" to be applied to foreign correspondents, which would allow them to censor and control foreign correspondents operating in their areas. The Soviet bloc nations, predictably, have urged on these endeavors as another way of establishing their solidarity with the Third World and encouraging antagonisms toward the Western nations. The Western governments and their media organizations have, of course, strenuously rejected these efforts to restrict free press activities.

Meanwhile, it has been revealed that the United Nations secured several million dollars from a wealthy Japanese businessman with which to pay for the preparation, printing, and distribution of newspaper supplements on Third World development issues and on the achievements of particular countries. These special sections, unidentified as to funding source, were distributed as regular portions of a number of major newspapers. The accuracy of the material seems not to have been seriously challenged, although it was clearly intended to present the advancement of the developing countries in an advantageous light and to counteract previous unfavorable publicity. Here again, the Western press, for the most part, protested this "buying" of approved media coverage as an interference with the traditions of a free press. The UN, although defending its actions, has indicated it will not again make this particular kind of attempt to redress the complaints from the Third World about Western media coverage.

At the same time, in the Third World press there can be found repeated evidence of slanted news that shows Western society in an unfavorable light, although most of it has come from Western sources. Moreover, the limitless appetite of television everywhere for program materials has provided markets throughout the Third World for American TV reruns, many of which cannot help but give a most deplorable picture of life in America.

The solutions, if there are any, to these troublesome communications problems surely will not be found in any form of censorship or in covertly "bought" news projects. But these problems do need to be addressed thoroughly in the interest of creating a climate of informed understanding in which cooperation between the developing and developed worlds can flourish. Private initiatives to that end are probably more likely to be productive than those directly undertaken by government.

Among some of the promising suggestions that have come forward related to these issues are the following:

- One or more nonprofit documentary film production service devoted to objective, comprehensive, in-depth reporting on various aspects of life in the Third World.
- Special training programs for Third World print and broadcast journalists so that they more promptly and adequately take their place among the worldwide corps of foreign correspondents.
- Special seminars on the developing countries and their problems for American editors, TV producers, and reporters, so that they will have greater knowledge, awareness, and understanding of the issues with which they must deal and, it would be hoped, greater resistance to the temptations of superficiality in handling Third World news.

For all such projects private funding, of course, would be desirable.

7. *Strengthening Local Educational Institutions in the Third World.* Historically, a very large portion of the private funds for foreign assistance made available by the Rockefeller Foundation, the Ford Foundation, and the Carnegie Corporation has gone to help develop universities, agricultural colleges, medical schools, teacher training institutions, management schools, and research institutes. From the earliest days of their overseas involvement they calculated that their most significant investments for development would be those directed to the education and professional training of local people to assume leadership roles in their societies. This meant expanding and upgrading small, struggling institutions created earlier by missionary societies or colonial governments. It also meant working with newly independent governments to create new schools and universities from the ground up.

American foundation grants have helped to build classrooms, laboratories, and libraries and to equip and staff them. They also have provided graduate training abroad for young men and women who would come home to become professors, administrators, and researchers. Such grants were seen as important contributions toward realizing the "institution building" and "nation building" goals of the emerging new countries.

Thanks to these private philanthropic activites and similar larger investments by various national governments, U.S. AID, and certain UN agencies, the developing countries have achieved a level of progress in training their own university-level professionals much more rapidly than might have been anticipated. Both private foundations and government funders have cut back substantially on their investments in "institution building." Nevertheless, education remains a critical factor for realizing the ambitions of developing countries.

Now the great challenge seems to be to find better ways to educate the great masses of people. Farmers need to learn how to increase their production of foodstuffs if severe local hunger problems are to be solved. More clerks, accountants, mechanics, and managers have to be trained if local businesses are to flourish and government agencies are to function. And if, eventually, more Third World countries are to realize their ambitions to industrialize and compete in the world market—which most of them are determined to do—they have to carry out a mass education movement that will bring their people to a level of skill and general competency comparable to that achieved by Korea, Taiwan, and Singapore—showcase examples of poor peoples who have achieved a high level of development in recent years. Grass-roots education increasingly demands attention and imaginative experimentation in the developing countries for the years ahead.

8. *Development Education.* Overlapping these various forms of international education is the newly emerging endeavor called development education, strongly favored by the PVOs and several foreign countries. It is a broad public information campaign to promote general adult understanding of the problems of the developing countries. With the Biden-Pell amendment, Congress has given official blessing to this effort.

Demonstrations Through Limited-Scale Experiments of How People Can Help Themselves

As the developing countries press ahead with their efforts to alter the current international economic order and to intensify their drive toward industrialization, they will undoubtedly continue to look to the World Bank, to various UN agencies, and to U.S. AID for major financial assistance with their key development programs. Nevertheless, in the slow, unspectacular improvement of the lives of the rural poor—still a great majority of the population in many countries—they need the help of individuals and organizations experienced in promoting community change. That experience is found most impressively among PVOs. Whatever the future patterns of development, they still have important work to do, both in the direct services they provide through experimental and demonstration projects they supervise and through their efforts to develop those indigenous PVOs that will eventually replace them.

For the foreseeable future the PVOs will continue to carry out a variety of development functions that draw support from AID and from certain international agencies and are directed toward improvements in farming and in the quality of rural and urban life. Meanwhile, they are intensifying their efforts to secure greater funding from foundations and corporations as well as from their traditional supporters—the churches and individual donors. How well they succeed in holding and increasing their precarious funding will depend on how well their real strengths are perceived and how effectively they can correct certain weaknesses. From this study, we have come to a few conclusions about both:

Strengths of the PVOs

1. Some of them are able to respond quickly to emergency needs because they already have in place, or on "inactive reserve," networks of volunteers who are experienced, dedicated, and can move promptly in gathering funds, clothing, medicines, and relief workers when a disaster strikes.

2. PVOs, including church groups, have trained workers with substantial foreign experience, with proven ability to adjust to strange and difficult living conditions, and who generally understand the subtle psycho-social problems of people in the developing countries and have the sensitivities required to function effectively in those environments.

3. PVOs generally operate on lower administrative budgets because they have never adopted the more elaborate structures and mechanisms of government agencies and the accompanying cost patterns. PVO personnel generally function on lower standards of living—sometimes very much lower.

4. In educating the general public about the needs of disaster-affected peoples and the problems and hopes of developing countries, the PVOs play a significant role. Their fundraising activities, their food and clothes collection drives, and their written reports and public speeches on the work being done abroad are ways of reaching large numbers of people directly and getting them personally involved in the foreign assistance enterprise. Thanks to the educational role of PVOs, they sometimes win over people who are strongly critical of "foreign aid," seen as a government activity, but

who can be very generous in their own voluntary support of private initiatives for foreign assistance. When they speak out as advocates they are more readily believed than journalists and government representatives.

5. In the recipient countries the PVOs are generally seen as nongovernmental entities and, therefore, are often more acceptable than official U.S. agencies. This is especially true where political passions have been aroused against the U.S. government and its foreign policies.

6. Because of their traditions of direct people-serving programs, and the scale and pattern of their work, the PVOs are uniquely fitted to carry out small, village-level experiments. If they succeed, they can be replicated under the same or other auspices. If they fail, lessons can be learned quickly from the failures, with minimum political cost.

7. Because of the high level of humanitarian motivation behind most of the PVOs, many of which are the outgrowth of some religious tradition or church institution, the PVOs have been unusually responsive to the needs of the poorest of the poor, and have demonstrated their abilities to function in the more isolated and primitive regions. Insofar as the "basic human needs" strategies to combat "absolute poverty" are significant parts of a nation's development plan, the PVOs have peculiarly important roles to play.

Weaknesses of the PVOs

1. Many need improved management. Depending heavily on volunteers who have been drawn into their work out of idealistic enthusiasm and often have no training and experience in administration, some PVOs suffer from poor organization, inadequate fiscal accountability, and sketchy record keeping. Some donors, recognizing these problems but believing they are soluble, have made grants especially for consultative services and training to improve management.

2. There is too little coordination among PVOs working in the same areas or on the same kinds of problems. There are inadequate provisions for their personnel to learn from each other, to engage in serious planning of shared activities, or to work out ways of avoiding unnecessary duplication and competition.

3. They are forever short of money. The tasks they confront are vastly greater than the resources available to them from all sup-

porters. Too much of their time and energies—and their scarce money, as well—go into not-too-effective efforts to raise money. Here again, some imaginative financial supporters have provided special funds for consultative services and training in the development of more effective fundraising techniques in approaching their natural constituencies.

4. They have not succeeded in creating adequate understanding and support for their work among foundations and corporations. What support they do receive from these sources tends to come because of the social concerns and religious ties of individuals and families related to the grantmaking organizations.

In the history of American private initiatives for relief and development, major roles have been played by these two types of institutions—foundations and private voluntary groups, including churches. Yet, the foundations most active in international development—Ford and Rockefeller, for example—have not had much to do with the PVOs. Traditionally, their pattern has been to work directly with the governments of the emerging new nations. At times they set up and funded special commissions or institutes to carry out programs on which their representatives and the appropriate government officials had agreed. At other times they made grants directly to government ministries, research institutes, or universities designated by the government. At a crucial period they were important factors in the "nation building" and "institution building" strategies of the developing countries. They may still have such roles, on a limited scale, to play in some countries. However, as the new nations—thanks in part to U.S. foundation support—have shaped their national development plans, have built universities and health care services, and have trained their own cadres of professionals, they no longer need or want American foundations' help on the scale and in the form they once welcomed. That does not mean that there are not plenty of important endeavors for foundations to support abroad—there are. But now they must look toward somewhat different channels through which to direct their funds to aid the developing world.

One of these channels has been there all the time: the PVOs created and staffed, for the most part, by North Americans and Europeans. Now, gradually, there are emerging related new institutional actors: the indigenous private voluntary organizations (IPVOs), established within the developing countries themselves. It could well be that one of the more important missions for American PVOs and American foundations in the developing world is to nurture the growth of local voluntary organizations that can be the long-term instruments of development as no foreign institutions can be from now on.

Emergency Relief and Food Aid

For all the obvious and irrefutable arguments about the desirability of moving beyond foreign relief to development assistance, relief problems, as such, have not gone away. With more than 10 million refugees (as of mid-1981) scattered through Thailand, Pakistan, Lebanon, Somalia, South Florida, and many other places in between, the most elemental human needs are paramount. Food, tents, blankets, medicine—these are the immediate essentials for survival. With hurricanes, earthquakes, droughts, and tidal waves the unpredictable but recurring experiences for various parts of our disaster-prone globe, emergency relief will always be required. That will be true even if the human propensities for inhuman violence that produce most refugees can be abated. And ways must be found, as emergencies pass, for the victims of disasters to rebuild their lives on a basis of self-supporting initiatives.

Likewise, in dealing with the problems of chronic and extreme poverty—whether in the Caribbean, Bangladesh, Somalia, Bolivia, El Salvador, or wherever—relief and development initiatives have to go hand in hand. As foreign assistance workers come into contact with the chronically poor, the first impulse is to bring in basic relief supplies. Because malnutrition is such a widespread phenomenon in certain regions, and because the malnourished need more food in order to have the strength and will to work at improving their lot, such supplies are often vital in speeding the broader, long-term strategies for development.

For gathering funds, supplies, and relief workers, the private volunteer groups are crucial. The Red Cross, the Salvation Army, countless church groups, and other private agencies can be counted on to rush to the rescue. They have to be sustained in some continuing state of readiness. They must also be supported promptly when disasters strike. Foundations and corporations, as well as churches and individuals, have demonstrated again and again their readiness to respond to emergency relief needs abroad, even though their policy guidelines and giving practices may theoretically bar them from giving for overseas projects. And all of them, donors and PVOs, need to develop more comprehensive strategies for phasing "relief" into "development."

In recent years it has become fashionable to disparage "relief" in favor of "development," and many PVOs that began as relief service agencies have proclaimed, with some pride, their advancement into the more highly valued field of development. There are good reasons to move beyond relief and try to help the recipients of relief break free of "charity." Yet it is not an either/or situation of relief versus development. From the recurring cycle of emergency relief situations, there is no escape. What we have not learned—and what needs learning—is how to handle emergencies, while they last, in the most creative, least demeaning, least destructive manner—and to end the emergency relief period as quickly as possible so that the people helped can become truly self-sufficient, not pauperized into permanent dependency.

In recent years, one of the most popular forms of relief has been the Public Law 480 program called "Food for Peace," or simply "Food Aid." It came out of humanitarian, charitable concern. It also has been a "good deal" for American farmers forever worried about price-depressing surpluses of farm products. It is no coincidence that some of the strongest political support for generous food relief abroad comes from the states that are heavy producers of corn, wheat, and dairy products. To admit this linkage of foreign aid generosity with economic self-interest is not to disparage "food for peace" programs to help poor people in times of acute food shortage, as during the famine in the Sahel region of West Africa during the mid-1970s. But there are serious questions to be raised about the American tendency to respond automatically to disasters abroad with shipments of PL480 corn and wheat. At times, it has been argued, such relief has had severely negative effects on the lives of the people being "helped."

For instance, immediately after the catastrophic earthquake in Guatemala in early 1976 (in which 14,000 people were killed in the Chimaltenango district), large quantities of PL480 corn, wheat, and dried milk were shipped from the United States and distributed, largely by CARE and Catholic Relief Services, free of charge. According to some local leaders and American resident development workers, that food was really not needed at that time. The earthquake struck at the end of one of the best local corn harvests in years, and the crop was not lost. The wheat had not been harvested, but most of it stood in the fields ready to be gathered. All of a sudden, hundreds of tons of free U.S. food were trucked into these rural villages. According to some of the experienced U.S. relief workers in the area at the time, the results were substantially counter-productive:

- standing in line to collect free food became a major occupation for a great many people, diverting them from completing their own harvesting and the repairing of their homes;
- the price level for local crops was severely depressed, sometimes below the cost of production; at a time when the farmers needed extra income to pay for house repairs, they had less cash than before;
- local quarrels broke out over the distribution of the free food, corruption was encouraged, and in many communities local leadership tended to pass into the hands of unscrupulous manipulators of the foreign food distributors and of their own people;
- promising development education projects to teach local poor people how to improve crop production and family nutrition collapsed in some communities because the people reasoned that the free food now took care of their basic needs;
- long-term self-help efforts to expand and improve local agricultural production were discouraged.

When the free food distribution was eventually stopped, the local people had severe problems of readjustment to the realities of their hard but manageable struggle to take care of their needs themselves.

Even more disturbing are the reports on the relationship between American food aid and the continuing severe poverty of millions of rural people in Bangladesh. Although often cited as the classic "international basket-case" country, sunk in virtually hopeless poverty, Bangladesh has the warm climate, abundant rainfall, and deep rich soil that should make it one of the most productive agricultural lands on earth. A U.S. Senate report, published several years ago, concluded that "the country is rich enough in fertile land, water, manpower, and natural gas for fertilizer, not only to be self-sufficient in food, but a food exporter, even with its rapidly increasing population size." Instead, according to the World Bank, more than half of the population eats less than the minimal 1,500 calories per day, and two-thirds of the population is said to be suffering from protein and vitamin deficiencies. Life expectancy is about forty-six years, and one-quarter of the children die before the age of four. Per capita annual income is the equivalent of about $100. The Bangladesh people, 90 percent of whom are rural, are poor indeed.

Understandably, American efforts to help, both by the government and private agencies, have focused on shipping large quantities of foodgrains and dried milk. Gifts to the government of this food, much of it supplied through the U.S. PL480 program, were in turn sold through the official rationing system. The bulk of the donated food has gone to government employees and the urban population; only about one-third of it reached the rural people who make up the vast majority of the nation's poor. That the distribution system is widely reported to be unfair is, of course, cause for concern. Yet even more troublesome is the effect of this free food on national food production policies and performance. According to a U.S. Embassy report in 1976: "The incentive for Bangladesh government leaders to devote attention, resources, and talent to the problem of increasing domestic foodgrain production is reduced by the security provided by U.S. and other donors' food assistance." As explained by Betsy Hartmann and James Boyce, who lived and did research work in a rural Bengali village in the mid-1970s under Yale University sponsorship, "food aid undermines domestic food production by reducing the government's need to procure grain from local farmers and thus support prices at harvest time."

The point of all this is not to say that American food distribution to impoverished countries like Bangladesh should be cut off. But there is unmistakable need to find additional, more reliable ways to see that the gift food actually reaches the most impoverished. And there is the continuing, long-term necessity to increase local food production. Efforts to that end are going to have to focus on raising the productivity of the small farmers. That requires a vast expansion of village educational programs. It also requires changes in credit arrangements for small holders.

It also raises the challenging question of how to carry through meaningful land reform programs. In Bangladesh, approximately one-third of all rural households are landless and another 30 percent try to survive on one acre of land or less.

At the United Nations Conference on Science and Technology, held in Vienna in 1979, it was reported that "The developing world is overwhelmingly a world of smallness. Four-fifths of the farms are of five hectares (twelve acres) or less. Nearly half are just a single hectare. . . . We know from the history of a few countries . . . that tools and machines can be designed for micro-enterprises that are more productive than traditional technologies, and that are low-cost and job-creating rather than labor-displacing."

PVOs such as World Neighbors, the Intermediate Technology Development Group, the International Rural Reconstruction Movement, the Heifer Project, Technoserve, and many others learned those lessons long ago. Their skills in working with local grass-roots organizations in stimulating fresh initiatives among the individual small farm families constitute a great strength for the whole international development enterprise. Expanding their activities and creating more organizations like them, both international and indigenous, may well be one of the most important tasks to which funders of private initiatives for development may want to give major attention in the years ahead.

A Non-American Voice on Food for the Developing World

The following observation is from *The Economist*, London, November 8, 1980:

> Nowhere is the contrast between rich and poor countries more grotesque than in the distribution of food. After crop failures in Africa (made worse by war in Uganda and the Horn), more than 150 million people in 26 countries south of the Sahara are hungry. Many of them will starve to death. On the other side is the EEC (European Economic Community), groaning under the weight of agricultural surpluses. To keep prices from falling, mountains of food are being stored. . . .
>
> Defenders of the EEC's common farm policy argue that surpluses can help build bridges to the third world. But food trade and aid are more complex than that. . . .
>
> The aim of disaster relief should be to save as many lives as possible, not to get shut of embarrassing surpluses that are a glut on the market. This aim is nearly always better sighted by giving the deserving poor cash rather than food. Money gets there faster, and it allows the recipient countries to buy the food they need most, at maximum speed, through efficient grain and commodity trading houses.

Food for Peace?

About 90 percent of food aid (worth $2 billion a year) goes not as emergency relief but to lighten the balance of payments burdens of poor countries. Cash would do that better, too.

The big American food for peace (PL 480) programme was introduced originally by the Eisenhower administration to subtract America's agricultural surpluses from the markets by distributing them to countries that are not commercial buyers. This programme allowed successive Indian governments to keep domestic food prices so low that Indian farmers had little incentive to expand production. This has happened in other countries, most spectacularly in Egypt, Burma and Mali. Handouts from rich men's tables have permitted governments to give the short-term interests of the urban masses cheap food priority over the interests of their farmers (and of all their citizens in the long run); this sort of aid has kept down the higher prices for peasants that would produce larger and more profitable domestic harvests. . . .

The International Food Policy Research Institute estimates that it would cost $12 billion a year in agricultural aid of all kinds (four times the 1977 figure) to make the third world self-sufficient by 1990. And this assumes the poor countries themselves meet half the capital costs and 80 percent of the recurrent costs. But it would be money well spent. . . .

Poor countries are not helpless. During the past five years, India, Pakistan, and Thailand have all raised their farm prices and been rewarded by a dramatic increase in their crops.

Epilogue

As this book goes to press, several developments of significance for the future of private foreign aid are unfolding. They should be noted in the interest of comprehensiveness and timeliness, although it is clear that we are dealing with an always changing subject. A brief description of some of these newer developments follows.

"Grantmaking International" Organized

In the late summer of 1981 there came into being a formal network of private foundations and corporations that support activities related to international purposes. Relief and development projects are high among those purposes. Called simply "Grantmaking International," it is intended to promote the exchange of information among organizations that fund programs of an international character, whether in the United States or abroad, and to assist other funding agencies that may be considering such activities.

For many years it has been widely recognized, and often deplored, that only a handful of U.S. foundations are engaged in any sustained giving for international purposes. It also has been noted, however, that more than one hundred additional grantmakers each year take part in such funding on a limited, occasional, and special-appeal basis. In times of high public sensitivity to some natural or man-caused disaster abroad, that number may be multiplied several fold. Repeatedly, there are expressions of international interests from the smaller and thinly staffed foundations, accompanied by comments on their inadequacies for making fully responsible and informed judgments about international projects.

With growing awareness that many domestic American problems are related to events and interests abroad, and that there is no neat dividing line between domestic and international problems, it is almost inevitable that the desire to be involved in international grantmaking will increase among U.S. funding organizations. And that, in turn, will underscore the desirability of some trusted source of information about the international grantmaking process and the needs, problems and complexities of the field.

Grantmaking International is designed to be a small, autonomous association of foundations, corporations, church bodies, and perhaps other private funders. Their interests and objectives are by no means identical, but they share a conviction that private grantmaking for a variety of international purposes can and should be improved and expanded—and that this can be facilitated through consultations and information exchange. The members of the group are committed to providing support for its modest budget. At least in its initial stages, GI is expected to be affiliated with the Council on Foundations, but neither financed nor controlled by it.

Transnational Cooperation in Private Philanthropy

The Hague Club is an association of more than forty private foundation executives, mostly from Western Europe. The Venezuelan Federation of Private Foundations, with about thirty members, is the largest group of foundations in Latin America. Both associations sponsored international conferences in 1981 in the hope of encouraging more private initiatives in dealing with development issues.

Under the title of "The Second International Conference of Foundations and Business Leaders," a four-day meeting was held in Caracas in March 1981, attracting almost 200 participants from fifteen countries. The discussions dealt with varying approaches to private philanthropy in the Western Hemisphere and the needs for increased funding of development programs. Among those attending were representatives of about thirty U.S. foundations and corporations. There were also foundation representatives from Great Britain and Spain.

Although many of the sessions were concerned with the technical and legal aspects of grantmaking in different countries, there were extended sessions devoted to basic social and economic problems that increasingly affect all societies: energy, food production, protection of the environment, housing, population planning, and rural development.

The response was excellent to this second effort to bring together private grantmakers in the Americas; the first such conference had been held five years earlier, also in Caracas. One tangible result was an agreement that some kind of ongoing association should be formed and that a third conference would be held in Santo Domingo, probably by 1984. It was further agreed that an occasional newsletter should be published to keep the various private grantmakers informed about program activities in North and South America that might be of more than purely local interest. It was also proposed that a few organizations explore the possibilities of joint transnational funding of certain types of development projects through grants from foundations in two or more countries.

The Hague Club, which holds general meetings twice a year, invited the chief executives of a dozen of the major U.S. foundations to join its members in April 1981 for a conference in Amsterdam on a number of the issues associated with the so-called North-South Dialogue. Within both the European and the American groups of grantmakers there were widely varying expressions of interest and program activity related to this topic. No commitments to ongoing collaboration were made, and no plans for a follow-up meeting were agreed upon.

One European foundation representative whose organization is heavily engaged in support of development projects in the less developed countries urged that all foundations pledge themselves to make grants equal to at least 10 percent of their annual expenditures for development projects in the Third World. That proposal was not acted upon, nor was there any agreement about the desirability of foundation cofunding across national boundaries. Nevertheless, out of the experience of sharing in the examination of some of the issues that affect the relations of developed and developing countries, there seemed to emerge a tacit understanding that the advanced countries will have to involve themselves more deeply in the development issues affecting the Third World, that the private sector in the advanced countries will have to play a larger role in development, and that communication among private grantmakers around the world is both necessary and desirable.

It remains to be seen how far collaboration may develop among private grantmakers internationally. But there are more favorable signs pointing in that direction than ever before.

New and Stronger Patterns of PVO Collaboration

Private grantmakers have long admonished many of the PVOs in the field of international development to improve their internal management, to broaden their base of support, to develop more coherent case statements in behalf of their programs, and to find more comprehensive ways to collaborate with each other. In 1980 and 1981 there was encouraging movement toward those objectives.

A group of PVOs did in fact get together on a joint statement of the nature and merits of the work they do in service to developing countries in various parts of the world, and published a brief, attractive brochure. This signaled the beginning of PAID (Private Agencies for International Development). A number of PVOs participated in the organizing and carrying out of an international development conference held in Washington in May 1981. Other PVOs assisted the foundations and corporations in the preliminary discussions leading up to the organization of Grantmaking International, then wisely backed away from direct membership so that the full responsibility for that new effort would rest upon the funding agencies themselves. Still another group of PVOs assisted in the establishment of Action for World Development to promote greater public understanding of development issues and to provide a continuous flow of information for influencing public policy formation on these issues, but without becoming a lobbying agent.

Perhaps the most significant signs of growing influence of the PVOs are to be found in their successful efforts in winning support despite broad funding reductions of the Reagan administration—coupled with increasing imaginativeness and resourcefulness in defining and experimenting with new options for development.

One illustration merits special attention. Partners of the Americas, ten years old in 1981, has launched a special project for training community leaders in both the United States and various Latin American countries to help build support for development projects. Funded by a grant of $490,000 from the Kellogg Foundation, Partners has undertaken a program of seminars for forty carefully selected fellows—men and women with proven interest in international relations and community development, half of them from the United States, half from the Caribbean and Central and South America. Some of the seminars were to be only for the North Americans, some only for those chosen from outside the United States. Some were to bring both groups together. In addition to lectures and discussion, the participants were to have extensive exposure to specific community projects and learn from direct involvement in their operation.

Potentially most important of all, the fellows in this project were to explore how they can help make the whole program a genuine partnership, not just another benevolent U.S. gesture toward poorer neighbors. This concept could possibly turn out to be the ultimate test of foreign aid.

Up to now, foreign assistance has, perhaps inevitably, been almost entirely a one-way proposition. The United States helps poorer, less advanced, less skilled people. Out of their riches of physical and human resources, Americans share some of their abundance with those less fortunate. It has been part of our national image to see ourselves as having achieved what others want to achieve but haven't been able to do on their own, and as being able and willing to show them how to make progress toward our level of attainment. Many other people have that same image of us — and of themselves. Whatever validity such superiority-inferiority stereotypes may have at certain stages in development, they are increasingly inaccurate and inappropriate. Benevolence and dependency are not a suitable basis for long-term fruitful and harmonious relationships. Foreign aid as a one-way form of charity is, in the long run, demeaning and resented. Perpetual gratitude for favors bestowed by richer neighbors is not a natural attitude that can be sustained.

Is a two-way sharing possible between the United States and the countries to which it has given assistance in the past or is presently helping? At first glance, to many, that will seem highly unlikely, if not absurd. Yet it is a possibility that must be explored. It is the ultimate goal toward which we must work. Foreign aid must become a partnership, or eventually it will be rejected by both sides.

The truth is that the United States has much to learn from developing countries — about the use of paramedics in health services, about the care of the aged, about intensive small-scale farming, about the preservation and development of traditional crafts and art forms. Countries we help with education programs can assist us in training our undergraduates and graduate students, just as we assist in the training of theirs. Their performing arts groups can entertain our people, just as ours can entertain theirs. We need to put real effort and imagination into finding legitimate ways in which to build our relationships upon a basis of reciprocity, of undertaking research and experimentation jointly — of truly helping each other. It may be that we will never balance the accounts exactly and neatly. But there are those concerned about the long future of development and about American influence in the world who think we can and must transform foreign aid into mutual assistance.

The Reagan Administration and Foreign Aid

Although some of the theoreticians of the Reagan administration had obvious difficulties with the whole concept of foreign aid, and although some of the initial pronouncements by Reagan officials sent great alarms throughout the development community, it has turned out that American assistance to the less developed countries is not threatened with extinction. On the contrary, there remains a substantial level of funding, although as in previous administrations, a very large percentage of the total goes to two countries, Israel and Egypt. Moreover, the use of private sector organizations and institutions to carry out government-supported foreign assistance programs continues on a high level.

The proposed major new thrust of the Reagan administration in the development field has to do with the search for an increased role for American business firms. As in other areas of government activity, it is believed that private entrepreneurs can, in many instances, more promptly and more effectively speed the social advancement of developing countries than can directors of government aid projects. Both officially and informally, encouragement has been given to private bankers and other investors, American manufacturers and trading companies, and engineering, marketing, and consulting firms to become more active in pursuing both their own profits and service to the developing countries through more energetic exploration of the economic opportunities of the Third World.

Tax and other incentives, it is hoped, will stimulate more private sector interest in Third World activity. So, it is believed, will direct and open advocacy by government leaders.

The Reagan administration has made clear that it will give particularly favorable attention in the allocation of its foreign assistance resources to those countries that are making energetic efforts to assist themselves, that shy away from doctrinaire commitments to socialist experimentation, that encourage their own private sector enterprises, and that welcome American investors and entrepreneurs. It is a point of view that has helped to shape Reagan policies in many fields of domestic activity. It is not surprising that it should be applied to international development questions as well; nor is it surprising that some developing countries suspect and oppose those policies.

In the long run, the achievements of the many diverse private initiatives for relief and development will depend upon the imagination, energy, and resourcefulness with which the various private organizations pursue their opportunities and concerns. Government policies and funds seem unlikely to guarantee either their success or their failure. The present pluralistic approach built into public policy and operating experience in the foreign aid field give to the champions of private initiatives significant encouragement but no guarantees.

What is important for the long future of international assistance activities is that the foundations, corporations, churches, and PVOs should see themselves as part of a vast, informal network of institutions and organizations that can make a great difference in the lives of many millions of people around the world—and in the relationships between the United States and those emerging new countries. And it is essential that they approach their shared tasks with an abundance of individual creativity and a will to cooperate more fully than they ever have before.

Annotated Bibliography

We have chosen to present these materials in a way we hope will be helpful in encouraging further study of this fascinating and complex field—both by listing in four broad categories existing published materials and by calling attention to those organizations that continuously gather information and publish fresh materials in occasional papers, annual reports, newsletters, and other periodicals.

1. PRIVATE VOLUNTARY ORGANIZATION ACTIVITIES ABROAD

The best source of information about the current activities of the United States PVOs is the Technical Assistance Information Clearinghouse (200 Park Avenue South, New York, New York 10003), an affiliate of the American Council on Voluntary Agencies in Foreign Service. TAICH was funded in 1978 by AID to produce and publish surveys on the broad range of activities of U.S. PVOs, as well as country-by-country reports of projects in specific underdeveloped countries. TAICH also has an extensive library on PVOs open to the public—but call first.

For information on PVOs not based in the United States, a better source is the Society for International Development, which has an information clearinghouse on nongovernmental agencies involved in development assistance (Palazzo Civilta del Lavoro, 00144 Rome, Italy). Another good source is the Geneva Headquarters of the International Council of Voluntary Activities (17 Avenue de la Paix, 1202 Geneva, Switzerland). Still another networking organization concerned with volunteer and exchange programs (many sponsored by governments) is the Paris-based Coordinating Committee of International Voluntary Service.

For information about any of the PVOs registered with AID there are extensive materials available from the AID Public Affairs Office (Agency for International Development, Washington, D.C. 20523). The best U.S. government library on the subject is at the State Department, Room 3239, Washington, D.C. 20523.

Some of the individual PVOs have excellent libraries, in-house publications, and records that relate to their own internal operations and histories as well as to their fields of activity. The library of the American National Red Cross (17th and D Streets, N.W., Washington, D.C. 20006) deserves special mention as an excellent depository of information on international relief. The Transcentury Corporation (1799 Columbia Road, N.W., Washington, D.C. 20009) has an information clearinghouse on the more technically oriented PVOs. The Overseas Development Council (1717 Massachusetts Avenue, N.W., Washington, D.C. 20036) also has extensive materials on PVOs as well as on many related public policy issues. In New York, the Foundation Center library (888 Seventh Avenue, New York, N.Y. 10019) has a broad collection of historical books on PVOs, as does the library of the Ford Foundation (320 East 43rd Street, New York, N.Y. 10017).

The following publications are particularly worth noting:

U.S. PVOs

Beyond Charity: U.S. Voluntary Aid for a Changing Third World. John Sommer, Overseas Development Council, Washington, D.C. (1977).

Final Report: Development Impact of Private Voluntary Organizations in Niger and Kenya. Development Alternatives, Inc., U.S. Government Printing Office, Washington, D.C. (1979).

Religious Private Voluntary Organizations and the Question of Government Funding: A Preliminary Report. Center of Concern, Washington, D.C.

Private and Voluntary Organizations in Foreign Aid. Elliot Schwartz, Special Studies Division, OMB, Washington, D.C. (November 15, 1978).

The Role of Voluntary Agencies in International Assistance: A Look to the Future. AID, The Advisory Committee on Voluntary Foreign Aid (1974).

Voluntary Foreign Aid Programs: Reports of the American Voluntary Agencies Engaged in Overseas Relief and Development Registered with the Advisory Committee on Voluntary Foreign Aid, 1979. AID, Washington, D.C. 20523.

U.S. Non-Profit Organizations in Development Assistance Abroad. Technical Assistance Information Clearinghouse (TAICH), 200 Park Avenue South, New York, N.Y. 10003 (1978). AID funds TAICH to profile the projects conducted by U.S. PVOs abroad. The aggregate data is published in this volume and there are separate "country reports" that show the extent of U.S. involvement in specific Third World countries.

Attention should also be given to the annual and occasional special reports published by most PVOs about their own activities.

International PVOs

ICVA News. International Council of Voluntary Agencies, 17 Avenue de la Paix, 1202 Geneva, Switzerland. The *News* is an informative periodical with articles on programs, conferences, policy issues, UN developments, and fundraising. ICVA, the only international association for private voluntary agencies, has strong ties with European PVOs and with intergovernmental agencies.

Nongovernmental Organizations in Consultative Status with the UN Economic and Security Council. UN Publications, New York (1980).

"The Role of U.S. NGO's in International Development Cooperation." D. H. Smith *et al.*, in *NGOs in International Cooperation for Development,* UNITAR, New York (1978).

World Statistical Directory of Voluntary and Development Services. United Nations Development Program, Division of Information, Room 1906, One UN Plaza, New York, N.Y. 10017.

Activities of Japanese Nonprofit Organizations in Southeast Asia. Japan Center for International Exchange (9–17 Minami-Azabu 4-Chome, Minato-Ru), Tokyo, Japan (1977).

Directory of Activities of International Voluntary Agencies in Rural Development in Africa. Economic Commission for Africa, United Nations, New York, N.Y. 10017 (1972).

Commonwealth Directory of Aid Agencies (Caribbean and Africa—1978). The Commonwealth Foundation, Marlborough House, London SWIY 5HY, U.K.

OECD-ICVA Directory: Development Aid of NGOs and Nonprofit Organizations (1967; new edition 1981). Organization for Economic Cooperation & Development, Publications Office, 2 Rue Andre Pascal, 75 Paris (16e), France.

2. INTERNATIONAL PHILANTHROPIES OF FOUNDATIONS AND TRANSNATIONAL CORPORATIONS

There is no really comprehensive library of information on the international activities of foundations in the United States. The best available collection is contained in the extensive holdings of the Foundation Center in New York City, which has a section devoted to national funding directories from several, but by no means all, of the countries that publish them. Most of the international funding directories are there, as are the annual reports of virtually all the U.S. foundations involved in international activities. The Foundation Center's other major collections and field offices are in Washington (1001 Connecticut Avenue, N.W., Washington, D.C. 20003); Cleveland (739 National City Bank Building, 629 Euclid Avenue, Cleveland, Ohio 44114), and San Francisco (312 Sutter Street, San Francisco, California 94108).

The libraries and the publication offices of the biggest foundations are also important sources of information. These include the Ford Foundation (320 East 43rd Street, New York, N.Y. 10017), Rockefeller Foundation (1133

Avenue of the Americas, New York, N.Y. 10036), Carnegie Corporation (437 Madison Avenue, New York, N.Y. 10022), and Kellogg Foundation (400 North Avenue, Battle Creek, Michigan 49016).

Among the best sources of information about European foundations are: the Agnelli Foundation (Via Ormed, 10125, Turin, Italy) and the Hague Club (Koninginnegracht 52, P.O. Box 1905, The Hague, Netherlands). The best source of information on Japanese corporate philanthropies is the Japan Center for Information Exchange, which has a New York office (c/o The Japan Society, 333 East 47th Street, New York, N.Y. 10017). For Latin American foundations a good resource center is the Venezuelan Federation of Private Foundations, Apartado de Correos 332, Caracas, Venezuela.

The United Nations Environmental Program (Nairobi, Kenya) recently commissioned a study of international foundation activity, which includes a listing of national associations and national directories of foundations in many countries.

For information about the philanthropic activities of transnational corporations, an important source of information is the Conference Board (845 Third Avenue, New York, N.Y. 10022). The board publishes annual studies with aggregate data (that is, with no reference to individual corporations), although its services and resources are intended for the board's members, which include the largest American corporations. Another good source of information is Business International (1 Dag Hammerskjold Plaza, New York, N.Y. 10017), a research service for its members, all of which are transnational corporations. For information on corporate social responsibility from a somewhat adversarial point of view, the UN Centre on Transnational Corporations (Room B21508, United Nations, New York, N.Y. 10017) is the most likely source.

The following books and periodicals on foundation and corporate giving abroad are among the more useful sources of information:

Foundations

Curti, Merle. *American Philanthropy Abroad*, Rutgers University Press, New Brunswick, N.J. (1963). A comprehensive review of giving by American churches, foundations, individuals, various private associations, and the U.S. government for relief and development purposes in foreign countries, from the beginning of the Republic through the early 1960's. A thorough, scholarly work by a distinguished professor of history at the University of Wisconsin. An indispensable historical guide.

Education and Development Reconsidered (The Bellagio Conference Papers). Published by Ford Foundation and Rockefeller Foundation, edited by F. Champion Ward, Praeger Publishers, New York (1974).

Fosdick, Raymond B. *The Story of The Rockefeller Foundation*, Harper and Bros., New York (1952). A highly readable history of the Rockefeller Foundation from its founding in 1913 to 1950, written with care and perception by its fourth president, who served from 1936 to 1948.

International Philanthropy: A Compilation of Grants by U.S. Foundations, Summary of Statistics from the 1977 Report. The Foundation Center, New York (1979).

Murphy, E. Jefferson. *Creative Philanthropy: Carnegie Corporation and Africa 1953–1973.* Teachers College Press, Columbia University, New York (1976). A detailed report on the deep involvement of Carnegie in efforts to strengthen the educational services in various parts of Africa, particularly in those countries that have been part of the British Empire as colony or commonwealth member.

Shaplen, Robert. *Toward the Well-Being of Mankind: Fifty Years of the Rockefeller Foundation.* Doubleday & Company, Garden City, N.Y. (1964).

"Will Philanthropy Meet Its International Challenge?" Alexander Hehmeyer, *Foundation News,* January–February, 1979.

Corporations

Beyond Money. Carol Sakoian and the BI/Public Policy Staff, Business International, 1 Dag Hammerskjold Plaza, New York, N.Y. 10017 (1979). Business International provides research services to its members, transnational corporations. This book is largely a compilation of case studies of various TNCs that have philanthropic programs in which technical assistance, products, and facilities, as well as money, are offered to overseas grantees. (It is heavily drawn upon for our chapter on corporate giving.)

Centre on Transnational Corporations' Reporter. Room B21508, United Nations, New York, N.Y. 10017. This small UN agency researches activities of TNCs and advises Third World countries on contract negotiations. It tends to reflect Third World suspicions of the transnationals.

The Corporate Examiner. Interfaith Center on Corporate Responsibility, 475 Riverside Drive, Room 566, New York, N.Y. 10027. This monthly newsletter ($25 yearly) monitors the activities of TNCs from a consumerist point of view.

Corporate Foundation Directory. Taft Corporation, 1000 Vermont Avenue, N.W., Washington, D.C. 20005. Includes the philanthropic programs of many transnational corporations.

Eells, Richard (Editor). *International Business Philanthropy.* Macmillan, New York (1979).

International Investment and Multinational Enterprises: Responsibilities of Parent Companies for their Subsidiaries. OECD, Suite 1207, 1750 Pennsylvania Avenue, N.W., Washington, D.C. 20006 (1980). Provides background information that is useful to understand the "corporate social responsibility" philosophies of transnational corporations and their grants policies.

Multinational Monitor. P.O. Box 19312, Washington, D.C. 20036. This monthly magazine, produced by Ralph Nader's organization, tracks the activities of transnational corporations with an eye toward exposing their practices, which it claims are contrary to the interests of Third World peoples.

3. DEVELOPMENT THEORY AND FOREIGN AID POLICY

The sources of development theory are the American research "think tanks"; the World Bank; the United Nations and other intergovernmental agencies (such as the Organization for Economic Cooperation and Development); American, European, and Third World universities; and academically inclined publishing houses. Their studies often help to set the framework for governmental policy regarding foreign aid. Today the most influential of these sources of information is the World Bank. Its social scientists produce a steady stream of reports and analytical studies published by the bank itself (World Bank Publications Unit, 1818 H Street, N.W., Washington, D.C. 20433).

The main source of information about the New International Economic Order (NIEO) is the United Nations; its publications are available at the Dag Hammerskjold Library (United Nations, New York, N.Y. 10017), or from the library of the United Nations Institute of Training and Research (801 United Nations Plaza, New York, N.Y. 10017). For extensive materials on the industrialized countries' response to the NIEO, an excellent source is the Washington library of the Organization for Economic Cooperation and Development (OECD) (1750 Pennsylvania Avenue, N.W., Washington, D.C. 20036).

A number of scholarly journals regularly carry important articles on foreign aid and development. Of these, perhaps the most widely read is *Foreign Affairs*, produced by the Council on Foreign Relations (58 East 68th Street, New York, N.Y. 10021). Another comparable quarterly is *Foreign Policy*, published by the Carnegie Endowment for International Peace (11 Dupont Circle, Washington, D.C., 20036).

The think tanks close to the Reagan administration all publish materials on foreign aid: the Heritage Foundation (513 C Street, N.E., Washington, D.C. 20002); the American Enterprise Institute for Public Policy Research (1150 17th Street, N.W., Washington, D.C. 20036); the Center for International and Strategic Studies (1800 K Street, N.W., Washington, D.C. 20036).

The research institute that is closest to the work of the PVOs is the Overseas Development Council (1717 Massachusetts Avenue, Washington, D.C. 20036), which publishes an annual survey of the development assistance issues faced by the United States and by the intergovernmental agencies. ODC also publishes analyses of the North-South issues.

Publications lists of Praeger Publishers, a major publisher on North-South issues, are available from its New York office (385 Madison Avenue, New York, N.Y. 10017). Another publisher heavily involved in scholarly publications on international affairs, including Third World development, is

Westview Press (5500 Central Avenue, Boulder, Colo. 80301).
There are numerous and diverse publications that usefully deal with the following basic issues:

Policy Questions

Catalog of World Bank Publications. World Bank Publications Unit, 1818 H Street, N.W., Washington, D.C. 20433 (1980). A free catalog of major works on international development and finance issues.

Development Cooperation Review. Organization of Economic Cooperation and Development (OECD), 1750 Pennsylvania Avenue, N.W., Washington, D.C. 20006. An annual publication on "development assistance" from each industrialized country.

Global 2000 Report to the President. Superintendent of Documents, U.S. Government Printing Office, Washington, D.C. 20402 (1980). (Full text: 800 pages; 50-page summary.) Result of three years' work of the Council for Environmental Quality and the Department of State, it offers a dismal portrayal of what the world will look like in 2000 if present policies aren't changed.

Industrial Policy and the International Economy. Trilateral Commission, 345 East 46th Street, New York, N.Y. 10017 (1979). How representative leaders of the developed world see the North-South dialogue.

International Development Review, Society for International Development, U.S. Chapter: 1834 Jefferson Place, N.W., Washington, D.C. 20036. Quarterly periodical of Rome-based association of development-related professionals.

Small is Beautiful: Economics as if People Mattered. E. F. Schumacher, Harper and Row, New York (1973). Almost by itself, this book helped shift the thinking of PVOs, AID, the international foundations, the UN agencies, and the World Bank toward stimulating small-scale income-producing projects in rural areas of the poorest countries.

Worldwatch Papers. Worldwatch Institute, 1776 Massachusetts Avenue, N.W., Washington, D.C. 20036. Lively and readable papers on several dimensions of the North-South dialogue.

The New International Economic Order

The New International Economic Order: A Selected Bibliography. Bibliographic Series #30, UN Publications, Room A-3315, United Nations, New York, N.Y. 10017.

North-South: A Program for Survival. Willy Brandt, MIT Press, Cambridge, Mass. (1980). The findings of the Brandt Commission on restructuring the world economy.

Policy Alternatives for a New International Economic Order. Edited by William Cline, Praeger Publishers, 512 Fifth Avenue, New York, N.Y. 10017.

"Philanthropy and the New International Economic order." Craig Smith in *Implementation of the New International Economic Order*, Pergamon Press, Fairview Park, Elmsford, N.Y. 10523 (1981). An examination of the potential of global private philanthropy for revamping the world economic system.

Seventeen Volume Library on the New International Economic Order. Pergamon Press, Fairview Park, Elmsford, N.Y. 10523 (1979–1981). This is an ambitious series of books prepared for the 1980 Special Session of the UN General Assembly, assessing progress on two decades of work toward the New International Economic Order.

Relief and Refugees

International Disaster Relief: Towards a Responsible System. Steven Green, 1980's Project, Council on Foreign Relations, McGraw Hill (1977). This book shows alarming trends in natural disasters and global relief efforts and reviews the range of organizations involved.

"New Forms of NGO Cooperation in World Conferences." Angus Archer in *NGOs in International Cooperation for Development*, UNITAR, New York (1978).

Report on U.N. High Commission on Refugees Assistance Activities in 1979–1980 and Proposed Voluntary Funds: Programmes and Budget for 1980. UN General Assembly, UN Publications, New York (1980). Summarizes the refugee dilemmas in fifty-one countries and describes UNHCR's strategy, as the coordinator of UN and private assistance efforts, to provide relief.

U.S. Development Assistance

Agenda. Agency for International Development Office of Public Affairs, 320 21st Street, N.W., Washington, D.C. 20523. Monthly free AID newsletter on AID's programs.

In Partnership with People: An Alternative Development Strategy. Inter-American Foundation, U.S. Government Printing Office, Washington, D.C. 20402 (1979).

The Making of United States International Economic Policy: Principles, Problems, and Proposals for Reform. Stephen Cohen, Praeger Publishers, 521 Fifth Avenue, New York, N.Y. 10017 (1980).

Serving Human Needs. Irene Pinkau, Charles F. Kettering Foundation, 5335 Far Hills Avenue, Dayton, Ohio 45440 (1979). This study comprehensively examines the extent and quality of what the author calls "developmental services" in the Third World. In addition to describing national and international government efforts in each world area, the study examines the different forms of voluntarism that are indigenous to different world areas.

The United States and World Development, Agenda 1981. John Sewell and the staff of the Overseas Development Council, Praeger Publishers, 521 Fifth Avenue, New York, N.Y. 10017 (1980). Each year the Overseas Development Council publishes an update of the latest issues that are confronting, or about to confront, policymakers concerned with global development.

PVOs' Relationship to U.S. Foreign Aid

Aid as Obstacle. Frances Moore Lappé, Joseph Collins, and David Kinley, Institute of Food and Development Policy, 2588 Mission Street, San Francisco, California 94110 (1980). The authors argue persuasively that foreign aid doesn't work when it is funneled through national governments that do not have effective development programs aimed at helping the poorest of the poor.

Foreign Assistance: A View From the Private Sector. Kenneth Thompson, University of Notre Dame Press, Notre Dame, Indiana (1972). A dated but useful study of AID/PVO "co-financing."

"Private and Voluntary Organizations in Foreign Aid." Elliot Schwartz, U.S. Office of Management and the Budget (1978). This government report discusses the question of how cost effective PVO funding is compared with AID's government-to-government funding.

"Religious Private Voluntary Organizations and the Question of Government Funding." Preliminary report by Jan Blewett, Peter Henriot, and Elizabeth Schmidt, Center of Concern, 3700 13th Street, N.E., Washington, D.C. 20017 (1980).

"Symposium on U.S. Foreign Policy and Private Philanthropy in Developing Countries: Problems of Incentives and Coordination, Summary Report." Brookings Institution, 1775 Massachusetts Avenue, N.W., Washington, D.C. 20036 (1979).

World Hunger Issues

Bread for the World. Arthur Simon, Paulist Press, 400 Sette Drive, Paramus, N.J. 17652 (1973). This book presents the philosophic underpinnings for Christian ecumenical lobbying on hunger issues.

The Challenge of World Hunger. Bread for the World Educational Fund, 32 Union Square East, New York, N.Y. 10003 (1980). A summary and analysis of the report of the President's Commission on World Hunger.

Overcoming World Hunger: The Challenge Ahead. Report of the President's Commission on World Hunger, Superintendent of Documents, U.S.

Government Printing Office, Washington, D.C. 20402 (1980). This comprehensive report summarizes the case for the United States' increased involvement in promoting relief and development in the Third World.

"A Shift in the Wind." The Hunger Project Newsletter, P.O. Box 789, San Francisco, Calif. 94101. Published quarterly. It includes articles on various hunger crises, reviews of new key books, and interviews with hunger experts.

Who's Involved with Hunger. World Hunger Education Service, 2000 P Street, N.W., Suite 205, Washington, D.C. 20036. An annotated bibliography and organizational directory.

World Hunger Actionletter. American Friends Service Committee, 15 Rutherford Place, New York, N.Y. 10003.

Educating the Public on World Affairs

Educating for the World View. Report of the Council on Learning, Change Magazine Press, 271 North Avenue, New Rochelle, N.Y. 10801 (1980). An excellent view of the new initiatives, both governmental and private, regarding global education in schools, colleges, and universities.

The Findlay Story. William Shaw and Edwin McClain, Charles F. Kettering Foundation, 5335 Far Hills Avenue, Dayton, Ohio 45440 (1979). Tells the story of what happened after fifteen civic leaders of Findlay went to East Africa and returned to educate Findlay citizens about Third World poverty.

President's Commission on Foreign Language and International Studies: Background Papers and Studies. Superintendent of Documents, U.S. Government Printing Office, Washington, D.C. 20402 (1979). Twenty-three interesting articles, including surveys of Americans' global attitudes and a discussion on how U.S. multinational corporations relate to foreign languages.

Schooling for a Global Age. Edited by James Becker, McGraw-Hill, New York (1979).

Strength Through Wisdom: A Critique of U.S. Capability. Report from the President's Commission on Foreign Language and International Studies, November 1979, Superintendent of Documents, U.S. Government Printing Office, Washington, D.C. 20402. Documents the declining quantity and quality of international curricula in the U.S. public schools.

Volunteer Services in the Global Learning Process: A Working Paper for Strategy and Action. Irene Pinkau, ACTION Contract No. 79-043-1016 (1980). This 250-page report, co-commissioned by ACTION and Kettering Foundation, is the most comprehensive assessment of past efforts and future proposals for global education.

4. INTERNATIONAL FUNDING DIRECTORIES

There is no single, all-inclusive directory of international funding for grant seekers. However, an assortment of directories provides much useful information on various aspects of the financing of international programs.

General International Funding Directories

Grants and Fellowships in International Studies. Edited by Angela Hardy, International Studies Association, University of Pittsburgh, Pittsburgh, Pa. 15260.

The International Foundation Directory, Revised Edition. Europa Publications, Ltd., 18 Bedford Square, London WCIB 3JN, United Kingdom (1979).

Directory of Financial Aids for International Activities. Office of International Programs, University of Minnesota, 201 Nole West, 315 Pillsbury Drive, SE, Minneapolis, Minn. 55455.

Grants for Graduate Study Abroad, 78–79. International Institute of Education, 809 United Nations Plaza, New York, N.Y. 10017.

Awards, Honors and Prizes, Volume Two (Third Edition, *International and Foreign*). This 450-page directory was published in 1975. Gale Research Co., Book Tower, Detroit, Mich. 48226.

CISP International Studies Funding Book (1979). Council on Intercultural Studies and Programs, 60 E. 42nd Street, New York, N.Y. 10017. Provides a list of organizations with area studies, plus a survey of funding sources for faculty, students, and institutions, as well as affiliated individuals.

Newsletters

Intercultural Studies and Programs. ISIS (Intercultural Studies Information Service), 60 East 42nd St., New York, N.Y. 10017.

International Programs Newsletter. American Council of State Colleges and Universities, Suite 7001, 1 Dupont Circle, Washington, D.C. 20036.

International/Intercultural Consortium Newsletter. American Association of Colleges and Universities, Suite 410, 1 Dupont Circle, Washington, D.C. 20036.

Foundation Directories for Different Regions and Countries

Guide to European Foundations, Third Edition (1978). Agnelli Foundation, Via Ormea 37, Torino, Italy.

Summary Guide to Educational Foundations, Vol. I, Europe, excluding U.K. (1976); Vol. II, United Kingdom (1978). A.A. Zimmerman, European Higher Education Unit, North East London Polytechnic, Longbridge Road, Dagenham, Essex RM8 2AS, U.K.

Latin American Foundations (1973). Fundacion Eugenio Mendoza, Apartado no. 332, Caracas, Venezuela.

Philanthropic Foundations in Latin America (1968). Russell Sage Foundation, 230 Park Avenue, New York, N.Y. 10017.

AUSTRALIA

Directory of Philanthropic Trusts in Australia, Second Edition (1979). The Association of Australian Philanthropic Trusts, Myer House, 250 Elizabeth Street, Melbourne, Victoria 3000, Australia.

CANADA

A Canadian Directory to Foundations and Other Granting Agencies, Fourth Edition (1978). Association of Universities and Colleges in Canada, 151 Slater Street, Ottawa, Ontario, Canada K1P 5N1.

DENMARK

Vejviser for Legatsøgende, 13th Edition (1970). J.H. Schultz Førlag, Gothersgade 49, Copenhagen K, Denmark.

FRANCE

Fondations (1970). Journaux Officiels, Ministry of the Interior, 26 rue Desaix, 75 Paris 15, France.

Traité des Fondations, d'Utilité Publique (May, 1980). Presses Universitaires, 108 Boulevard St. Germain, Paris, France.

GERMANY (FED. REP.)

Deutsche Stiftungen für Wissenschaft, Bildung und Kultur (1969). Nomos Verlagsgesellschaft m.b. H. & Co., Kommanditgesellschaft, Baden-Baden, Germany.

Vademecum, Deutscher Lehr und Forschungsstatten. Stiftverhand für die Deutsche Wissenschaft, 4300 Essen, 1 Bredeney, Postface 23 03 60, Germany.

ITALY

Le Fondazione Italiane (1973). Franco Angeli Editore, Milan, Italy.

JAPAN

Philanthropy in Japan, Revised Edition (1978). Japan Center for International Exchange, 9-17, Minami-Azabu 4-chome, Minato-ku, Tokyo, Japan.

Activities of Japanese Non-profit Organizations in South-east Asia (1977). Japan Center for International Exchange, 333 East 47th Street, New York, N.Y. 10017.

NEW ZEALAND

Directory of Philanthropic Trusts, Second Edition (1978). New Zealand Council for Educational Research, Education House, 178-182 Willis Street, Wellington 1, New Zealand.

PHILIPPINES

Philippine Directory of Foundations (1974). The Association of Foundations, c/o The S.C.C. Development & Research Foundation, Manila, Philippines.

SPAIN

Directorio de Fundaciones Espanolas (1978). Centro de Fundaciones, Calle Don Ramon de la Cruz 36, Madrid-1, Spain.

SWEDEN

Svenska Kulturfonder, Third Edition (1977). Kurt Lehsmann & Wilhelm Odelberg, Norstedts Tryckeri, Stockholm, Sweden.

TURKEY

Foundations in Turkey (1978). Development Foundation of Turkey, Kennedy Cad., 33/7 Kavaklidere, Ankara, Turkey.

UNITED KINGDOM

Directory of Grant Making Trusts, Sixth Compilation (1979). Charities Aid Foundation, 48 Pembury Road, Tonbridge, Kent TN9 2JD, England.

UNITED STATES

The Foundation Directory, Seventh Edition (1979). The Foundation Center, 888 Seventh Avenue, New York, N.Y. 10019.

VENEZUELA

Fundaciones Privadas de Venezuela (1974). Fundacion Eugenio Mendoza, Apartado no. 332, Caracas, Venezuela.

Index

Chile, 27, 81
China, 14, 15, 18, 48, 49–50, 52,
    55–56, 97
  Communist, 20, 50, 53, 56, 90,
    172, 270
China Medical Board (New York),
    50, 93–94
Cholera Research Laboratory
    (Bangladesh), 70
Chollar, Robert G., 88
Christian Action for Development
    in the Caribbean (Barbados),
    87
Christian Children's Fund, 178
Christian Service Corps, 96
Churches
  financial contributions, 39–40
  foreign, 88, 240
  and foreign assistance, 1, 2, 3,
    12, 14, 15, 35–40, 45, 178,
    248
  and war relief, 10, 13
Churchill, Winston, 20
Church of God, 84
Church of the Savior, 38
Church World Service, 3, 36, 39,
    43, 159, 178–179, 232
CIAT. *See* Center for Tropical
    Agriculture
CIDA. *See* Canadian International
    Development Authority
CIMMYT. *See* International
    Maize and Wheat
    Improvement Center
Citizen Action Network, 204–205
Clark, Edna McConnell,
    Foundation (New York), 95
Claussen, A. W., 214, 217
Cleveland, Harlan, 207, 247
Cloud seeding program, 164
CODEL. *See* Coordination in
    Development, Inc.
Cold War, 20, 23
College of the Holy Family
    (Egypt), 92
Colombia, 49, 58, 59, 61, 70,
72, 82
Colonialism, 6, 26, 79–80. *See
    also* United States, and
    colonial powers
Columbia University, 84, 94, 97.
    See also American Assembly
    of Columbia University
Columbus (Ohio), 247–248
"Columbus in the World, the
    World in Columbus," 247
Commerce, Department of, 186
Commission for Polish Relief, 16
Commission of Belgian Relief, 10
Committee for Economic
    Development (Australia),
    67, 69
Commonwealth Fund, 11
Commonwealth Program, 78–79
Communications Workers, 227
Communism, 13, 20–21, 22
Community involvement
    program, 114
Compton Foundation, 45
Conference Board studies
    (1973, 1976), 102–103
"Conference for Continuous
    Mediation," 9
Conference on Human
    Settlements (UN) (1976), 210
Conference on Population (UN)
    (1974), 210
Conference on the Environment
    (UN) (1972), 210
Congress, U.S., 2, 15, 198, 200,
    259
Congress for Cultural Freedom
    (Paris), 67
Congressional Staff Forum on
    Food and International
    Development, 90
Consortium for Community
    Self-Help, 188
Contraception, 61, 181. *See also*
    Population programs
Cooperative League of the United
    States of America, 188

voluntary sector, 246–247
war relief, 10–13, 15–18, 19
See also Dartmouth
Conference; Global
education; Pluralism
United Steelworkers, 227
United Way, 171, 250
Universities, 1, 3
University College Hospital
School (London), 51
University of Bologna, 67
University of California, 75, 97
University of Chicago, 65, 97
University of Dacca (Bangladesh),
73
University of London, 84
University of Louvain (Belgium),
11
University of Manchester, 69
University of Michigan, 65, 97,
247
University of Missouri, 90
University of Naples, 67
University of Notre Dame, 84
University of Paris, 67
University of Pennsylvania, 84
University of Pittsburgh, 84
University of Texas, 84
University of the Americas
(Mexico), 84
University of the Witwatersrand
(Johannesburg), 79
University of Washington, 97
UNRRA. *See* United Nations
Relief and Rehabilitation
Administration
Upper Volta, 24, 70, 164
Urban shanty-town slums, 28
"U.S. Non-profit Organizations in
Development Assistance
Abroad" (TAICH), 40, 182
U.S./South African Leadership
Exchange Program, 79

Venezuela, 2, 49, 87, 213, 255,
261, 273

Verona Fathers Mission (Uganda),
92
Versailles Peace Treaty (1919),
14
Vietnam, 27, 44, 156, 176, 177,
183, 228, 263
VISTA. *See* Volunteers in Service
to America
VITA. *See* Volunteers in
Technical Assistance
Vogler, Richard, 41
Volunteer Development
International, 188
"Volunteer Services in the Global
Learning Process" (Pinkau),
246
Volunteers in Service to America
(VISTA), 246
Volunteers in Technical
Assistance (VITA), 83, 180,
183, 188

Waldheim, Kurt, 230
Walk-a-thon, 44
Wallace, Henry A., 56
Wall Street Journal, 260
War bonds, 16
War Relief Control Board, 16, 17
War Relief Services. *See* Catholic
Relief Services
Warri (Nigeria), 109
Wassadou Agricultural
Development Program
Consolidation (Senegal),
175
Water programs, 109, 112, 164,
231
Wellesley College, 84
West, Harold, 96
West, Hilda, 97
West, Richard, 97
Western Europe, 19, 20, 21, 82
Western Samoa, 60
West Foundation (Indianapolis),
96–97
West Germany, 82, 222
West Indies, 78, 79, 87